THE CHURCH AND THE SECULAR
ORDER IN REFORMATION THOUGHT

THE CHURCH AND THE
SECULAR ORDER IN
REFORMATION THOUGHT

JOHN TONKIN

1971

COLUMBIA UNIVERSITY PRESS
NEW YORK AND LONDON

John Tonkin is Lecturer in European History at the University
of Western Australia.

Copyright © 1971 Columbia University Press
ISBN: 0-231-03374-5
Library of Congress Catalog Card Number: 73-143390
Printed in the United States of America

PREFACE

THIS STUDY of the problem of the institutional Church in the thought of the Protestant Reformers appears in print at a time when ecclesiology, for some years the most lively and interesting topic of discussion among theologians and Church historians, has yielded its central place to other issues. In writing this book I have been conscious of this shift in contemporary preoccupations, but I have not found it a substantial problem, since my primary concern throughout has been to understand the thought of the Reformers rather than to comment on current issues. I am convinced that the question of the institutional Church is an issue of central importance in the intellectual history of the Reformation period, and that an understanding of this issue is fundamental to a proper assessment of the significance of the Reformers' thought. The discussion of such historical issues is clearly in no way affected by shifting patterns of contemporary preoccupations.

To say this is not to disavow an interest in the present theological relevance of the Reformation. As I have tried to indicate briefly in the final chapter of this book, the issues raised in the Reformers' understanding of the Church seem to me to be of perennial importance for those who regard themselves as heirs of the Reformation or those who welcome dialogue with the Reformation tradition. We are now, I believe, in a better position to see these issues in their proper perspective.

Moreover, it is worth pointing out that the wider preoccupations of more recent theological discussion are by no means alien to the ecclesiological concerns of the Reformers. What the Reformers thought about the Church was intimately and inextricably bound up with their understanding of the secular order and of human society, with their historical hopes and their eschatological expectations. For that reason I have found it necessary, for the sake of historical accuracy, to avoid a narrow ecclesiastical reference and to cast the whole discussion of the Reformers' ecclesiology within this broader intellectual context. If, by so doing, I have also linked up with issues of contemporary interest, then so much the better.

Since this work is primarily an interpretation of the Reformers' thought, I have attempted to maintain throughout in the notes as full and precise a reference as possible to the original texts and the standard translations of the works of the three Reformers. Citations from the Weimar edition of Luther's works include not only volume and page number but also the number of the line on which the relevant passage begins. Letters and extracts from the *Table Talk* are further identified by number. References to the volumes of Calvin's works in the *Corpus Reformatorum* edition include the volume number of the *Corpus* in parenthesis, since the two sets of numbers are often confused. Citations from commentaries and sermons include, wherever possible, the relevant Scriptural references. A full listing of these texts and translations appears in the bibliography and a note concerning the abbreviations employed follows this preface.

The issues with which this book is concerned first engaged

my attention when I had the opportunity to pursue studies in Church History at the Graduate School of Drew University, and I am conscious at this time of a great debt to those who assisted me in many ways—to Dr. Colin Williams, now Dean of Yale Divinity School, who was my first teacher in theology at Queen's College, Melbourne, and helped make possible my visit to Drew; and to the faculty of the Graduate School who gave unsparingly of their advice and assistance during very difficult times—especially to Karlfried Froehlich, now of Princeton, under whose guidance the project was originally conceived; to Gordon Harland, now of the University of Manitoba, who pointed me on many occasions toward crucial questions which I might otherwise have overlooked; to Will Herberg, whose breadth of historical knowledge and contagious personal excitement about historical study I found so thoroughly stimulating; and above all to Bard Thompson, now Dean of the Graduate School, whose wise counsel, incisive criticism, and painstaking attention to detail I found invaluable at every stage. Far different, but no less valuable, was the contribution of my wife Barbara, whom I thank for reminding me at all times that nothing in this world—not even the writing of books—ought to be taken with ultimate seriousness.

John M. Tonkin

Department of History
University of Western Australia
July, 1970

CONTENTS

ABBREVIATIONS

WA.	*D. Martin Luthers Werke:* Kritische Gesamtausgabe
WA. Br.	*D. Martin Luthers Werke: Briefwechsel*
WA. DB.	*D. Martin Luthers Werke: Deutsche Bibel*
WA. TR.	*D. Martin Luthers Werke: Tischreden*
LW	*Luther's Works* (American Edition)
PE	*Works of Martin Luther* (Philadelphia Edition)
CR	*Iohannis Calvini Opera Quae Supersunt Omnia* (*Corpus Reformatorum*)
Inst.	*Institutio Christianae Religionis* (1559) (Corpus Reformatorum, vol. 2)
LCC	*Institutes of the Christian Religion* (Library of Christian Classics, vols. XX–XXI)
CNTC	*Calvin's New Testament Commentaries*
MML	*Commentary on a Harmony of the Evangelists: Matthew, Mark and Luke*

COT   *Commentaries on the Old Testament*

TT   *Calvin's Tracts and Treatises*

Letters *Letters of John Calvin*

Op.   *Opera Omnia Theologica of Alle de Godtgeleerde
         Wercken van Menno Symons*

CW   *The Complete Writings of Menno Simons*

ME   *The Mennonite Encyclopedia*

MQR   *The Mennonite Quarterly Review*

INTRODUCTION

CIVILIZATION is inconceivable without the participation of the human community in institutions of various kinds—political, economic, social, and religious—yet no age has been without those who have questioned and criticized the institutions around which human life is structured. At times, this questioning has been tentative and muted; in our own time it has been insistent and searching, and religious institutions find themselves in an analogous position to other institutions, subjected to radical criticism. At the heart of this criticism is the conviction that institutions stultify or even negate the dynamic impulses which gave them birth, freezing them into static, self-perpetuating systems, and becoming thereby the masters rather than the servants of man.

Institutionalism, therefore, is in one respect a sociological problem, and the Christian Church as a human institution is as subject as any other institution to this kind of analysis. Within the Christian tradition, however, there is a far more profound criticism of institutions, of which the fundamental motivation is theological rather than sociological, and it is the intention of this study to focus on the theological criticism of institutions within the Christian, and especially the Protestant, tradition.

The selection of Protestantism as the focus of interest is neither accidental nor arbitrary for, while the criticism of the institutional Church is as old as the New Testament,[1] it acquired a special significance at the time of the Reformation and became in the thought of the Reformers a point of sharp contrast with the central tradition of medieval Catholicism.

The dangers of generalizing about medieval Catholic ecclesiology ought not to be overlooked, since it was by no means a static or uniform tradition but rich in the variety of its manifestations. The preoccupations of the mystics and pietists, for example, differed sharply from the concerns of those in positions of institutional power and responsibility. In the first chapter of this book, I have attempted to give appropriate recognition to the diversity of medieval ecclesiology.

Nevertheless, it is possible to speak meaningfully of a central or official tradition, in contrast to those other currents of thought which were on the whole either unconcerned with institutional matters, condemned as heretical, or marginal in their influence. At the heart of this central or official tradition of medieval ecclesiology was the conviction that the visible, hierarchical institution, in communion with the vicar of Christ, embodied in an unqualified way the reality of the Church. The Protestant Reformers, by contrast, characteristically avoided a full identification of the Church's inner reality with her outward institutional expression. Whereas the Catholic tradition placed the institution beyond basic theological criticism, the Protestant position made that criticism imperative.

The development of a distinctive doctrine of the Church within the Protestant tradition must be understood not as rationalization of a state of schism, but as a genuinely theological development arising out of medieval themes and problems but not bound to medieval solutions. The source of the issue

within the medieval period is the Augustinian dialectic between what may be termed an "eschatological" and an "immanental" understanding of the Church—that is, between a
view which sees the Church's true nature as something to be
realized in the future and one which sees it as fully realized
within the present institution. These two impulses present
together in Augustine's thought became radically separated
for the greater part of the medieval period, and the unresolved
problems resulting from this separation formed the common
inheritance of the Protestant Reformers and set the stage
for their approach to the problem of the Church and its institutional embodiment.

The central focus of this book is a comparative study of the
ecclesiological thought of Martin Luther, John Calvin, and
Menno Simons, each the major representative of a distinct and
enduring tradition of the Protestant Reformation. It attempts
to give proper weight both to their significant unity and to
their remarkable diversity. Their unity inheres chiefly in two
shared theological perspectives derived, respectively, from their
reflections on Christology and eschatology. In their Christology
a marked shift is evident from abstract to personal categories
of understanding and issues in a reinterpretation of the Church
in thoroughly personal terms, as a community gathered around
Christ. In their eschatology, there is a firm reappropriation of
the dynamic, forward-looking dimensions of Christian hope,
and a consequent recognition of the institutional Church as an
ambiguous and imperfect historical institution.

Despite these common general perspectives, however, the
three Reformers' interpretations of the institutional Church are,
in the last analysis, highly diverse, and this fact is attributable
to far-reaching differences in the detailed content of their
Christology and eschatology and in the basic structure of their
theological thought.

Enough has been said here already to indicate that the sig-
ficance of the Reformers' doctrines of the Church cannot be

adequately understood except in the context of wider issues; and it is for this reason that the reader will not find in these pages a narrow or exclusive preoccupation with ecclesiology as such. How the Reformers approached the theological task, and what they thought about creation, the secular order, history, and human destiny is as significant for understanding their attitudes to the institution as anything they ever said about the Church itself.

The extent of the differences between the Reformers, the degree of continuity which each maintains with the medieval tradition, and the fact that the whole discussion takes place in an atmosphere of controversy make it highly problematical to speak of any solid or enduring "achievements" of the Reformers in relation to this issue. What may be discerned, rather, is the emergence—often struggling and hesitant—of certain theological tendencies which they derived from the Biblical tradition, yet approached with a freshness and origi- nality which made their work influential far beyond their own time, and by no means exhausted in its implications even now.

The most significant of these theological tendencies are dis- cussed in the concluding chapter of this book. The core of the work, Chapters II, III, and IV, is an intensive examination and comparison of the theology of the three Reformers, with em- phasis on the way in which their understanding of Christ and of the Christian hope informs their distinctive interpretations of the role of the institutional Church in the world. Chap- ter I, which deals with the medieval period, is not a full-scale account of the medieval doctrine of the Church but is a thematic study of those aspects of ecclesiology which are in- dispensable for understanding the work of the Reformers.

I · THE MEDIEVAL HERITAGE

"CITY OF GOD" AND "CATHOLIC CHURCH"

THE AUGUSTINIAN TENSION

THE SPECIFIC problems with which medieval ecclesiology was to concern itself are first clearly set in focus by Augustine of Hippo in his work *De Civitate Dei,* where we may discern the emergence of a theme destined to pervade medieval ecclesiological discussion—the implicit contrast between the "city of God" and the "Catholic Church," between the Church understood as an invisible community on the march to a goal beyond history and the Church understood as a concrete, visible institution within history.

The work originated as an occasional pamphlet answering charges of Christian responsibility for the fall of Rome, but it developed into a theological masterpiece of profound significance not only for Christian theology but for the whole Western intellectual tradition, especially in the fields of ethics and political theory. It is important to remember, however, that its significance in such areas derives from the profundity of the analysis of grace and salvation which is Augustine's principal concern throughout the work.

For all their bewildering diversity, the twenty-two books of *De Civitate Dei* have an impressive unity. This unity lies in Augustine's interpretation of history, which comprehends in one magnificent sweep the destinies of heaven and earth from the time of the original harmony of the angels with God, through the perplexities and contradictions of human history to the final fulfillment of history in the last judgment, the resurrection, and the eternal bliss of the city of God.

The core of this vision of history lies in Augustine's interpretation of the image of the "two cities," a fundamentally Biblical image which had had considerable currency in the early Church but which Augustine invested with a distinctive meaning.[1] Human history, he declares, has its origin in the defection of the angel Lucifer, since man is created to fill the vacuum in heaven caused by the departure of Lucifer and his band. The city of the Devil, thus inaugurated, has its earthly foundation in the figure of Cain, whose disobedience and fratricide are a profound paradigm for all subsequent history. The city of God has its foundation in Christ, the eternal Logos, and as Cain is the archetype of the earthly city, so Abel is the archetype of the heavenly city, and all his spiritual descendants are citizens of this community, in anticipation of the historical advent of Christ.[2]

Accordingly, humanity may be divided without remainder into two parts,

the one consisting of those who live according to men, the other of those who live according to God. And these we mystically call two cities, or the two communities of men, of which one is predestined to reign eternally with God, and the other to suffer eternally with the Devil.[3]

We may note, in this brief definition of Augustine's, three significant clues to the nature of the two cities. First, membership in each city is not by personal choice or human designation, but by God's gracious predestination. Secondly, the distinguishing feature of each city is not any quality which it possesses but the direction of its allegiance, toward God or the Devil. Thirdly, the two communities are not formal institutions but "mystical" communities of men, bounded neither by time nor space, invisible yet real.

All three factors imply that the two cities cannot be identified with the visible institutions of Church and State. Identification of the earthly city with the State is impossible, because the *civitas terrena* transcends historical bounds to include the dead and unborn as well as the living, while the State is a purely historical institution. On the other hand, complete differentiation is out of the question for, although the State is not in itself the earthly city, when a particular State orients its life in opposition to the true worship of God, then it becomes by that bondage to Satan an expression of the earthly city.[4]

A simple identification of the city of God with the Church is also impossible, although at this point we have to reckon with a greater ambiguity in Augustine's position. As a mystical community, the city of God could never be equated with a purely historical institution. But the ambiguity enters because the institutional Church is never for Augustine a purely timebound reality like the State but is joined to the Church triumphant. That is to say, the contrast between a mystical community and a strictly historical institution, which adequately explained the relationship between the earthly city and the State, will not hold so easily for the relationship of the city of God and the Catholic Church. The ambiguity is of great significance, and we shall have occasion to return to it.

Each of the two cities represents the complete antithesis of the other, but in the present age they remain radically mixed together, the boundaries of each being known only to God. The end or goal of the two cities, like their origins, is suprahistorical. It is the coming of Christ at the last judgment, at which time the two cities, mixed together in the present age, will be separated for their final destinies, and the kingdom will be delivered up to God.[5]

It is apparent that eschatology in *De Civitate Dei* is not one doctrine among others but the fundamental theological motif. In fact, so much does the eschatological motif predominate that Christology is left with an equivocal and uncertain role. For, while Augustine speaks of the grace of Christ as the source of man's redemption, and sees Christ as founder of the city of God, it is difficult to ascribe any crucial significance to the historical advent of Christ in the ongoing drama of the two cities. The figure of Christ seems to function rather as the universal Logos than as the historical Messiah, and one is tempted to say that the story of the two cities would not change essentially if the historical appearance of Christ were disregarded altogether. That would be pressing the matter too far, however, since Christ plays a central role in the Church, and the latter is closely related to the city of God. Yet it remains true that eschatology rather than Christology provides the fundamental theological motif of *De Civitate Dei,* and it is in that motif that we must seek the basis of Augustine's understanding of the Church.

The fact that Augustine's whole approach to the Church is governed by the eschatological thrust of his thought means that he does not indulge in timeless definitions of the Church's nature or accounts of her hierarchical structure. His mode of thought points him away from static, spatial categories toward dynamic, temporal categories so that, when he discusses the Church, he is preoccupied with its existence and destiny in time and history. Accordingly, the "city of God" may be recognized as his primary ecclesiological category. It is the community of the predestined, in an alien land, on pilgrimage toward their heavenly goal. It is no earthly institution, for the present age is interim, provisional, and destined to pass away, and its institutions are essentially impermanent. But the city of God is everlasting, for it is founded on the eternal predestination of God and runs its course through history, under His providence, toward the resurrection and the judgment.

If the eschatological orientation of Augustine's thought precludes granting any ultimate significance to historical institutions, we may still ask legitimately what significance they do retain, and how his vision of the pilgrimage of the city of God relates to his understanding of human society on the one hand and of the institutional Church on the other. Augustine's understanding of the world as God's creation, over which He rules in His sovereign providence, requires that he take seriously life in human society. Moreover, it is through this life that the eschatological community pursues its pilgrimage. "How could the city of God . . . either take a beginning or be developed or attain its proper destiny, if the life of the saints were not a social life?" [6] Yet, while Augustine gives occasional hints that life within society has its own intrinsic significance, the overall impression which he conveys is that the order and government of human society derives its necessity from man's sin, and that the manifold activities of man in society play a totally subordinate role in the context of his vision of history. While the Christian must take part in history and its processes, these have no enduring significance, for the only meaningful historical progress is the inexorable movement of the city of God toward the fulfillment of its historical destiny.[7]

Since that progress is realized in history, however, the question still remains: what is the relationship, if any, of this mystical community to that visible, hierarchical institution which calls itself the Christian Church? We have already taken note of the ambiguity which enters Augustine's thought at this point. For him, the Church is never a merely historical, time-bound institution. Augustine's sense of the Catholic Church's deep resources of grace, combined with the historical necessity of defending the Roman institution against its heretics and its pagan accusers, led him to articulate a position which at times seems to imply an identification of the city of God with the Roman institution. Thus, in Book XX, he declares that "the Church even now is the Kingdom of Christ and the Kingdom of heaven." [8] God has acted for man's salvation, and the visible, sacerdotal Church is the ark of salvation, for it bears within it those two essentials of salvation—an authoritative center of truth, and the riches of sacramental life, through which salvation flows to the believer. In his earthly pilgrimage, the Christian is sustained by these anticipations of glory.

Ernst Benz, in his recent work *Evolution and Christian Hope,* has clearly articulated this Augustinian emphasis on the institutional Church, and he sees Augustine as the final stage in the transformation of Biblical eschatology into "the doctrine of the institutional Church as the present Kingdom of God." [9] That Augustine sees the Church as an "advance-effect of the Kingdom on history" and a "present pledge" of salvation is certainly true. It is true also that Augustine eliminates apocalyptic thought and associates the millennium closely with the present life of the Church, where God's Kingdom is already being realized through the impartation of divine truth and through the sacramental life. But it is most important to recognize that the elimination of apocalyptic and millenarian thought by Augustine did not mean a loss of eschatological perspective, and that his outlook remains strongly "futuristic" in orientation. History from Adam is seen in terms of seven ages, corresponding to the days of creation, and the Church lives just preceding the seventh day, the Sabbath of man. However, the seventh day is not the final stage of history. Beyond it lies the eighth and eternal day, when the Kingdom will be delivered up to God at the last judgment, and the temporal process brought to fulfillment. [10]

When Benz asserts that in *De Civitate Dei* Augustine "took

it for granted that the Church represented the Kingdom of God on earth," [11] he is in danger of making too simple a resolution of what remains in Augustine a point of strong tension. The emphasis on the Church as the ark of salvation remains muted in this work and it is made clear that the identification of the *civitas dei* with the institutional Church is never complete. In the same chapter of Book XX to which reference has already been made, Augustine stresses the incompleteness of the present Church. The saints now reign "otherwise than they shall reign thereafter." The wheat and the tares will continue to grow together. The "Church as it is now" is clearly distinguished from "the Church as it is destined to be when no wicked person shall be in her." [12] The possibility of complete identification is precluded by the consistently eschatological framework.

Benz has taken practically no account of the persistence of this future-oriented eschatology in Augustine, and his statement that the Church has "taken the place of the future Kingdom," and that eschatology has been "devaluated to a doctrine of the last things" [13] is a serious misunderstanding of Augustine. Eschatology is not a "final chapter of Church dogmatics" for Augustine but remains his fundamental mode of thought. The institutional Church, for all the riches of its present life, stands under the judgment of its final goal. The tension remains between the city of God and the Catholic Church, between futuristic and realized eschatology, between the kingdom as a final goal and the kingdom as a present experience. While Augustine would never have regarded these two emphases as implying any contradiction, the fact that they are not easily harmonized in his thought sets the stage for subsequent medieval discussion about the Church and supplies some of its basic issues and problems. Augustine's significance, despite Benz, lies not so much in a process which he concluded as in a debate which he inaugurated.

2

THE INSTITUTION IN THE ASCENDANT

THOMAS AQUINAS, MARSILIUS OF PADUA,

DIETRICH OF NIEM

As the Middle Ages unfolded, these two themes which Augustine maintained in tension became separated. Eschatology ceased to exercise any fundamental role in the understanding of the Church and, in its absence, institutionalism attained a position of dominance. The change was gradual, and the causes were complex, but several factors stand out as being of special importance in contributing to this development. One of these was the revival of Roman jurisprudence, beginning in the early twelfth century, which led to a corresponding development of ecclesiastical law into a system of great subtlety and comprehensiveness. The first substantial expression of this development of canon law was Gratian's *Decretum*, issued in the year 1140, and the result of this revival of interest in law was not only an unprecedented growth of administrative unity, but also an increasing preoccupation with the Church as a legal and ecclesiastical structure. The never-ending battles of the Papacy with emperors and kings only reinforced this development by concentrating attention on the issue of jurisdiction and sovereignty over the visible institution.

Of even greater significance, however, was the influence of the revival of Aristotelian philosophy and its use in Christian theology. It is most instructive to observe, in this connection, what happens to the Church in the theology of *Thomas Aquinas,* who consciously tried to wed Augustinian theology and Aristotelian philosophy within his system of thought.

Thomas, like Augustine, speaks of the Church as the mystical community of the predestined, dispersed through the ages, on pilgrimage to the heavenly country.[14] But such verbal correspondences with Augustinian themes cannot disguise the fact that a basic methodological shift has taken place. Whereas Augustine's eschatological emphasis prevented him from ascribing much intrinsic significance to human society, Thomas's use of Aristotelian philosophy impels him to begin with the analysis of human society and to argue inductively from this analysis rather than deductively from Biblical or speculative propositions. Accordingly, the origin of human society is located in the creation rather than the fall—that is to say, in human nature as such rather than in human sin. Society thereby gains a measure of autonomy and intrinsic significance, though all authority remains subject to God, and Thomas assumed that Church and State would support each other.

When Thomas turns from civil society to the Church as the society of Christians, the analysis becomes more complex, and two important methodological factors preclude any description of the Church as a natural human community. First, Thomas adds to the Aristotelian structure of nature the supernatural realm. Secondly, his ecclesiology has no independent locus in his theology but is actually a part of his Christology. These two factors are closely related, for the Incarnation of Christ is conceived of as the point at which nature and supernature became joined. In his commentary on the wedding at Cana recorded in the second chapter of the Gospel according to John, Thomas says:

Mystically, the wedding-feast means the Church. . . . That marriage began in the Virgin's womb, when the Father espoused the Son to human nature in unity of person. . . . It was solemnized when the Church was joined to him by faith. . . . It will be consummated when the bride, that is, the Church, shall be brought into the bridal chamber of heavenly glory.[15]

While this text appears to suggest that the consummation is still to be achieved, the weight of Thomas's emphasis falls on the reality of the union of nature and supernature within the Virgin's womb. As Christ joined two natures indissolubly in one person, so that community which bears his name is a divine-human community. Thomas's empirical approach, applied to the Church, leads him from nature to supernature, so that the Church is recognized not as a natural human society but, by analogy with the God-man, as a divine-human society and, by analogy with the perfection of Christ, as a perfect society.

Consequently, when Thomas persists in affirming the Church as a heavenly reality which God alone knows, and when he continues to employ words like "pilgrimage" and "consummation," these no longer carry the same meaning as they had in Augustine's thought. For eschatology, which was the basis of Augustine's perspective and therefore defined the meaning of such descriptions of the Church, has become in Thomas a doctrine of the last things, which exercises no ecclesiological function. Thomas replaces eschatology as an all-embracing system of thought with an Aristotelian ontology, an hierarchical structure of being. Supernature is added to nature, the Incarnation is interpreted as the uniting of both, and in that union the Church finds its origin. The temporality which was so basic to Augustine's thought has receded into the background, and it is replaced by an emphasis on corporeality, and the preoccupation of ecclesiological thought is with the question of the Church's nature, essence, and structure rather than her historical destiny. There is no historical dichotomy to be resolved, for the Church on earth is a perfect reflection of her heavenly, supernatural reality. The teaching office guarantees the preservation of truth, while the fullness of the Church's life is bestowed here and now in the Sacraments, above all in the Eucharist, through which Christ's true body is communicated to the faithful.[16]

In Thomas, therefore, we have to reckon not with a modification of Augustinian thought on the Church but with a completely transformed frame of reference. The basis of ecclesiology is no longer eschatology but Christology, interpreted within an Aristotelian structure of being. Since eschatology is thereby relegated to an incidental role, an institution-centered understanding of the Church becomes dominant. The Church is no longer defined by its destiny as the eschatological community but by its nature as the divine-human institution, whose hierarchical form reflects the rule of God Himself, and whose resources of grace embody the fullness of the divine life. Thus the institution is sanctified, and the Augustinian note of eschatological judgment is no longer to be heard.

Thomas's understanding of the institutional Church was, of course, only one of several options, and we need to consider other influential views as well. Another writer very much preoccupied with the institutional Church was the fourteenth-century publicist **Marsilius of Padua.** Like Thomas, he was an Aristotelian, but medieval Aristotelianism was diverse in its expressions, and it is no cause for surprise that it assumed a radically different form in the thought of Marsilius. One significant difference is on the question of faith and reason. Thomas, as we have seen, was able to establish and maintain an harmonious relationship between them. The Averroist school of Aristotelian thought, on the other hand, interpreted the relationship of faith and reason more in terms of opposition, and accorded the priority to reason. Marsilius stands somewhere between the two. While he saw no essential conflict between faith and reason, he was unable to move easily between them. Accordingly, in the structure of his major work, *Defensor Pacis,* reason and revelation are not interwoven in the argument but stand alongside each other, the task of revelation being to confirm the arguments of reason. In the opening chapter he indicates clearly his intention of keeping these two approaches separate in the discourses.

In the first, I shall demonstrate my views by sure methods discovered by the human intellect, based upon propositions self-evident to every mind not corrupted by nature, custom, or perverted emotion. In the second discourse, the things which I shall believe myself to have demonstrated I shall confirm by established testimonies of the eternal truth, and by the authorities of its saintly interpreters and of other approved teachers of the Christian faith, so that this book may stand by itself, needing no external proof.[17]

The twofold and independent appeal to reason and revelation results in a dual definition of the Church. The analysis of the Church according to reason takes place within the framework of Aristotelian political analysis. It is immediately apparent how drastically Marsilius differs from Thomas, for there is no equivalent of the latter's supernatural realm, and man is understood not in terms of nature and grace but in terms of the natural ordering of his biological desires. Politics is developed out of natural necessity, and no theological or ethical criteria define in any way its goals. Its end, by analogy with the healthy animal, is "the good disposition of the city or state whereby each of its parts will be able perfectly to perform the operations belonging to it in accordance with reason and its establishment." [18] Man's fulfillment, therefore, is a worldly one, through the processes of well-ordered government. Gewirth clearly and aptly sums up the basis of Marsilian politics when he remarks that

the biological, therefore, is not merely the initial mainspring of the political realm, soon surmounted by ethical and theological values; it is rather the sufficient context which sets all the problems to whose solution politics is directly addressed, and which, moreover, also provides the essential criteria for the functioning and evaluation of political institutions.[19]

The radicalism of Marsilius' thought in the medieval context is apparent when we recognize that he is not merely asserting the autonomy of the political realm but expounding a unified view of the world equally as inclusive as that of the Papacy, but one in which the structural order of papal power is decisively reversed and supremacy is accorded to the "human legislator" rather than the Papacy. Accordingly, while theological criteria are eliminated from politics in the first discourse, the Church as an institution is not. Indeed, it functions as an integral part of the political organism in helping to advance the goal of peace. Priesthood is established "for the worship and honoring of God, and for the benefit resulting therefrom for the status of the present or the future world." Religious laws make it possible to ensure "the goodness of human acts, both individual and civil, on which depend almost completely the quiet or tranquillity of communities and finally the sufficient life in the present world." [20]

Marsilius' preoccupation here is clearly not the truth of religion but its utilitarian value for society, and it is understandable, therefore, that he has been portrayed as a thoroughgoing cynic, condoning the use of religion as a tool for manipulating man in society. To advance such a claim, however, is to neglect his understanding of revelation and, therefore, to misinterpret him altogether. For Marsilius, though a staunch critic of the Papacy, is a churchman who regards the Christian religion as the result not of human invention but of divine revelation. If reason indicates that belief in God and the future life is socially and politically useful, faith knows it to be eternal truth. It is important to recognize that, while the politicizing of the institutional Church is often assumed to be Marsilius' chief aim, he evinces no special enthusiasm for this point of view and even introduces it by the literary device of posing as a reporter for the views of another; whereas when he approaches the subject of the Church as a reality of revelation, he adopts an argumentative stance, as if to indicate that he is dealing with something far more important to him than the recognition of the civic function of religion.

The "truest and most fitting" description of the Church, according to revelation, is "the whole body of the faithful who believe in and invoke the name of Christ, and all the parts of this whole body in any community." [21] The Church is intrinsically a spiritual reality, and believers are connected by the ties of a common faith and by common participation in the sacramental life.

The description of the Church as the body of the faithful is in itself neither novel nor radical since it was a common definition of the time and had been used even by Thomas.[22] In the tradition, however, the term had no content apart from the hierarchical, institutional Church, but functioned as an alternate description of it. In no way did it indicate any questioning of the indispensability of such a visibly ordered body. Marsilius, however, openly denied the absolute necessity of the institutional order, and therefore his description of the Church as the "body of the faithful" has no essential institutional connection. Thus, while his description of the Church according to revelation is not antireligious in any way, it is equally inimical to the assumptions behind papal power as is his description of the Church according to reason. There is no coercive authority vested in the priestly hierarchy, and Church authority is located in the residual power of the congregation. It is the faithful who ultimately control the Church in the same way that the citizen body ultimately controls society. The power of the congregation is exercised over excommunication, election of priests, bishops, and even Pope, and over the definition of articles of faith through the elected General Council, which most fully represents the whole body.[23]

The parallel between Church and State is not a complete one. For, while the State, having received its authority from the body of citizens, exercises a coercive power upon that citizen body, the Church is restricted to teaching and sacramental functions and denied such coercive power. There is hierarchical inequality within the Church, but that is a matter of human decision and not of divine necessity.

What, then, is the relationship of this community of faith to the institution which functions within the structure of the

State? Marsilius' stated intention of using revelation to confirm reason seems to indicate that he intended to speak not of two churches but of one church seen in different ways. There is no reason to doubt that he saw the community of citizens and the community of the faithful as coextensive realities. But at this point his thought becomes highly problematical, for he fails to follow through his methodological intentions. The Church defined by revelation does not confirm the Church defined by reason. Rather, it stands beside it, with no self-evident connection between the two. Any attempt to articulate this relationship becomes in some degree a matter of conjecture, but some general, if tentative, conclusions may be drawn. First, the fact that his arguments from reason and revelation respectively have no positive relation to each other means that he cannot finally avoid a dichotomy in his description of the Church. On the one hand is the Church according to reason, which acts as a subordinate arm of the State for the attainment of secular goals and, on the other hand, the Church according to revelation, which concerns itself with faith and salvation.

Secondly, any possibility that the latter could function analogously to Augustine's "city of God" in radical tension with the sacerdotal institution is ruled out. Although Marsilius speaks of the community of faith as a body distinct from the world and characterized by the negation of all secular values,[24] the secularistic ground plan of his thought is unable to accommodate an eschatological outlook like that of Augustine. There is no sense of man participating in a divine drama in history. Faith and salvation in Marsilius is finally reduced to a legal and cultic system. "Christ," he declares, in describing the salvation of man,

handed down the evangelical law, containing commands and counsels of what must be believed, done, and avoided. By observance of these, not only are men preserved from sensory punishment . . . but also through God's gracious ordainment they merit, by a certain congruity, eternal happi-

ness. And for this reason the evangelical law is called the law of grace, both because through the passion and death of Christ the human race was redeemed from its guilt and from the penalty of losing eternal beatitude which it had incurred as the result of the fall or sin of its first parents; and also because, by observing this law and receiving the sacraments established with it and in it, we are given divine grace, after it is given it is strengthened in us, and when we lose it it is restored to us. Through this grace, by the ordainment of God and the passion of Christ, our works come by a certain congruity (as we have said) to merit eternal happiness.[25]

The recurrence of traditional Christological and soteriological phrases within this passage cannot disguise the fact that when Marsilius speaks of grace, it is understood not as a transcendent mystery pervading the Church's life but as the natural result of proper observance of the law and cult of the Church. The horizons of his outlook never transcend this basically empirical, secularistic context, and in that respect he differs radically from Thomas.

Yet it is most interesting to observe that, in terms of the problem which we have posed, the ultimate result of Marsilius' position is not very different from that of Thomas. In the discussion of Thomas, it was noted that, despite his preoccupation with the supernatural, the loss of the Augustinian eschatological perspective resulted in a thoroughgoing identification of the Church with its visible, institutional expression. Marsilius, for all his clear differences from Thomas, finally achieves the same result, and for the same reason, the discarding of eschatology as a decisive element. Therefore, though he describes the community as being ordered "toward the best life of the future world," [26] this concept is purely formal and has lost its dynamism, for the community of faith is no longer the eschatological community on pilgrimage toward its goal. It is no longer defined by its origin in the mystery of grace or by its transcendent destiny beyond history but by its empirical character as a body observing the law of Christ.

The Marsilian distinction between the community of faith and the ecclesiastical institution, therefore, is a weapon of attack against aspects of the ecclesiastical institution—specifically, against papal power—but in no way does it represent a radical criticism of the institutional Church as such. It bears no resemblance to the Augustinian dialectic of the "city of God" and the Catholic Church. The dynamic, eschatological perspective is as absent from Marsilius as from Thomas, and though the secularism of the former seems diametrically opposed to the supernaturalism of the latter, both finally identify the reality of the Church completely with the visible institution.

During the late fourteenth and early fifteenth centuries, concern over the institutional Church took on an added dimension, at the time of the Great Schism (1378–1417). This concern was to an extent a very practical response to a desperate situation, yet the Conciliar theory which came into full flower at the time of the schism was more than a reaction to an immediate crisis; it represented the fruition of a couple of centuries of scholarly preoccupation with the problem of the institutional Church.

Recent scholarship has provided an important corrective to the view that Conciliar thought derived chiefly from Marsilius and William of Ockham, and it has stressed the importance of the Church's rich traditions of canon law in the formation of Conciliar ideas.[27] Much of the attention of the earlier canonists was directed toward the problem of the relationship of spiritual and temporal power. From the time of John of Paris, however, increasing attention was given to the internal structure of the Church, and the most important aspect of this development was the application of corporation law to Church government. Corporation theory was first employed in relation to the individual Church, and its revolutionary potential did not become clear until it was applied to the Church as a whole. Hostiensis had asserted that the head of a corporation has more authority than any one member, but not more than the whole body together. John of Paris made use of such well-accepted tenets of canon law theory and combined them in such an original way that he posed a serious threat to papal authority. He located authority in the Church as a whole and interpreted the Pope as a *dispensator*, who derives his authority from God and from the people.

These ideas were increasingly used within the Church by individuals and groups to justify their own interests against the Papacy, and the theories attained a measure of greater sophistication in the thought of Cardinal Zabarella, who developed a consistent view of Christendom as a corporation presided over by the Pope, who normally exercises the power inherent in the Church, but who derives that authority from the consent of the congregation of the faithful. Canon law, therefore, was decidedly two-sided in its impact. It lay behind not only the development of an elaborate doctrine of papal supremacy but also the beginnings of a constitutional view of Church government which bore fruit in the Conciliar movement of the late fourteenth and early fifteenth centuries.

The Conciliar movement posed a serious threat to the papal understanding of authority in the Church. The struggle for power which developed out of the situation of the Great Schism was motivated in many cases by a genuine pastoral concern and a fear that the schism had placed in jeopardy the soteriological function of the Church. It is our task here to ask whether this movement offered in any significant way a fresh approach to the understanding of the Church itself.

The most significant propagandist of the Conciliar movement was the German curial official **Dietrich of Niem,** whose treatise *De Modis Uniendi Ac Reformandi Ecclesiam,*[28] sheds some important light on this question. Dietrich makes a distinction, which bears a superficial resemblance to that of Augustine, between the "universal Church" and the "apostolic Church." The former is headed solely by Christ and is made up of members of all nations, classes, and cultures; and within this Church Pope, Cardinals, prelates, clerics, kings, princes, and commoners occupy their various positions. This Church cannot err, or suffer schism or heresy. Within it repose the means of salvation, which maintain their power even without a Pope, since the sacramental life flows from Christ the Head to the faithful, and not by hierarchical guarantee. Unity of faith is the fundamental reality of the universal Church, and the hierarchical order which exists within it is contingent and not absolute.[29]

The "apostolic Church" is found within the universal Church and consists of the Roman ecclesiastical hierarchy. Headed by the Pope, it is subject to error, schism, and heresy. It functions as the operative arm of the universal Church and exercises only that authority which is delegated by the universal Church through its General Council. That is to say, the universal Church is related to the apostolic Church as genus to species, as the source of authority to its executive arm. By implication Pope and hierarchy are ultimately dispensable.[30]

While Dietrich's point of view involves radical implications for the structuring of ecclesiastical authority, it is clear that this distinction which he articulates bears no strong resemblance to Augustinian thought. He is not speaking of the mystical community of the elect over against the visible institution, for such a distinction is entirely foreign to his way of thinking. Moreover, we must not be misled by Dietrich's emphasis on the Lordship of Christ and on the direction of the Holy Spirit into thinking that he thereby places the ecclesiastical institution under radical judgment. For in fact the opposite is the case—both the Lordship of Christ and the activity of the Holy Spirit are thoroughly institutionalized. Not only is the Council vested with supreme powers, beyond which

there is no appeal, but we are informed that the acts of the
Council are "like the Gospels of Christ which admit of no
dispensation and over which the Pope has no jurisdiction,"
and that its orders and decisions are "made by the Holy
Spirit." [31] Here Dietrich reflects the secularized empiricism of
Marsilius, for the eschatological dimension is entirely absent,
and in no sense is the institution placed under judgment.

While there is a dramatic shift in the role of the Papacy,
therefore, there is no basic change in the understanding of the
Church and its institutional embodiment. The Conciliarists'
failure, theologically, is that they had no distinctive ecclesiology. Dietrich's distinction between the universal Church
and the apostolic Church amounts finally to a rationale for
undercutting papal authority in favor of the Council. The
movement as a whole, however highly motivated, was in the
last analysis a struggle for power within a substantially similar
ecclesiological framework. The Papacy regarded itself and its
institutional structures as the immanent embodiment of the
Lordship of Christ and the authority of the Spirit, and it
thereby exempted its institutional life from transcendent judgment. Dietrich's intention is to reverse the roles of Papacy and
Council. His concern is not with the nature of the Church; it
is with the priority of authority and power within the institution. For him, the Council embodies the truth as surely and
unambiguously as the Papacy conceived itself to do.

That Conciliarists like Dietrich had no basic ecclesiological
argument with the Papacy finds some confirmation in the fact
that those at the Council of Constance who were leaders in
the Conciliar cause were the very ones who carried through the
prosecution and trial of John Hus so vehemently. Contemporary accounts of the Council indicate no interest in de-
bating the ecclesiological issues raised by Hus and no inclination toward accepting his criticism of the papal Church. The
question was not whether he ought to be condemned, but who
exactly ought to declare his condemnation.[32]

Dietrich and the other Conciliarists were interested in renovating and changing the structure and government of the sacerdotal institution, not in questioning its basis. If Dietrich rejects both the present structures of papal power and Marsilius' politicizing of the Church, he nevertheless reflects to perfection in his ecclesiology the same "immanental" viewpoint which we have already observed in figures as diverse as Thomas Aquinas and Marsilius of Padua. Common to all is the loss of the dynamic Augustinian eschatology, which leads in each case to a thoroughgoing identification of the Church with its institutional form. The Augustinian tension between the Catholic Church and the city of God, between what is now and what is to be, is nowhere present. Accordingly, while there can be specific criticisms of aspects of institutional life, there can be no radical criticism of the institution as such. For the institutional Church now stands in the very center of ecclesiology, beyond the judgment of a transcendent norm.

3
THE INSTITUTION UNDER FIRE
JOACHIM OF FLORIS, JOHN WYCLIF, JOHN HUS

If the predominant trend of medieval ecclesiology was toward a loss of eschatological perspective and an increasing tendency to absolutize the institutional Church, this did not develop without protest. The eschatological impulse found frequent and diverse expression throughout the period in such a way as to call radically into question the trend toward an institution-centered ecclesiology.

An important expression of this protest came through the writings of *Joachim of Floris* (1131–1202), a Calabrian monk who was born almost a century before Thomas Aquinas. Although his work was largely disregarded in his own time, the extent of its influence on subsequent Western thought is yet to be adequately measured and is certainly substantial.[33] While we lack a critical edition of his works and do not know how much of what we have represents later interpolation, the significance of his basic thought for the question of ecclesiology is relatively clear.

Joachim is important not just because he revived the eschatological impulse but because he wove it into a consistent pattern of thought, a trinitarian structure of the succession of the ages. History is seen as a progressive self-manifestation of the divine Trinity. The age of the Father was the Old Testament period; the age of the Son was the period extending from the New Testament into the present time of the Church. But this age, Joachim believed, would in turn yield to the coming age of the Spirit, a new epoch in which the Eternal Gospel would make obsolete what had gone before (including the revelations of Old and New Testaments), and bring mankind to full enlightenment.

The three ages are based, respectively, on Law, Grace, and Love in the Spirit, and the characteristic representatives of each are, respectively, the married man, the cleric, and the monk. Joachim conceives of an overlap between the ages, so that the third age is seen as already present in foretaste in the figure of Saint Benedict. The Church of the monks is already being formed in the midst of the Church of the clerics.[34]

Joachim was more preoccupied with his theories than with concrete criticism of the contemporary Church, and his work was little noticed in his own time. Nevertheless, the implications of his views for the doctrine of the Church were profound. Within the tradition of the Church, the "eternal Gospel" was the faith committed by Christ to the Church, whose task it was to continue and to guard that Gospel on earth as Christ's representative, until the end of time. By contrast, Joachim's understanding of the eternal Gospel points to the age to come, and the implication is that the present Church which began with Christ is not an everlasting foundation but a passing phase in the history of salvation, an imperfect prefiguration of the Church of the future. Papacy, hierarchy, preaching, sacraments, and the whole mediatorial role of the institution of salvation are confined to the second epoch, for when the age of the Spirit dawns, man will know the eternal Gospel by direct vision with no need of any mediator. Saint Peter will yield to Saint John the Evangelist and the bishops to the new order of "spiritual men."

The effect of Joachim's eschatological perspective, therefore, is to undercut the role of the institutional Church from the far side, by a vision of the future. Because the age of the Spirit is coming, in which the present institutional structure will have no place, the claim of the institution to be the embodiment of salvation for all time is radically denied.

To say that Joachim revived the eschatological impulse is, of course, not to suggest that he reasserts Augustinian thought as such. On the contrary, his view of constant progress and re-creation is essentially utopian in character and a far cry from Augustine's theology of the two cities. What Joachim and Augustine have in common is simply the formal tendency to think eschatologically, and therefore, by implication, to deny absolute validity to the present institution.

The revolutionary implications of Joachim's thought were taken over by others, who applied his prophecies directly to their own time and stressed the imminence of the third age in a way which Joachim had not done. In 1254 there appeared a work by Gerard of Borgo San Donnino entitled *Introduction to the Eternal Gospel,* in which the author calculated that the age of the Spirit would dawn in six years, in the year 1260. While this viewpoint stirred immediate reaction and was swiftly condemned, the Joachimite impulse became the dominant drive behind the Spiritual Franciscans, or *fraticelli,* who identified Saint Francis as the *novus dux* of the third age and Joachim as his "John the Baptist" who heralded his coming. Moreover, they regarded themselves as heirs to the spiritual functions formerly exercised by the Papal hierarchy and strove to return to apostolic simplicity. They attempted to put into practice the third age of Joachim, living in poverty and humility, hoping thereby to transform the Church into a community of the Spirit, without Pope, hierarchy, Scripture, sacraments, or theology.

The movement was finally quelled by the Roman Church and its theologians, led by Thomas and Bonaventura, who affirmed that the Church as an institution of salvation would endure until the second coming of Christ. The impulse of protest endured, however, and emerged again in different ways in the various sectarian movements of the later Middle Ages.

If the role of the institutional Church as the embodiment of salvation was implicitly undercut by Joachimite theology from the "far side," it was equally threatened from the "near side" by another tendency, through which the doctrine of predestination became once more the key to understanding the Church. That is to say, Joachimite theology called the institution into question by a perspective of the future which looked beyond it to the age of the Spirit, while the predestinarian ecclesiologies called it into question by a perspective of the past, searching behind it to a recognition of the secret and eternal will of God. This latter tendency is seen in its most pronounced form in the writings of John Wyclif (1328–1384) and John Hus (1369–1415), both of whom depart from the general medieval pattern and treat the doctrine of the Church as a direct and specific theological issue. While it will not be possible in this introductory essay to treat their ecclesiologies comprehensively, we shall attempt to discern the nature of their protest against the prevailing patterns of medieval ecclesiology and their effectiveness in offering a viable option.

John Wyclif [35] not only directly attacks the abuses in the life of the Church but explicitly rejects the papal claim to primacy, on the basis of Scripture. Even more basic, however,

than his use of the scriptural norm is the way in which he re-
defines the Church so as to shift the whole discussion away
from the sacerdotal institution.

*When people speak of holy Church, they understand there-
by prelates and priests, monks and canons and friars, and all
men that have crowns,[36] though they live never so cursedly
against God's law, and call not nor hold secular men to be of
holy Church, though they live never so faithfully after God's
law and die in perfect charity. But nevertheless, all that will
one day be blessed in heaven are members of holy Church,
and no more.[37]*

By the last phrase—"all that will one day be blessed in
heaven"—Wyclif intends to indicate very clearly that membership is not by human choice or institutional affiliation but by
divine predestination. The Church is the whole body of the
faithful who are predestined by God (*universitas fidelium pre-
destinatorum*).[38] It has three parts, the angels and the blessed
triumphant in heaven, the saints sleeping in purgatory, and
the Church militant on earth.[39]

When he speaks of the Church of the predestinate, Wyclif
quotes Augustine freely, and indeed the resemblance of his
thought to that of the Latin father is at points striking. He
suggests at times a concept which is close to Augustine's understanding of the "two cities," though it does not play such a
central role in his thought. Over against the community of the
predestined, he speaks of the "foreknown" or the reprobate as
"a body of which the Devil is head." [40] While the two communities will be finally separated at the last judgment, in the
present age they are radically mixed together. There are tares
among the wheat, those who are in the Church but not of it
and who, like excrescences in the human body, are destined to
be finally purged from it.[41] Since predestination is God's pre-
rogative, the elect are known only to Him, and no man can distinguish the wheat from the tares. Nor can he assert his own

election with certainty, even if he be Pope—he can only believe it by faith.

Despite his obvious dependence on Augustine, Wyclif ties
his concept of the body of the predestined to Christology more
than Augustine ever did. Christ alone is Head of the predestined, extrinsically in his divinity, intrinsically in his humanity. His marriage to the Church was predestined from all
eternity. The Incarnation represents the "second nuptials," and
the marriage will finally be consummated at the last advent,
when the Church will be crowned queen.[42] The Pope does not
even know if he is of the elect, and to call him Head of the
Church would be to make the Church into a two-headed mon-
ster when, rightly speaking, Christ is its only true Head. The
Pope may be regarded as head of the particular Church in
Rome, but even then only insofar as he conforms to Christ.

Christology informs ecclesiology at an even deeper level than
the affirmation of Christ's headship, for Wyclif sees the humanity of Christ as the form and organic principle of the
Church's life. The Incarnation of the humble Christ is the
reversal of Adam's pride, and his life and teaching represent
the pattern to which the Christian's own life should conform.
This pattern is in strong contrast to the concern for worldly
splendor which characterizes the lives of prelates and priests.
Accordingly, Wyclif regards the Constantinian settlement as a
disastrous day for the Church, since it turned away from the
pattern of Christ, whose poverty and humility represent the
only true pattern for the Christian to emulate.[43]

Wyclif, therefore, represents more than a protest against
ecclesiastical corruption. His ecclesiology is a reappropriation
of the Augustinian emphasis on the Church as an invisible
community of the predestinate on pilgrimage to its eschatological goal. However, the predestinarian emphasis is not qualified, as in Augustine, by an emphasis on the hierarchical institution of salvation which brings the promises of the future into the present. Both the predestinarian emphasis and the vision

of the humility of Christ stand radically opposed to the institution. Wyclif, therefore, runs directly counter to what we have described as the "immanental" outlook of medieval ecclesiology. The Church defines itself not by its institutional expressions but by God's gracious election and the vision of Christ's humility.

Despite the possibilities inherent in this view for a fresh and creative approach to the Church and its institutional life, Wyclif is unable to follow through these possibilities, and his failure can be seen at two specific points. First, having eliminated the institutional test for membership in the Church of the elect, he tends to set up in its place a moral test—conformity to divine precepts—so that the elect may be identified as those who achieve a certain quality of life rather than those who participate in the ecclesiastical institution. The definition is different, but the effect is the same: divine election loses its transcendent character and becomes increasingly a matter of human determination.[44]

More serious is the fact that, despite some evidence of a sense of the corporate nature of faith, especially in his doctrine of the Eucharist, the understanding of the Church which finally emerges from his works is strongly individualistic. So pessimistic is he over the visible Church as the "pretending Church," and so concerned is he to deny the necessity of priestly mediation, that the understanding of salvation which he articulates tends to focus on the individual rather than on the body of the faithful. Liberation from sacerdotalism, which might have brought him to a fresh apprehension of the Christian community as the locus of the life of salvation, led him rather to emphasize the free access of the individual to God.[45]

John Hus, the Bohemian reformer who met his death at the Council of Constance, was deeply influenced by Wyclif's teaching, and stands to some extent within the same tradition. He deserves consideration in his own right, however, for he was by no means a mere echo of the English reformer, as

Johann Loserth asserted in the last century.[46] Hus used Wyclif's thought always in a free and critical manner and probably owed less ultimately to him than to the native Czech reform tradition.[47]

Hus, like Wyclif, relies heavily in his arguments on quotation from Augustine, and in his work, the Augustinian eschatology once more finds powerful expression.[48] The Church is described as the "totality of the predestinate," and this predestination is seen as the sole ground of the Church's life.

Every one who is predestined is one of her members, and consequently a part of this Church which is Christ's mystical body, that is, hidden body, ruled by the power and influence of Christ the Head, and compacted and welded together by the bond of predestination.[49]

Hus employs the Biblical images of the wheat and tares and the dragnet to indicate that the Church on earth is a radically mixed body of the elect and the foreknown. While affirming that the identity of the elect is known only to God, he follows Wyclif in introducing a moral test, so that life in conformity with God's laws makes possible a qualified inference of membership among the elect.

Hus is as uncompromising as Wyclif in affirming the sole Headship of Christ over the body of the Church, from all eternity outwardly and, since the Incarnation, inwardly.[50] Christ is the Church's true foundation and the apostles can be described as foundations only so far as they point toward faith in him.

At two points in particular, Hus goes beyond Wyclif. First, he uses the concept of predestination not only to look backward to the eternal will of God but to point forward to the fulfillment of that will. While this is not entirely absent in Wyclif, Hus lays greater stress on the fact that the Church is always "becoming." The Church is the virgin Bride of Christ who has fornicated with the Devil yet is destined to become

finally a chaste virgin by the grace of adoption.[51] By interpreting predestination in this dynamic way, he provides a two-
pronged attack against any tendency to identify the reality
of the Church with the present institution. No only is the
Church the company of the elect known only to God, but this
community has no resting place; it is constantly pressing forward toward the destiny to which it has been called. The resemblance of Hus's "Church of the elect" to Augustine's "city
of God" is clear and striking.

Hus goes beyond Wyclif also in his stress on the scriptural
norm. Every Christian, he said,

*is expected to believe explicitly and implicitly all the truth
which the Holy Spirit has put in Scripture, and in this way
a man is not bound to believe the sayings of the saints which
are apart from Scripture, nor should he believe Papal bulls,
except in so far as they speak out of Scripture, or in so far
as what they say is founded in Scripture simply.*[52]

Scripture, therefore, becomes the touchstone by which every
pronouncement of saints, fathers, and Popes is to be judged.
In his use of Scripture, Hus generally avoids the proof-texting
methods common among his predecessors and, in asserting the
scriptural norm over Christian life and doctrine, he forshadows
the work of the Reformation theologians.

Unfortunately, Hus's stern attack on the papal institution is
not matched by any positive achievement in clarifying the
role of the Church as a visible body in the world. He is almost
exclusively preoccupied with the Church of the elect and says
little of the visible Church beyond recognizing it as a mixed
body. While he is not as individualistic in orientation as Wyclif,
the end result of his ecclesiology is that the eschatological impulse which he, like Wyclif, appropriated from Augustine
tends to swallow up or eclipse the institutional Church rather
than to provide a perspective from which positive renewal
might be forthcoming.

4
THE LEGACY

These brief studies in the medieval ecclesiological tradition have indicated above all the crucial importance of the eschatological motif. When this is dominant, the institutional Church remains under transcendent judgment; when it is lost or subdued, the institution tends to be absolutized.

It was the latter tendency which became dominant as the medieval period unfolded. The loss of the eschatological perspective permitted Thomas Aquinas to describe the Church as a supernatural reality, reflecting perfectly in its earthly form the supernatural world, dispensing rather than standing under judgment, developing not by repentance and renewal but by the natural growth of its immanent life. In Thomas, the *eschaton* stands not over against the Church but in the Church; the institution is no longer an earthen, but a heavenly vessel. In the case of Marsilius and Dietrich, where a secularistic rather than a supernatural reference prevailed, we noted that the result was finally the same—an unambiguous identification of the *ecclesia* with the visible institution. Eschatology no longer exercised its critical judgment over the Church's institutional life.

On the other hand, while the note of transcendent judgment is sounded in the apocalypticism of Joachim and the predestinarianism of Wyclif and Hus, its potential is dissipated because it leads to a rejection of the visible institution rather than to its creative renewal as an eschatological community.

The ecclesiological legacy of the Middle Ages is clearly one of unsolved problems, but the issue which Augustine had implicitly raised is no less genuine or important because of its inadequate treatment by the medieval theologians. For what is at stake in the Augustinian dialectic of "city of God" and "Catholic Church" is really the fundamental problem of the Christian Church in every age—the need for the Church to be a visible community in the world without regarding itself as the Kingdom of God, to have concrete and particular forms without absolutizing them, to be a renewing force in the world yet always open to renewal, and to be at once worldly and transcendent.

The unfinished business of one generation is always high on the agenda of the succeeding generations, and this case is no exception. The doctrine of the Church, far from being a peripheral concern, is one of the most critical issues in the Reformation controversy, and the Reformation as a theological event is not an individualistic protest against churchly Christianity but a struggle between two opposing understandings of the Church.[53]

While the unresolved problems of the Middle Ages provided the Reformers with many key issues, their ecclesiology represented far more than a mere footnote to the medieval debate, for it involved a thoroughgoing reconsideration of the Church on a theological basis. The two principal foci of this reinterpretation are eschatology and Christology. Eschatology is as basic for their doctrines of the Church as it was for the medieval theologians, but this point of formal continuity with the medieval tradition became their most important point of departure from it. Their preference for an historical rather than a metaphysical mode of thought, and above all their rediscovery of the Biblical understanding of the living God, active in creation and history, made eschatology once more a matter of immediate relevance for the life of the world, and therefore for the Church.

What made their ecclesiology more than a return to Augustinianism was their reinterpretation of the Church on the basis of Christology—not the Christology of Aristotelian metaphysics, or even that of the traditional Catholic creeds, but a Christology more "existential" in orientation, deeply dependent on Biblical imagery, and pointing to a dynamic and personal relationship between Christ and his people as the foundation of the Church's life.

Martin Luther, John Calvin, and Menno Simons deserve special consideration because each represents an important and distinctive type of response to the issue before us. Anything which may be said of their common achievement must await a full consideration of each in his own right.

II · MARTIN LUTHER

MARTIN LUTHER must be reckoned by any reasonable measure as one of the epoch-making figures of world history—yet there was nothing in his upbringing and early life to indicate such a prodigious future. Born of peasant stock in a small and unimportant town, nurtured within the narrow and shadowy confines of popular folk-religion, and oblivious to the expanding horizons of the world of culture and learning, he seemed destined for anonymity rather than fame. Nevertheless, he showed from an early age unmistakable signs of academic promise, and his ambitious father saw to it that he had every chance of advancement.

The story of his progress to maturity—his philosophical studies in the Nominalist tradition, his plans for a career in law, cut short by his entry into the Augustinian monastery, the long and painful struggle for faith leading finally to his emergence as a reformer—all this is so well known as to need no repetition here. Suffice it to say that in the mature Luther, as Gerhard Ritter notes,[1] there was a unique conjuction of the man of action and the deep thinker, the impassioned prophet riding on the waves of popular unrest and the profound religious genius whose own inward struggles touched a sensitive nerve in the depths of the German spirit.

The man and the occasion, in fact, were admirably matched. For Germany in the early sixteenth century was a country marked by sharp contrasts and standing at the crossroads. Signs of hope and renewal were evident on every hand. The economy was buoyant and prosperous; trade, industry, and towns were expanding; and cultural life was flourishing under the impact of the Renaissance after 1450. Erasmus voiced a common sentiment when he hailed his own time as the dawning of man's greatest age. The world, he declared, was at last coming to its senses, as if awakening from a deep sleep, shedding its ignorance, and entering into maturity.[2]

Signs of renewal were evident also in the Church, above all in a singular flowering of popular piety; and if this movement was in some of its manifestations motivated by fear and despair and preoccupied with externals, it showed at its best a thoroughly healthy trend toward a more genuinely spiritual and inward apprehension of Christian faith. The spirit of the "new devotion" found expression in the writings of Tauler, and of the *Theologica Germanica,* and in the art of Dürer and Grünewald, and one who drank deeply from this source was the young Luther himself.

If German religious life was characterized by a fundamental strength and vitality, the same cannot be said of the Roman Papacy, despite its outward splendor. After centuries of conflict with emperors and kings and the more recent internal struggles of the Conciliar period, the Papacy had emerged from battle apparently strong and triumphant. Yet it was, after all, a hollow triumph. The Popes had recognized frankly the strength of the rising national monarchies, and had taken the course of dealing with them individually by negotiation and concordat. It was an expedient course of action but also a dangerous one, for it had obliged the Papacy to become increasingly a genuine monarchical state, in a manner which threatened the credibility of its spiritual authority, created political enemies, and brought with it the necessity of developing a system of administration and taxation to match its new political position. Those forces which might have brought urgently needed reform to the Church had been rendered powerless, and in any case any meaningful reform would have struck precisely at those points on which the Papacy rested its power. As abuses and taxes multiplied, it was hardly surprising that the late fifteenth century and early sixteenth century saw the development of intense resentment against Rome, especially in Germany.

Strong as this anti-Roman feeling undoubtedly was in Germany before the Reformation, there were deeper currents of thought at work in society and in the Church and, most notably, an upsurge of apocalyptic fervor. The apocalyptic tradition in medieval thought had never enjoyed official approval, but it was no less strong on that account, and though its impact varied from place to place and from time to time, it had remained a factor of considerable influence throughout the later Middle Ages. We have had occasion to consider already the work of some of the more notable exponents of the apocalyptic tradition—Wyclif and Hus, who introduced the theme of the Antichrist into theological discussion in a very powerful way, and Joachim of Floris, whose prophecy of the age of the Spirit called into question the whole present order. Their influence was far more than that of a passing episode. Wyclif and Hus both left behind them devoted bands of followers who carried on their work, while Joachim's influence continued to be felt, especially among the Spiritual Franciscans who applied his prophecies directly to social, political, and religious life.[3]

Nor was this apocalyptic thought confined in its influence to theological speculation. Some classes had been left behind by the rapid social and economic expansion of Germany, most notably the peasants, who still numbered some three-quarters of the total population. Norman Cohn has shown in his study of medieval apocalyptic thought [4] how it was precisely in such times of rapid expansion that the bewilderment and anxiety of those dislocated by social change provided fertile soil for apocalyptic and spiritualistic ideas to take root and to flower. In the latter part of the fifteenth century, there were numerous peasant risings of an apocalyptic character in Germany, among them the celebrated people's crusade of Hans Böhm, the drummer of Niklashausen, only seven years before Luther's birth. This feeling of apocalyptic excitement was rarely absent in the late fifteenth and early sixteenth centuries, and it was only intensified by the entry of the Turks into the European orbit, with their capture of Constantinople in 1453 and the subsequent advance westwards. By 1529, they had penetrated as far west as the gates of Vienna, and they remained a direct and continuing threat to European security throughout the time of Luther's reform. There were many, moreover, who saw in the Turkish menace a deeper symbolic meaning, as a clear sign of the advent of the last days and of God's impending judgment on Christendom.

1
THEOLOGICAL FOUNDATIONS: THE PATTERN OF DIALECTIC

As a child of this world, Luther was open to its manifold influences, yet he was never wholly governed by any of them. He was deeply appreciative of the linguistic work of the humanist scholars, especially of their provision of Biblical texts in the original languages, and he shared their concern for a return to the sources, but he remained almost entirely unaffected by humanist presuppositions and intellectual notions. By training, he stood squarely in the intellectual tradition of late medieval Nominalism, and he derived from that tradition many of his basic perspectives and preoccupations; yet he came through his inward struggle for faith to repudiate some of the central Nominalist doctrines. He was profoundly influenced by the spirit of the "new devotion" in its German manifestations, but at no time was he wholly under its spell. His mind, in short, was far more than a mirror of external events and currents of thought. It was a profoundly creative mind and, when all the influences upon it have been discerned, its character remains authentically his own.

The distinctiveness of Luther's thought inheres in its dialectical character. That is to say, it proceeds by means of the bringing together of opposites into a meaningful unity. The significance of this basic pattern is best understood not by abstract definition and analysis but by observation of its actual impact on the structure and content of his theological exposition.

ESCHATOLOGICAL DIALECTIC: THE WORLD. One of Luther's key dialectical images is his doctrine of the *two kingdoms,* which he employs in a direct way chiefly in his discussion of the relevance of the Christian ethic in the world and in his interpretation of the relationship of church and state. The doctrine is implicit in his whole theological outlook, however, and an understanding of it provides an important clue to the meaning of his eschatology.[5]

The dualistic terminology of the doctrine of the two kingdoms is reminiscent of the long medieval battle between the Papacy and the secular rulers over the relationship of the two swords of spiritual and temporal power and, indeed, of Augustine's distinction between the two cities. While recognizing such influences on the formation of this distinction in Luther's thought, however, our chief concern must be not its historical pedigree but the significance which it takes on within the pattern of his own theology.

Luther's fullest treatment of the concept is found in his

treatise of 1523, *Temporal Authority: To What Extent It Should Be Obeyed,* where, over the course of several pages, he maintains the necessity of the distinction between the two kingdoms in the following manner:

. . . we must divide the children of Adam and all mankind into two classes, the first belonging to the kingdom of God, the second to the kingdom of the world. Those who belong to the kingdom of God are all the true believers who are in Christ and under Christ, for Christ is King and Lord in the kingdom of God. . . . All who are not Christians belong to the kingdom of the world and are under the law. . . . If this were not so, men would devour one another, seeing that the whole world is evil and that among thousands there is hardly a single true Christian. . . . For this reason, God has ordained two governments: the spiritual, by which the Holy Spirit produces Christians and righteous people under Christ; and the temporal which restrains the un-Christian and wicked so that— no thanks to them—they are obliged to keep still and to maintain an outward peace. . . . Both must be permitted to remain; the one to produce righteousness, the other to bring about external peace and prevent evil deeds. Neither one is sufficient in the world without the other.[6]

While Luther's terminology is not identical with Augustine's, the similarity between their viewpoints is at times striking. The two communities into which the human race is divided are distinguished by different principles of loyalty. Augustine contrasts *amor dei* with *amor sui,* while Luther separates them in terms of belief or nonbelief in Christ as king and Lord. The two communities are recognized as being necessary to each other, but are distinguished sharply in terms of their functions, and any attempt to confuse them is regarded by Luther as evidence of the work of the Devil himself, who is constantly "cooking and brewing these two kingdoms into each other." [7]

God's kingdom is a kingdom of grace and mercy, not of wrath and punishment. . . . But the kingdom of the world is a king-

*dom of wrath and severity. . . . Now he who would confuse
these two kingdoms—as our false fanatics do—would put
wrath into God's kingdom and mercy into the world's kingdom; and that is the same as putting the devil in heaven and
God in hell.*[8]

Luther's determination to keep the two kingdoms sharply
separated, and his description of the functions of the worldly
kingdom in predominantly negative terms, should not lead us
to believe that he deprived the worldly realm of its positive
significance. Indeed, in his exposition of Psalm 101, he pictures
the worldly kingdom as a kind of parable of the spiritual kingdom, a "symbol of true salvation and of His kingdom of
Heaven, like a pantomime or a mask." [9] In his treatise *Whether
Soldiers, Too, Can Be Saved,* he points out that the worldly
realm, like the spiritual, is established by God and serves His
purposes. Its weapon is the sword, rather than the Word, and
its goal temporal blessing rather than everlasting life; yet it
is, like the spiritual realm, "a divine thing entirely." [10]

But what is the relationship of the Christian, made righteous
by faith, to this divinely willed world order? At this point,
Luther appears to give a number of different answers which
cannot easily be reconciled. In the treatise *On Worldly
Authority,* Luther suggests that the life of the Christian is such
that he has no need of worldly authority.

*If all the world were composed of real Christians, that is,
true believers, there would be no need for or benefits from
prince, king, lord, sword or law. They would serve no purpose,
since Christians have in their hearts the Holy Spirit, who both
teaches and makes them to do injustice to no one, to love
everyone, and to suffer injustice and even death willingly and
cheerfully at the hands of anyone. . . . For this reason, it is
impossible that the temporal sword and law should find any
work to do among Christians, since they do of their own accord
much more than all laws and teachings can demand. . . . I
would take to be quite a fool any man who would make a*

book of laws and statutes for an apple tree, telling it how
to bear apples and not thorns, when the tree is able by its own
nature to do this better than the man with all his books can
describe and demand. Just so, by the Spirit and by faith all
Christians are so thoroughly disposed and conditioned in their
very nature that they do right and keep the law better than
any one can teach them with all manner of statutes; so far as
they themselves are concerned, no statutes or laws are needed.[11]

No passage of Luther's writings is more open to misunderstanding than this one. We should note at the start that the
whole statement is predicated on his oft-repeated assertion that
"there are few true believers, and fewer still who live a Christian life," and that the world and its masses will always be un-
christian.[12] Nor did Luther mean by such a qualification that
there was in fact a group of people, however small, who had
achieved such perfection that they could be exempted from all
worldly authority. In the same treatise, he explicitly denies that
any man can be called truly Christian, in the sense which he
has given to the term, and insists that all men must be placed
under restraint.[13]

The key to the issue is Luther's understanding of Christian
righteousness as "alien" righteousness. Righteousness is not a
possession of man but a characteristic of Christ, and it becomes
man's only by faith. Therefore, it is an eschatological reality,
for the Christian remains *simul justus et peccator*, with no
expectation that this tension will be resolved in this life.[14]

The meaning of the concept of the two kingdoms is considerably clarified by comparison with Luther's treatment of
the Law-Gospel and Flesh-Spirit dialectic in his commentary
on Galatians 3:23. After distinguishing between Law and
Gospel historically in terms of the time before and the time
since the advent of Christ, Luther turns immediately to a
dialectical interpretation of the distinction in relation to the
Christian life. The distinction should be applied, he declares,

*not only to the time but also to feelings; for what happened
historically and temporally when Christ came—namely, that
he abrogated the Law and brought liberty and eternal life to
light—this happens personally and spiritually every day in
any Christian, in whom there are found the time of law and
the time of grace in constant alternation. . . .*

*Therefore, the Christian is divided this way into two times.
To the extent that he is flesh, he is under the Law; to the extent that he is spirit, he is under the Gospel. . . .*

*The fear of God is something holy and precious but it
should not be eternal. It must always be present in a Christian,
because sin is always present in him. But it must not be alone;
for then it is the fear of Cain, Saul and Judas, that is, a servile
and despairing fear. By faith in the Word of grace, therefore,
the Christian should conquer fear, turn his eyes away from the
time of the Law, and gaze at Christ Himself and at the faith
to come. . . .*

*Thus Paul distinguishes beautifully between the time of the
Law and the time of grace. Let us learn to distinguish the
times of both, not in words, but in our feelings, which is the
most difficult of all. For although these two are utterly distinct, yet they must be joined completely together in the same
heart.*[15]

Luther's distinction between the two kingdoms must be interpreted in the same dialectical fashion as the distinctions of
Law and Gospel and Spirit and Flesh in the above passage.
They are "joined completely together in the same heart." Although utterly distinct in their principle of life and mode of
operation, they are dialectically related in the life of the
Christian. For the Christian does not live in a pure community, separated from the world. He is a citizen of both kingdoms. Insofar as the righteousness of faith is being created in
him, he is of the spiritual kingdom, living by faith in the world,
and in this respect *justus*. But since faith is an eschatological
reality, he is still *peccator*, and to that extent he lives ac-

cording to the worldly realm and remains subject to its authority.

The same dialectical pattern of thought is evident when Luther turns from the Christian as citizen of the two kingdoms to a consideration of the destiny and the significance of the secular order. For at this point we find in Luther a coincidence of two apparently opposite impulses—*apocalypticism and secularity.* On the one hand he anticipates the swift and immediate disintegration of the secular order, and on the other hand he affirms it as God's creation and the sphere of man's vocation.

Reference has already been made to the profound stirrings of apocalyptic speculation in Germany in the generation preceding Luther. During the Reformation era itself, of course, this apocalyptic tradition is most clearly recognizable in figures like Thomas Münzer and Jan of Leyden, the kind of figures whom Luther dismissed as fanatics and visionaries. Yet Luther's opposition to such prophetic revolutionaries as these can all too easily blind us to the fact that the apocalyptic strain of thought was very strong in Luther himself.

Indeed, it is no exaggeration to say that Luther lived his whole life with a vivid consciousness of the swift approach of the last day, and he interpreted the events of his time as signs of its imminence. Although he rarely attempted to speculate concerning the exact time of Christ's return, he was convinced that the judgment would come suddenly to an unheeding world, that the angels were already girding on their swords to prepare for the final battle, and that the opportunity to escape the penalty of judgment was already slipping out of man's hands.[16] This note of urgent warning is unmistakable in Luther's address of 1524 to the Councilmen of the German cities.

Germany, I am sure, has never before heard so much of God's word as it is hearing today; certainly, we read nothing of it in history. If we let it just slip by without thanks and honor,

I fear we shall suffer a still more dreadful darkness and plague. O my beloved Germans, buy while the market is at your door; gather in the harvest while there is sunshine and fair weather; make use of God's grace and word while it is there! For you should know that God's word and grace is like a passing shower of rain which does not return where it has once been. It has been with the Jews, but when it's gone it's gone and now they have nothing. Paul brought it to the Greeks; but again, when it's gone, it's gone and now they have the Turk. Rome and the Latins also had it; but when it's gone, it's gone and now they have the Pope. And you Germans need not think that you will have it forever, for ingratitude and contempt will not make it stay. Therefore, seize it and hold it fast, whoever can. . . .[17]

Luther likened the world to a creaking old house, on the verge of falling down.[18] "All things," he wrote to Nicholas Hausmann in October, 1526, "are boiling, burning, moving, falling, sinking, groaning." [19] But while he looked for signs of the last day in the stirrings of nature, even more did he see those signs appearing in the progress of the Gospel over against the Turk and the Pope, interpreting even its most encouraging advances as analogous to the last brilliant flaring up of a candle about to be extinguished, or the last rallying moment of a sick man about to die. Caspar Heydenreich reports a conversation with Luther in 1542, in which Luther remarks:

I hold that judgement day is not far away. I say this because the drive of the Gospel is now at its height. And the Gospel acts like a light. When it is about to go out, it flares up as if it still wants to burn for a long time, and so it is extinguished. It now appears as if the Gospel wanted to spread out far and wide. But I fear that it will now go out in a twinkling and judgement will come. . . . A sick person, too, acts in this way. When he is about to die, he usually acts very lively at the end, just as if he were about to recover again; but in a twinkling, he is gone.[20]

Unlike Calvin, therefore, Luther had no optimistic projection that the world would be transformed by the light of the Gospel—he expected rather the snuffing out of the light, which would lead to a period of wild abandonment until Christ should appear to bring all things to their fulfillment.[21]

The same image of the candle is used again in 1530, in a letter to John Frederick of Saxony, in which Luther suggests that the last day might well come before the Scriptures were fully translated into German.[22] This letter was written at a time of considerable optimism for the Reformation cause, and it is apparent from this kind of reference that Luther's apocalyptic expectation was not born of despair in the later years of his life, as a rationalization for limited success, but was present with him from the beginning, even in his moments of greatest triumph and achievement.

The apocalyptic motif finds its clearest and most forceful expression in Luther's interpretation of the Papacy and the Turkish Empire by the apocalyptic symbols of the book of Revelation—the Antichrist and the Beast. While he believed initially that a Council might clear up the misunderstanding between himself and the Pope,[23] as early as March, 1519, he confided to his friend Spalatin in a letter: "I do not know whether the Pope is the Antichrist himself or whether he is his apostle, so miserably is Christ . . . corrupted and crucified by the Pope in the decretals." [24] By February of the following year he was less hesitant about making the identification, and if any doubt remained, it was dispelled by the papal bull of 1520, *Exsurge Domine,* in response to which Luther unequivocally identified the Pope as the "true Antichrist." [25]

Luther's description of the Pope as the Antichrist was not an impulsive term of abuse but a precise theological judgment, based on his reading of Scripture, developed early in his career as a reformer, and maintained consistently until his death. He was not the first to make this identification, for both Wyclif and

Hus had anticipated him in this respect.[26] But while they were preoccupied with the wicked life of the Papacy, Luther's central concern was not the moral issue but the theological issue of corruption of the faith, or apostasy from the Word. The heart of his charge against the Papacy was that it had usurped the place of Christ and added the necessity of works and ceremonies to faith.[27] That the Antichrist should be none other than the occupant of the chair of Saint Peter did not amaze Luther, for he saw it as the fulfillment of Scripture. Just as Lucifer was the brightest of angels before he rebelled, and just as the Son of God had been betrayed by an apostle and crucified in the holy city of Jerusalem, so it was only to be expected that the greatest corruption should issue from the city of Rome. Antichrist, Luther declared, "takes his seat not in a stable of fiends or in a pigpen or in a congregation of unbelievers, but in the highest and holiest place possible, namely in the Temple of God." [28]

If the Papacy represents the Antichrist who corrupts the faith from within, the Turk represents for Luther the beast of Revelation 13 who, like the pagan Roman Empire in New Testament times, threatens the Church from without by open hostility.[29] As King Herod was the farewell token of the Jewish kingdom, heralding Christ's incarnation, so the Turk is the farewell token of the Roman Empire, heralding Christ's return in judgment.[30] Pope and Turk, therefore, are the "dual murderers" of the Church, and the more fearfully they rage, the more clearly do they indicate the imminence of the last day, when the Antichrist and the beast will be finally destroyed.[31]

The return of Christ, according to Luther, would be an event of decisive significance for both Church and world. While he rejects the notion of a millennial rule of Christians before the end, Luther does conceive of the last day as a day of hope for Christians, a day of redemption which they should await with patient assurance.[32] In the time of waiting, the Church need fear nothing, confident that Christ will finally crush the Devil, and that his resurrection will bear fruit in the resurrection of the whole Church.[33]

There is no corresponding hope, however, for the world's resurrection. The wicked would be harvested for the "wine-press of God's wrath" and separated from the righteous by the divine alchemy. The full redemption of the Church would come only by deliverance from "this shameful, sick, diseased, wretched world . . . from the Devil and his slaves." [34] The Biblical promise of a new heaven and a new earth, Luther believed, would be fulfilled only out of the ashes of the old one, after a return to primal chaos.[35]

In speaking of the coming judgment, Luther declared that God would "knock over heaven and earth onto one heap and make another new world," [36] and similar phrases recur in his writings. In the commentary on the second epistle of Peter, written in 1523, this same notion appears in the context of a radical distinction between man's time and God's.

Since, then, in God's sight, there is no reckoning of time, so must a thousand years be before him, as it were, a day. Therefore the first man, Adam, is just as near to him as he who shall be born last before the last day. For God sees time not lengthwise but obliquely. . . . We can, through our reason, look at time only according to its duration; we must begin to count from Adam, one year after another, until the last day. But for God it is all in one heap; what is long for us is short for him; and again, with him there is neither measure nor number.[37]

No term expresses more aptly the characteristic features of Luther's eschatology than this curious phrase "in one heap." For we do not find in Luther that measured historical perspective so characteristic of Calvin's outlook in which the whole world is seen as being enfolded in the divine plan of restoration and renewal. There is a plan in history, but the last day comes not as the fulfillment of an already begun restoration of the world, not as the last act of an ordered drama, but as the sudden and radical judgment of God on a world already falling in ruins.

Finally, this eschatological perspective governs Luther's approach to the question of the Church's proclamation of the Gospel in the world. He comes to terms with this issue in his three Ascension sermons on Mark 16:14–20, from the Church Postils. In the first sermon, for example, he insists that

the Gospel, properly speaking, is not something written in books, but an oral proclamation, which shall be heard in all the world and shall be cried out freely before all creatures, so that all would have to hear it if they had ears; that is to say it shall be preached so publicly that to preach it more publicly would be impossible. For the Law which was of old, and what the prophets preached, was not cried out in the world before all creatures, but it was preached by the Jews in their synagogues. But the Gospel shall not be thus confined; it shall be preached freely unto all the world . . . it shall be cried out before the whole creation so that earth shall not have a nook or corner into which it shall not penetrate before the last day.[38]

The proclamation to all creatures, therefore, is part of Luther's eschatological vision, but we need to be careful in assessing its importance within his whole theological outlook. We may note first of all that, apart from these sermons where the Ascensiontide text itself called on him to speak directly of the "great commission" of Christ to his disciples, the theme is almost entirely absent from his theology. Moreover, several factors in his exposition of the issue within this context are worthy of special note. Even within the framework of this missionary text, he spends most of the time in discussing the content of the Gospel to be proclaimed rather than the necessity of its proclamation to all creatures.[39] Secondly, when he does speak of the command to preach, his emphasis lies not on the conversion of the heathen but on carrying the message of Christ's Lordship before the rulers of the nations.[40] Finally, any urgency in his exhortation is muted by his conviction that the Gospel will work its own way inexorably in the world. For it is "like a stone thrown into water, producing ripples which circle outwards from it, the waves rolling always on and on, till they come to the shore." [41] While Luther clearly acknowledges the validity of the eschatological demand to proclaim the Gospel to all creatures, it is not a major concern of his theology and takes second place to the responsibility of steadfast witness by the true Church against the Antichrist during the last days.

No analysis of Luther's thought is adequate which does not recognize the importance of the apocalyptic outlook in his stance toward the present world. But if that were all that could be said of him, there would be no reason to devote more attention to him than to other figures in that curious procession of apocalyptic and millenarian visionaries who have appeared briefly on the stage of Western history and passed unheeded into obscurity. Luther's distinctiveness inheres in the fact that his apocalyptic outlook is conjoined with a remarkably positive secular affirmation; and it is in the dialectical relationship of these two postures that the essence of his outlook on the secular order becomes clear.

Luther's positive acceptance and affirmation of the secular order may be discerned in his attitudes to the natural world, to government, and to vocation. In each case, his stance is rooted in theological conviction, but its consequences transcend narrow theological limits. Nature is understood as the good Creation of the transcendent God, and nowhere is this more tellingly or profoundly articulated than in the 1521 treatise on the words *Hoc est corpus meum,* where Luther firmly insists on the bodily presence of Christ in the Supper.

It is God who creates, effects, and preserves all things through his almighty power and right hand, as our Creed confesses. For he dispatches no officials or angels when he creates or preserves something, but all this is the work of his divine power itself. If he is to create or preserve it, however, he must be present and must make and preserve his creation both in its innermost and outermost aspects.

Therefore, indeed, he himself must be present in every single creature, in its innermost and outermost being, on all sides, through and through, below and above, before and behind, so that nothing can be more truly present and within all creatures than God himself with his power.[42]

That God is present in all his works, even to the leaves of the trees, does not mean that he can ever be enclosed within creation, for "the same majesty is so great that neither this world nor even a thousand worlds could embrace it and say, 'See, there it is.'"[43] Not even in his most extravagant statements does Luther approach pantheism. God remains the transcendent Creator, Lord over all his works. While he is apprehended through Creation, it is no unmediated presence. Rather, God is hidden in his creatures. They are the masks (*larvae*) which veil the divine majesty, and by which God confronts man in his hiddenness. "In this life," Luther declared in his commentary on Galatians 2:6, "we cannot deal with God face to face. Now the whole Creation is a face or mask of God."[44]

It is clear, therefore, that Luther's solemn outlook on the decaying and collapsing world in no way prevented him from taking a thoroughly positive and even joyful attitude toward the created world. Although his faith was rooted in a reading of the Scriptures, it was never an arid, "scholastic" affair, and it never developed in isolation from his apprehension of the natural world, "that most beautiful book or Bible in which God has described or portrayed himself."[45] The processes of nature, the dumb animals, man himself, and especially children were all living parables of the life of faith, smaller miracles retained by God to point to the greater miracle of the Word made flesh.[46] Indeed, so closely is Luther's theology oriented toward the natural world that he can interpret redemption on occasion in explicitly worldly terms, as the restoration of the proper understanding and use of the created world.[47] For the man of faith who discerns the presence of God in his creatures is pointed thereby to the Word who created all things and who became flesh in Jesus Christ.

While Luther's approach to nature is grounded in his theology, his orientation is neither narrow nor restrictive. That is to say, he does not use nature merely to illustrate doctrinal and moral presuppositions. The reader of Luther can scarcely avoid recognizing in him a genuine, at times lyrical, delight in nature itself, its sheer beauty and its wonderful intricacy. Both in conversation with friends and in polemic against his enemies he was quick to grasp for analogies and illustrations from the natural world.[48] Nor did he indulge in the kind of fantastic, allegorical and legendary use of nature common in medieval preaching. Nature was for him the world before his eyes, and he could wax lyrical over the dew on the grass, the carefree flight of the birds, and the strength and condition of his dog.[49] In a fascinating passage in the *Table Talk,* Luther takes the humanist Erasmus to task for his blindness to the natural world. Erasmus, he declares sadly, is uninterested in the structure of the peach stone or the formation of the fetus in the womb. He looks at the creatures "as a cow stares at a new gate." [50] For all his apocalyptic fervor, therefore, the picture of Luther which emerges from his writings is the picture of a man who firmly embraced secular life—the world of nature, of eating and drinking, of whining dogs and screaming children, of married love and intimate friendship.

Luther's positive affirmation of the secular order may be discerned, secondly, in his view of worldly government. Its positive nature is not immediately obvious, for his outlook, like Augustine's, is predicated on the assumption that man has brought disorder into creation through his own sin, and that the world has become, accordingly, "the kingdom of Satan," the "enemy of Christ," and the "Devil's property." [51]

The Devil's rule is evident in the "unbelief, disobedience, sacrilege, blasphemy towards God, cruelty and mercilessness towards one's neighbour, and love of self in all the things of God and of man" which shows itself on every hand.[52] Yet the Devil is, despite everything, God's Devil, who roams abroad only as far and as long as God permits, and who is used by God to fulfill his purposes. The structures of worldly authority, likewise, are instruments of God's rule, even if they do not know it. Their purpose is to restrain evil, to preserve the decaying world, to patch and mend it while the present age endures.[53]

What seems at first to be a very narrow and restricted understanding of government becomes in Luther's exposition the means of breaking sharply with the theocratic ideal and according to temporal authority its own authentic role. This may be seen most clearly in Luther's treatment of the role of the prince. He had little time for the princes as individuals and regarded most of them as "fools," "scoundrels," or god-children of the Devil.[54] Yet he prized the office highly because of its central role in upholding worldly law and order and insisted, in accordance with the Christian tradition since Paul, that the ruler acts as God's servant, whether he be Roman Emperor, Turkish Sultan, or German prince.

Luther claimed that none had glorified the office of prince as much as he, and some of his statements, taken at face value, lend credence to the view that perhaps he glorified it far too much. In his exposition of Psalm 82, for example, he describes the princes as "gods." [55] Yet it is quite clear from the context that he means only that the prince acts as instrument of God in maintaining order. He specifically repudiates the idea that their authority is absolute and insists that they are answerable to God at all times.[56] He would have regarded with horror the tendency of later Lutheranism to make the prince a law unto himself.

Luther's recognition of the integrity of secular government

is shown in his insistence that the prince, even if he be a
Christian, should not try to rule the world by the Gospel. He
must act in wrath, not love, content to be a hangman and not
a shepherd. If he needs wisdom in knowing how to rule, his
best guide is not the Gospel but the wisdom of the pagan
philosophers, whom God has given to be the "prophets,
apostles, and theologians or preachers" for earthly government.[57] The prince, therefore, does not rule at the direction
of ecclesiastical authority but by reason and common sense.

The high function assigned by Luther to natural reason in
the government of earthly society is rarely recognized, and this
is not surprising, in view of his careless and intemperate language on the subject which has both embarrassed his advocates and provided a handy arsenal of weapons for would-be
detractors. Luther's writings abound with highly colorful and
derogatory references to Aristotle and descriptions of reason as
the "Devil's whore" and "enemy of God"—and it is hardly surprising that writers like Maritain, relying largely on the out-
dated polemics of Denifle and Grisar, have written off Luther
as the arch enemy of reason and a creature of appetite.

Brian Gerrish, however, has demonstrated conclusively the
distortions inherent in Maritain's position. He shows that
Luther's attitude to reason is, in fact, strangely ambivalent,
that his unqualified opprobrium is balanced by an extravagant
praise of reason as the instinct which separates man from the
animals and in accordance with which life ought to be lived.
Gerrish shows that what Luther opposes is not the faculty of
reason itself but a particular opinion of natural reason—the
notion that man can stand before the righteous God on some
ground other than God's grace. When reason trespasses in this
way in the spiritual realm, she is the Devil's whore, but when
she keeps to her proper task she is the Empress.[58] As a
guide for the business of society and government, she is sur-
passed by none.

When the prince does happen to be a Christian, Luther sees

it as especially important that the roles of prince and preacher should not be confused. "Why should I teach a tailor how to make a suit?" he declared. "He knows it himself. I shall only tell him that he should act like a Christian." [59] The preacher may not tell the ruler how to govern, but he may instruct him as a man in the Christian faith. In this way the proper distinction between the two kingdoms is maintained.

The autonomy of worldly government is, of course, not absolute. While the ruler is not responsible as ruler to the Gospel or to ecclesiastical authority, Luther insists that he exercises his role under God's judgment. This is a distinction of fundamental importance. The "secular" role of government would be drastically compromised by ecclesiastical control, but it is in no way jeopardized by "subjection to God" as Luther uses the term. For the concept of "subjection to God" in the context of Luther's philosophy of government has more immediate political than religious significance. It applies equally to Christian, non-Christian, and pagan rulers, regardless of their theistic or atheistic convictions. It signifies, on the part of the ruler, a clear recognition of the contingent, fallible, and human character of his rule. Subjection to God, in this sense, therefore, attempts to guarantee the secular character of government by precluding the open or implied pretension to infallibility and ultimacy which has characterized absolutist regimes from the ancient Oriental despotisms to the totalitarian regimes of this century. [60] The fact that "subjection to God" does not seem such a vital political concept in the context of modern representative democracy should not lead us to underestimate its secular significance in the context of the hereditary and authoritarian political system of Luther's Germany.

It has to be added, of course, that it was easier to make these strictures against absolutism than to translate them into concrete checks on the power of secular rulers, and that, in practice, Luther's strong support of the princes often tended to reinforce their absolutist aims. But whatever may have been

the political results of Lutheranism, it needs to be recognized
that the aim of Luther's philosophy of government is to secure
and preserve the proper secular status of worldly rule.

The secular order is affirmed, thirdly, in Luther's understanding of vocation. To deny that the prince can rule the
world by the Gospel is not to exclude the Gospel from the
world, but to free it for creative expression in the world
through the Christian's vocation. Luther stripped the word
Beruf (calling) of its exclusively ecclesiastical associations and
applied it to all honorable human tasks in whatever station
of society. The work of farming, of domestic service, of making
a home and rearing children, is accorded an equal dignity with
the work of the preacher.

*For I am not only a prince or the head of a household, a man
or a woman, who administers an office or vocation as the
others also do; but I am also baptized and washed with the
blood of Christ. . . . Wherever there is such faith and assurance of grace in Christ, you can also confidently conclude with
regard to your vocation and works that these are pleasing to
God and are true and good Christian fruits. Furthermore, such
temporal and physical works as governing a land or people,
managing a house, rearing and teaching children, serving, toil-
ing, etc., also develop into fruit that endures unto life everlasting.*[61]

Thus man's faith, in which he stands *coram deo* in the spiritual
kingdom, becomes active in love toward the neighbor in the
worldly kingdom. "Whatever face he has inwardly towards
God, he shows outwardly." [62]

The engagement of the Gospel with the world, therefore, is
to be understood in terms of the relation of faith to works.
Creation is the sphere of faith's works. The proper fruit of
faith is seen not as monastic devotion but as love toward the
neighbor in the world. Freedom from the law issues in freedom
for life within the secular order. This is the burden of Luther's
great treatise of 1520, *The Freedom of the Christian,* where he

articulates very clearly the relationship between the faith which unites man to God and the love of neighbor which flows properly from that faith.

Although I am an unworthy and condemned man, my God has given me in Christ all the riches of righteousness and salvation without any merit on my part, out of pure, free mercy, so that from now on I need nothing except faith which believes that this is true. Why should I not, therefore, freely, joyfully, with all my heart, and with an eager will do all things which I know are pleasing and acceptable to such a Father who has overwhelmed me with his inestimable riches? I will therefore give myself as a Christ to my neighbor, just as Christ offered himself to me; I will do nothing in this life except what I see is necessary, profitable, and salutary to my neighbor, since through faith I have an abundance of all good things in Christ.[63]

The Reformer's own movement from the cloister to the world became paradigmatic of the pattern of life which emerged in the communities shaped by the Reformation. Christian discipleship became flesh in the context of ordinary human life. Secular vocation acquired a new dignity. Radical commitment to God no longer precluded but implied radical involvement in the world.

The preceding discussion has wandered at times far from those matters which are considered to be directly relevant to ecclesiology. It is only within this broader theological context, however, that we may begin to apprehend Luther's understanding of the Church and its institutional form. Luther's understanding of the world is complex, but its fundamental direction is clear. Although the world hastens toward its final collapse, because it is God's creation and because its destiny remains within his hands, it remains a meaningful order for the life of man. Luther's apocalyptic, therefore, did not ultimately imply world denial, but rather it defined the nature and the limits of world affirmation.

We have referred to the "secularity" which characterizes Luther's understanding of the world, and it is appropriate at this point to define the term more accurately. It is intended to indicate the freeing of the world from dependence on a religious framework of understanding. Because Luther expected no transformation of the world by the Gospel, because he denied any redemptive significance to the world as such, he freed it to become a secular reality with its own integrity. Thereby, implicitly, he affirmed a sphere of free, creative, and responsible activity in which the Christian might participate simply as a man alongside other men in the common tasks of social life and civilization, not cherishing utopian hopes of perfection but seeking to regulate and to build according to the common human gift of reason.

In thus "de-sacralizing" the world, however, Luther was not making way for the introduction of a secularist idolatry in which the world is sanctified and deified, for the world remains God's creation, and exists under the sign of finitude and eventual dissolution. The Christian's life is a worldly life, but his allegiance is not to the world but rather to the Word of God who created it and who rules it in judgment and mercy.

Such is the power of this Word, wherever it is heard, that man may confidently let it be and not seek to add his own works to it. Luther was confident that God's Word would work its will unrestricted in both kingdoms, in different ways but with equal power, putting to rout both Pope and Devil. Something of this sublime confidence is reflected in the second Wittenberg sermon of 1522, where Luther comments on the early progress of the Reformation.

I simply taught, preached, and wrote God's Word; otherwise I did nothing. And while I slept, or drank Wittenberg beer with my friends Philip and Amsdorf, the Word so greatly weakened the Papacy that no prince or emperor ever inflicted such losses upon it. I did nothing; the Word did everything. Had I desired to foment trouble, I could have brought great bloodshed upon

*Germany; indeed, I could have started such a game that even
the emperor would not have been safe. But what would it have
been? Mere fool's play. I did nothing. I let the Word do its
work. What do you suppose is Satan's thought when one tries
to do the thing by kicking up a row? He sits back in hell and
thinks: Oh, what a fine game the poor fools are up to now.
But when we spread the Word alone and let it do the work,
that distresses him. For it is almighty and takes captive the
hearts, and when the hearts are captured the work will fall of
itself.*[64]

Luther's dynamic understanding of the Word of God as the
expression of His rule over all creation and over the world of
man does not resolve the dialectical tensions within his eschatology, but it comprehends them within a greater unity.
It is this same Word of God which provides the key to Luther's
understanding of the reality of the Church.

CHRISTOLOGICAL DIALECTIC: THE CHURCH

*Thank God, a seven year old child knows what the Church is,
namely, holy believers and the sheep who hear the voice of
their Shepherd. So children pray, "I believe in one holy Christian Church." Its holiness does not consist of surplices, tonsures, albs and other ceremonies of theirs which they have
invented over and above the Holy Scriptures, but it consists of
the Word of God and true faith.*[65]

Word and faith—in these words, according to Luther, the
whole essence of the Church was contained, and it was a
reality so simple that a child could understand it. Wherever the
Word of God and true faith joined in mutual embrace, there
the Church was to be found. Within this polarity, priority remains always with the Word, for the Word creates the Church
and remains the whole source and substance of its life.[66] It was
by this criterion of the Word that Luther came to reject the
Papacy as a body based on merely human traditions. The
Christian Church, he declared in a sermon of 1539, "should be

a house in which only the Word of God resounds. Therefore, let them shriek themselves crazy with their cry, 'Church! Church!' Without the Word of God it is nothing." [67]

What is this Word of which Luther speaks, and on which he lays such emphasis? Clearly, he identifies it closely with the Word of Scripture. In a sermon of 1528 on Matthew 12:46–50, for example, Luther attacks the Roman Church for confessing Scripture to be God's Word and then presuming to sit in judgment on it.

> . . . *whatever has moved the Christian Church so to contradict God, to silence Him and to say: we confess that Scripture is Thy Word, but it is to be in force and is to be followed only when we say so? What, think you, will God say on His judgement-seat? He will say: Sir Pope, ye bishops and princes and whoever you are, did you know Scripture to be my Word? We did. Why, then, did you not observe it? Why, because the Christian Church had not so decreed. So I hear, do I, that your Church is to control and rule my Word? I thought people were to consider final and determined what I said and spurn everything to the contrary, though all the world said it.*
>
> *How would you like it if your servant whom you had bidden to do something were first to go and ask a maid or a fellow-servant whether it pleased her or him?*
>
> *The Christian Church is God's maid and servant. It listens to and does nothing but what it knows to be His Word and command. Yet our adversaries are trying to force us for their sake to deny and surrender God's Word under the specious name of the "Christian Church." Therefore we are to know that the Church which undertakes this sort of thing is not the Christian Church, but the Devil's whore instead.*[68]

During the Diet of Augsburg, Luther stated the same point with more precision in a number of theses, in which he declared that the Church of God does not confirm the Scriptures but is confirmed by them, and that insofar as the Church approves of the word of Scripture, it does so with the endorsement of an inferior and not the authorization of a superior.[69] Holy Scripture, Luther insisted in his Galatians commentary, is queen over the Church, and within the Church there are no judges and arbiters over the Word but only witnesses, pupils, and confessors. Scripture is the mother of the Church and not her daughter, the begetter and not the begotten.[70]

As creature of the Word, therefore, the Church stands always under the authority of Scripture. But Luther's understanding of the Word is too dynamic to be limited to the written book, or even to the book as it is made alive in the word of preaching.[71] The Word is a living voice to be heard, and the whole life of the Church consists fundamentally in hearing that voice. Luther recognizes that the Church is constantly in peril of hearing the wrong voice, for the Devil is always trying to seduce the Church by appearing in the form of Christ and claiming his authority, and the Church must be constantly on guard to exclude all Satanic or merely human voices. How may the true voice be distinguished from the false? Luther answers that God Himself, through His Spirit, enables man to discern the true Word. Without the Spirit, the Word effects nothing.

The Holy Spirit reveals and preaches that Word, and by it he illumines and kindles hearts, so that they grasp and accept it, cling to it and persevere in it. Where He does not cause the Word to be preached, and does not awaken understanding in the heart, all is lost.[72]

Just as the Church endorses Scripture, so it recognizes the Spirit, not as an immanent possession subject to the Church's direction but as a transcendent reality by which it is directed.[73]

The Word, as Luther understands it, therefore, represents nothing less than the whole creative and redemptive activity of God toward sinful man, revealed in Christ and operative through the Spirit. It is never an empty or impersonal Word, echoing in a void, but a personal Word addressed to man and demanding from him an answer of recognition. That answer is faith, which grasps the Word and holds to it firmly. The Church is created by the Word, and springs to life as faith answers the Word. It is that company of people who "rely on nothing else than God's grace and mercy," who "believe on Christ and want to be saved through Him, not through their works or merit." [74] And since faith, like the Word itself, is a sheer gift, man cannot possess or manipulate the reality of the Church. He can only answer and affirm the creative activity of God.

Luther's interpretation of the Church on the basis of Word and faith effected a transformation of major proportions in ecclesiology, and it is instructive to reflect at this point on what this change represented. It meant, above all, that Christology became the basis of the doctrine of the Church. Formally, this was no new departure, nor was it strange to the medieval period. We have already noted how Thomas Aquinas' doctrine of the Church is based on Christology. Materially, however, Luther's contribution was distinctive, and this may be shown by comparing his formulation of the issue with that of Thomas. For Thomas, the Church was a divine-human society reflecting perfectly the union of God and man, supernature and nature, which came about in the person of the incarnate Word. For Luther, the Word represented not an ontological union of nature and supernature but a personal address of God to man, awakening faith. The impersonal, ontological framework gives way to one which is thoroughly personal, even existential, in orientation.

This represented a major shift in ecclesiology and implied a different understanding of the institutional Church. We have noted how Thomas brought together two paradoxical tendencies—a supernaturalism which looked to the world beyond, and a recognition of the earthly institution as a structure impregnated with divine substance. Luther's articulation of the polarity of Word and faith leads to an inversion of both sides of the paradox. For, on the one hand, it issues in a profound

concentration on the personal and human dimensions of existence, in which faith meets the Word. On the other hand, just
because the Church is so thoroughly "humanized," it can no
longer pretend to divine status but must recognize itself as
standing under the judgment of the transcendent Word to
whom alone it owes its origin. This was no incidental modification of medieval ecclesiology, no mere change in minor detail,
but a dramatic shift of orientation with radical implications for
the exposition of ecclesiology and for the evaluation of the
institutional Church.

This shift of orientation is reflected very clearly also in
Luther's treatment of the traditional ecclesiological imagery,
and especially in his interpretation of the creedal phrase which
became his central definition of the Church—the *communion
of saints.*

In searching for an adequate translation of the Biblical word
ecclesia, Luther rejected the German word *Kirche* as "meaningless" and "obscure" and suggestive of a public building,[75]
and he preferred instead the word *Gemeine.* In so doing, he
recognized that he had chosen a "civic and worldly word"
which could be used to describe, for example, a city or national
community under its head.[76] He chose it because, in its
Christian context, it pointed to a close personal relationship between Christ and his people. "Thus the Christian Church, or
Christendom, is called a communion, a gathered multitude of
many Christians and believers who cleave to Christ as their
Head." [77]

Accordingly, the creedal term *communio sanctorum* became
for him the central and sufficient definition of the Church. "The
Creed indicates what the Church is, namely a communion of
saints, that is, a group or assembly of such people as are
Christian and holy." [78] Noting that the phrase did not originally
appear in the Creed, he explained it as an explanatory gloss
which later, by chance, became incorporated into the text.
When the Christian confesses belief in the communion of
saints, therefore, he is not affirming a separate article of faith,

but clarifying and reaffirming what it means to confess the holy Christian Church.[79]

There was nothing essentially new or radical in Luther's singling out of this term, for it had enjoyed considerable currency in the medieval period as an ecclesiological term, in both papalist and antipapalist circles. What is significant is not his selection of the term, but the content which he gave to it. It became in his writings a point of confluence for all the distinctive lines of his new understanding of the Christian faith.

Rome could certainly agree with Luther's description of the communion of saints as "a crowd or assembly of people who are Christian and holy." [80] But the point of difference, as Luther saw it, was on the meaning of the two words "Christian" and "holy." In his opinion, the Papacy was not a holy Christian people but a "holy Roman people," for it had invented a holiness supposedly superior to Christian holiness,

found in the prescription of chasubles, tonsures, cowls, garb, food, festivals, days, monkery, nunning, masses, saint-worship and countless other items of an external, bodily, transitory nature. Whether one lives under it without faith, fear of God, hope, love and whatever the Holy Spirit, according to the first table, effects, or in misbelief, uncertainty of heart, doubts, contempt of God, impatience with God, a false trust in works (that is, idolatry), not in the grace of Christ and his merit . . . all that is of no consequence, because a man may be holier than Christian holiness itself. . . . Just throw a surplice over your head and you are holy in accordance with the Roman Church's holiness, and you can indeed be saved without the Christian holiness.[81]

Luther, therefore, was unable to see in Rome's understanding of holiness anything but a concentration on outward and superficial things and a consequent neglect of holiness as a gift of the Holy Spirit who bestows faith and writes his law on the Christian's heart.

For Christian holiness, as Luther understands it, is, strictly speaking, not an attribute of the Church at all, but an attribute of Christ in which the Church shares. It is not a finished reality but only the first fruits of what will finally be hers by the gift of the Spirit.[82] The saints, accordingly, are not those who have earned the title by their devotion or asceticism, or by ecclesiastical promotion. They are nothing but justified sinners who have heard the Word of God by faith and are daily being sanctified and renewed by the regenerative activity of the Holy Spirit. Their holiness is a matter of grace and has nothing to do with works or merit. To describe the Church as a communion of saints, therefore, is to see it as a solidarity of persons bound together by faith in Christ and led by the Spirit toward the eschatological fulfillment.[83]

Moreover, the common relationship of the saints to Christ in faith issues in a new and profound relationship of communion with each other. The meaning of the priesthood of all believers is not primarily that each Christian may assert his independent way to God but rather that he may act and pray on behalf of his neighbor.[84] Luther expressed this understanding of the communion of saints as a brotherhood in his 1519 sermon on the Lord's Supper.

In this we are all brothers and sisters so closely united that a closer relationship cannot be conceived. For here, we have one baptism, one Christ, one Sacrament, one food, one Gospel, one faith, one Spirit, one spiritual body (Eph. 4:4–5); and each person is a member of the other. No other brotherhood is so close and strong.[85]

We do not adequately apprehend the depth of Luther's understanding of the "communion of saints" unless we appreciate both the personal and the corporate dimensions of the term.

While the *communio sanctorum* was, for Luther, the sufficient definition of the Church, he did make use also of other traditional terminology, which was similarly purged of many

of its medieval associations and filled with his new understanding of the Gospel. He interpreted the term "people of God"
in the sense of a people under God's command rather than a
people possessing the sacred mysteries, and he clarified the
meaning of the Church as "mother" of the faithful by indicating that the birth of Christians is by the Word and through
the witness of the Spirit.[86]

It is even more instructive to see Luther's use of the term
"body of Christ." Like his medieval predecessors, he ties the
term very closely to the sacrament of the altar. Christ and the
Christian become in the body one flesh and blood, and all the
spiritual possessions of Christ and the saints are communicated to him who receives the sacrament.[87] Yet Luther effects
a transformation of the concept along the lines of his reinterpretation of the communion of saints. While the mystical
dimension of the term is not excluded, it is more than balanced
by a stress on personal communion, of each member with
Christ and with all other members. Whatever happens to the
Christian happens to Christ himself and to the whole body.
The members of the body are like kernels of grain milled
together or wineberries crushed into one dish—they become in
Christ's body bread and wine to each other.[88] Consequently,
when the Devil assails the Christian he will "bite his own
tongue and burn his own fingers," because he meets the combined forces of the whole body.[89] When one Christian suffers,
all suffer. When one dies, he is not alone in death.

*Therefore, when we feel pain, when we suffer, when we die,
let us turn to this, firmly believing and certain that it is not
we alone, but Christ and the Church who are in pain and are
suffering and dying with us. Christ does not want us to be
alone on the road of death, from which all men shrink. Indeed, we set out upon the road of suffering and death accompanied by the entire Church. Actually, the Church bears it
more bravely than we do.*[90]

Luther's use of the image of the "body of Christ" is clearly very similar to his understanding of the Church as the "communion of saints." Both terms are vessels for his fresh understanding of ecclesiology on the basis of Word and faith.

The thoroughgoing reinterpretation which Luther carried through in reference to the traditional ecclesiological imagery indicates that the distinctiveness of his ecclesiology is not located in his direct and sometimes vituperative polemic against the Papacy but in the way in which he shifts the whole discussion to a new focus. He follows through his Christological starting point in such a way that the whole paraphernalia of the papal hierarchy becomes peripheral to the main issue of obedience to Christ the Head of the Church.

What is the Christian Church? What does it say and do? They reply: The Church looks to the Pope, cardinals and bishops. This is not true! Therefore we must look to Christ and listen to him as he describes the Christian Church in contrast to their phony shrieking. . . . Christ says . . . There must be a people that loves me and keeps my commandments. Quite bluntly, this is what he wants.[91]

The shift which Luther effects is from outward to inward. The Church is no longer defined in terms of its structure and hierarchy but in terms of its inner life—the relationship of Christ the Lord to his faithful people, nourished by the Word, renewed by the Spirit. "The essence, life and nature of the Church is not a bodily assembly but an assembly of hearts in one faith."[92]

The distinctiveness of Luther's ecclesiology may be seen most clearly in his employment of a further image, which he found in the Bible, and to which he gave his own authentic stamp—the image of the **hidden church.** An understanding of this image provides the best avenue of approach to his interpretation of the ecclesiastical institution.

What Luther meant by the "hidden Church" is not to be comprehended adequately in terms of the dichotomy of "visible and invisible Church," so commonly applied to ecclesiology

from the time of Augustine. In most cases, the employment of
these categories is more confusing than enlightening. In the
case of Luther, it represents the application of an ontology
alien to his way of thinking and obscures the true meaning
of the Church's hiddenness.[93]

The hidden Church is not to be understood as a Platonic
idea or ideal existing beyond the substantial world. Luther
was charged with having such a view, and he vehemently
repudiated it in his reply to Emser in 1521. "When I called
the Christian Church a spiritual assembly, you mocked me as
if I would build a Church like Plato's city, which could be
found nowhere." [94] What Luther did mean by the hiddenness
of the Church can be understood only on the basis of his
Christological starting point, the relationship of Word and
faith. To begin from the side of faith, the hiddenness of the
Church meant to Luther that the true Church was not an
object of sight but of belief. The Church, he said, "is a high,
deep, hidden thing, which nobody can perceive or see, but only
grasp and believe in baptism, sacrament and Word." [95] In his
preface to the Apocalypse in 1530 and again in 1545, he draws
a distinction between the knowledge of faith and reason and
denies the ability of the latter to discern the Church.[96] The
same point is made in the 1521 tract against Emser, where the
analogous distinction between faith and sight is used to compare Rome and the true Church.

*Now compare them, the holy Church of Christ and the crazy
Church of the Pope. The holy Church of Christ says: I believe
a holy Christian Church. The crazy Church of the Pope says:
I see a holy Christian Church. The former says: The Church is
neither here nor there. The latter says: The Church is here and
there. The former says: The Church depends not on a person.
The latter says: The Church depends on the Pope. The former
says: The Church is not built on anything temporal. The latter
says: The Church is built on the Pope.[97]*

To understand the Church as a reality known by faith alone
brings us back to the other side of Luther's polarity, the Word

of God. For the Church is discernible only by faith because it is the community of the Word, Jesus Christ, whose glory likewise was discernible only by faith. The contempt of the world for the Church reflects its contempt for Christ, the Man of Sorrows. In the coming of Christ, God passed over the greatest and highest and came through the simple, the plain, and the weak, showing his majesty in vanity and weakness.

The whole world has nothing better, more precious, or nobler than the Church, in which the voice of God is heard and God is worshipped with true forms of worship, that is, with faith, invocation, patience, obedience, etc. Yet the Church is so hidden from view by the Cross, by afflictions, by dishonor, by contempt that the world concludes that nothing is more detestable and baneful.

Indeed, look at Christ Himself. What is more wretched than He? "We saw Him full of scabs," says Isaiah, "so that we turned our faces away from Him." Yet He is the Son of God, the king of glory and the salvation of all men.[98]

As the Lordship of Christ was veiled in his earthly appearance as a humble servant, obedient to death, so too the true life of the Church is veiled in weakness and poverty. As Christ could be known as Lord only by faith, so now that his Lordship is hidden in the Church, the Church can be known only by faith. And since this Lordship is destined to be revealed and unveiled, the Church is an eschatological community whose true nature also will be revealed at the last day. It is the most precious thing in the world, but is not recognized as such. It is holy, without spot and wrinkle, but "God conceals and covers it with weaknesses, sins, errors and various offences and forms of the Cross, in such a way that it is not evident to the senses anywhere." [99]

It is here that Luther's position stands in clearest contrast to the position of the Papacy. For the latter had emphasized its role as guarantor of truth and dispenser of sacramental grace. Accordingly, the true Church was seen to exist in the authority of the hierarchy, which was not hidden but clearly visible and tangible. Rome had transformed faith into sight and resolved the eschatological tension in the Church's life.

It is important to recognize that Luther's concept of the hiddenness of the Church was not born of his controversy with the Papacy, nor was it a rationalization after the event of his separation from Rome. As Karl Holl pointed out many years ago,[100] Luther's doctrine of the Church was present in all its essential elements in his early lectures on Psalms and Romans, before the outbreak of the Reformation. Already in these early lectures, Luther speaks of the true Church as a communion rather than a visible organism, and he locates the Church's real continuity not in the hierarchy but in the hidden, uninterrupted continuity of believers. In Psalm 103, for example, the Church is described as "invisible, known through faith," and in Psalm 17 as "hidden from the world but manifest to God." [101]

As the controversy with Rome developed, Luther did not adopt a new position but rather drew out further the consequences of the position which he had already established in its essentials. Increasingly he came to assert or to imply that there were no higher ecclesiastical vocations; that while the Pope's jurisdiction in the Church exceeded that of other clergy, he was essentially only a priest; and that the gift of the keys was primarily the command to preach the Gospel, and was entrusted to the whole Church rather than restricted to the Pope.[102] What emerged from the early controversies and came to fuller expression in the later writings was not a rationalization of revolt but a clarification of the position which he had held from the time of his earliest writings.

It would be entirely incorrect, however, to see Luther's understanding of the hiddenness of the Church as being opposed to the notion of a visible Church. On the contrary, Luther consistently recognized that the Church had to appear bodily in the world and had to have place and form, as Christ himself had had during his earthly life. Both Christ and the Church are understood dialectically, in terms of their outward and their inward reality. Christ was the glory of God, hidden under the form of a servant. He had outward form, but his true nature remained hidden. By analogy, the Church also is understood dialectically as being both hidden and visible. It has outward form in the world, but its true nature is hidden. The former precludes any spiritualized or disembodied conception of the Church, the latter, any tendency to define the Church by the face which it presents to the world.

The recognition that the Church is both a hidden reality and a body having outward form points us toward the goal of our study—the determination of the relationship between the Church's inward nature as the communion of saints and her visible embodiment as an institution living in the world.

2

THE INSTITUTION IN THE WORLD

HIDDENNESS AND VISIBILITY. While the Church is a hidden reality which can be known only by faith, faith is not left groping in the dark, for there are visible *signs of the true Church* by which its presence may be discerned. That the Church may thus become visible is due not to the power of human perception but to the miracle of divine condescension, for

God in His divine wisdom arranges to manifest Himself to human beings by some definite and visible form which can be seen with the eyes and touched with the hands, in short, is within the scope of the five senses. So near to us does the Divine Majesty place Itself.[103]

The meaning of Luther's description of the signs is not always entirely clear for, while in this passage he emphasizes strongly the sensual apprehension of the signs, in other

places he makes very clear that the "seeing" and "hearing"
of which he speaks is the inward seeing and hearing of faith.[104]
The latter meaning seems to be more basic for, while the
visible signs are the normal means by which this inward apprehension takes place, the mere possession of the visible signs
without the eyes and ears of faith means nothing. While they
are clear expressions of the divine condescension, God remains
master of His signs and does not deliver them into human
control.

These visible signs, moreover, are eschatological realities for,
while they truly convey the reality which they signify, they also
point forward to a time when such masks will no longer be
necessary.

*When we get to heaven we shall see God differently; then no
clouds and no darkness will obscure our view. But here on
earth we shall not perceive Him with our senses and our
thoughts. No, here we see Him, as St. Paul states (I Cor.
13:12) "in a mirror dimly," enveloped in an image, namely in
the Word and the Sacraments. These are His masks or His gar-
ments, as it were, in which He conceals Himself. But He is
certainly present in these. . . . For now we cannot bear to see
and look at His brilliant majesty. Therefore, He must cover and
veil Himself, so to speak, behind a heavy cloud.*[105]

In his treatise of 1539, entitled *On the Councils and the
Church*, Luther lists seven of these signs of the true Church.
First among them is the Word of God, "the holiest of holy
possessions by reason of which the Christian people are called
holy . . . the true ointment that anoints unto life eternal." [106]
Next to the Word are the signs of Baptism and the Lord's
Supper, when truly used according to Christ's ordinance, and
by these signs the Holy Spirit sanctifies and preserves the
Church.[107] The fourth sign is the power of the keys, or pastoral
absolution, given to and exercised by the whole congregation,
and not merely by the Pope (who, according to Luther, had
turned his keys into lock-picking tools for foreign treasure

chests). The keys were given to all Christians "for the comfort of our consciences," and St. Peter, like every other Christian, was the servant of the keys and not their master.[108] The ministry of the Word, consecrated and called for the sake of good order and according to Christ's institution; the Church's offering of prayer, praise, and thanksgiving; and a life of suffering and cross-bearing were the three further testimonies to the presence of the communion of saints in the world.[109]

The list is interesting, because it shows how Luther's understanding went beyond that of the Augsburg Confession in emphasizing as well as Word and Sacrament the pastoral function of the whole congregation and the quality of its life and worship. Yet even this list of seven signs is not to be taken as a neat definition by which the reality of the Church could be precisely located or reduced to a formula. There is, in fact, no uniformity at all in Luther's description of the signs or marks of the Church. At times, he speaks of Word, Baptism, Eucharist, and Absolution; on another occasion he adds the Lord's Prayer and the Creed; often he identifies simply Baptism and Gospel as signs of the Church; while at other times he speaks only of the Word.[110] The flexibility and absence of uniformity testify clearly to Luther's conviction that, while there were sure and visible signs of the Church, the reality of the Church could by no means be encased in a formula.

Despite this diversity of expression, however, there is a unified theological purpose evident in Luther's approach to the matter of the Church's signs. It is apparent, and by no means unexpected, that the Word, or the Gospel, occupies a place of paramount importance as a sign of the Church, and that all the others are, in a sense, derivative of it. Thus, in his reply to Ambrosius Catherinus, Luther insisted that the Gospel is

the one most certain and noble mark of the Church, more so than Baptism and the Lord's Supper, since the Church is conceived, fashioned, nurtured, born, reared, fed, clothed, graced, strengthened, armed and preserved solely through the Gospel.

In short, the entire life and being of the Church lie in the Word of God, as Christ says.[111]

In his exposition of Isaiah 2 in 1527–1529, Luther reaffirmed the Word as "the one constant and infallible mark of the Church," [112] and attacked the Papacy for holding that there were more. In the same year in which he wrote the treatise *On the Councils and the Church,* with its sevenfold pattern of the Church's signs, he declared in a sermon on Matthew 23:37 that

the only mark of the Christian Church is following and obeying the Word. When that is gone, let men boast as much as they please, "Church! Church!" There is nothing to their boasting anyway. Therefore, you should say: Do the people have the Word of God there? And do they accept it too . . . ? Wherever one hears the Word of God, there is the Church of God, though it be in a cow stable, the place where Christ was born.[113]

There is no contradiction here, for the Word or the Gospel as a sign of the Church is an inclusive and not an exclusive term. Because the Gospel is the "true treasure of the Church," then Baptism, the Eucharist, the Keys, and all the others are also marks of the Church, because they are expressions of the Word. They are not separate marks, but aspects of the fullness of the Gospel, which is the one true mark. That is why they so often appear in Luther's writings in appositional relationship to the Word.[114]

The inclusiveness which characterizes Luther's doctrine of the Word should warn us against misinterpreting those passages in which he assumes a close identification of the Word with "pure doctrine," as he does, for example, in his 1535 *Commentary on Galatians.*[115] While it cannot be denied that Luther often identified the Word with pure doctrine, and could be firm to the point of obstinacy in his doctrinal controversies, he cannot be charged with having made a rigid doctrinal

standard into a mark of the Church, after the manner of some
of the seventeenth-century dogmaticians. For not only is the
Word a far more inclusive concept than pure doctrine, but
also, just as faith is inseparably bound to the Word in creating
the Church, so the Word as a mark of the Church is inseparable from the response which it evokes. He emphasized not
doctrine in itself but "one plain, pure, Gospel doctrine and an
outward confession thereof," and identified true belief with
"being made righteous" rather than the mere acceptance of
doctrinal formulae.[116]

We may conclude that the strong personal dimension which
we have already noted in Luther's understanding of the basis
of the Church informs also his interpretation of the signs or
marks of the Church. When he uses the formula of Word and
Sacrament, it is characteristic of him not to be preoccupied
with ecclesiastical ordinances but to speak of the place of
pulpit, font, and altar in the ongoing life of the Christian congregation and of the Christian man.[117] Thus, it is in the
union of the Word as God's gift and faith as man's response
that the true Church comes into being. Accordingly, the signs
of the Church are not self-evident but are recognized only
through that new quality of perception which faith provides.
The Church, moreover, must be constantly on guard against
the Devil, who builds his chapel alongside God's Church and
copies those signs which God has given with his own crude
imitations to corrupt the faith and deceive the faithful.[118]
Christians should accept only those signs which God has
given, and they should do so with humility, recognizing them
not as substitutes for faith but as gifts by which faith may be
confirmed and nourished.

Since the signs of the Church are pointers to faith and not
insignia of membership which man may grasp as a guarantee
of belonging to the true Church, it follows that the boundaries
of the true Church cannot be drawn with any precision. If adherence to the Pope is ruled out as a standard of measure-

ment, it is not in order to introduce other manageable human standards but to recognize that only God knows the membership of the true Church.

Accordingly, despite his condemnation of the Papacy as the Antichrist, Luther willingly acknowledged the presence of true Christians within the Roman Church, because the signs which God had given were present even there. The Church, he believed, had never disappeared entirely, but had existed in continuity since the time of Adam and Eve, through the Old Covenant and under the Papacy.[119] On the other hand, he recognized also that the evangelicals were and always would be a mixed body of wheat and tares. He expressed a wish to be delivered from a church in which there were only pure saints, and even denied that such a church could exist.[120] It was only to be expected that, as heresy arises out of the interpretation of Scripture, so rascals will be found within the Church. Luther explained their presence in the Church by employing the same distinction which John Hus had used between what is in the body and what is of the body.

The body is a beautiful and noble creation of God. Yet what comes out of it but a secretion from the eyes, sweat, excrement, urine, snot, pus and sores? I must say that although sores and pus are in the body, the body is not evil because these things come out of it. For if these things were good, they would remain in the body, as other things do. But since the body, together with its members, is sound and healthy, the filth must come out and be thrown away. If you want to reject your body because snot, pus and filth come out of it, you should cut your head off. Thus Christendom, too, is a living healthy body of the pious little flock, God's children. Yet filth and stench are mixed in. They must be cast off.[121]

It is clear from this passage that Luther recognized the importance of discipline within the Church, although this never attained the same status as in the Reformed tradition. The function of discipline is carried out not by the clergy but by the whole congregation. The congregation may exclude a person from the outer communion of the Church but not from its inner communion, for since God alone makes members of the Church, He alone may exclude them from it. The purpose of all disciplinary action by the congregation is not to create a completely pure Church but to bring the erring brother to a knowledge of his sin, that he may renounce it; not to deprive him of his inheritance, but to make him aware of the danger that he may lose it by his own folly.[122]

While acknowledging the necessity for a judicious use of the ban, Luther never forgot that such judgments are relative ones. The signs of the Church indicate where the Church is, but they do not permit anyone to judge a particular person's membership.

For many a man has been baptized, hears the Gospel and goes to the Sacrament with others and is none the less a rogue and a non-Christian. A man's spirituality can only be recognized by that faith within the heart which considers Christ its Good Shepherd. But who recognizes the people who have this faith? You will not see this faith on me nor I on you, for no one can look into the heart of another. And so, no doubt, the situation will remain what it is; no one can know and designate the sheep and the flock but this shepherd Christ alone.[123]

This inevitable uncertainty, however, does not paralyze the Church by promoting speculation about who is and who is not of the Church. In *The Bondage of the Will*, Luther employs a distinction between a "judgment of faith" and a "judgment of charity." While God alone can judge faith, Christians can affirm by charity that those who are of the Church's outward fellowship share also in the membership of the true Church.

I mean that charity, which always thinks the best of everyone, and is not suspicious, but believes and assumes all good of its neighbour, calls every baptized person a saint. There is no danger involved if she is wrong; it is the way of charity to be deceived, for she is open to all the uses and abuses of every man, as being handmaid of all, good and bad, believing and unbelieving, true and false. Faith, however, calls none a saint but him who is proclaimed such by divine sentence; for the way of faith is not to be deceived. Therefore, though we should all look on each other as saints as a matter of charity, none should be declared a saint as a matter of faith.[124]

While Luther affirmed the function of discipline, therefore, he refused to become involved in drawing the boundaries of the true Church. He showed little interest in defining the Church's circumference and contented himself with pointing clearly to its true center.

Luther's preoccupation with the Church's inward reality, his refusal to allow for any signs which would unmistakably identify the Church or define its boundaries, and his insistence that the Church would remain though all forms were dissolved are clear indications that he regarded the question of the institutional *form of the Church* as secondary and derivative in importance. It was not, however, an unimportant question, for he clearly recognized the necessity of outward and visible forms and took pains to establish proper criteria for judging and evaluating those forms.

The criteria which he employed in institutional matters may be discerned most clearly in his approach to the issue of the relationship of the Church community to the general community. The question is raised in the Preface to Luther's *German Mass* of 1526, where he appears to envisage, in addition to the Latin and German services, a third kind of service which

should be a truly evangelical order and should not be held in a public place for all sorts of people. But those who want to be Christians in earnest and who profess the Gospel with hand and mouth should sign their names and meet alone in a house somewhere to pray, to read, to baptize, to receive the sacrament, and to do the other Christian works. According to this order, those who do not lead Christian lives could be known, reproved, corrected, cast out or excommunicated according to the rule of Christ (Matt. 18: 15–17). Here one could also elicit benevolent gifts to be willingly given and distributed to the poor according to Saint Paul's example (2 Cor. 9). Here would be no need of much and elaborate singing. Here one could set up a brief and neat order for baptism and the sacrament and center everything on the Word, prayer and love.[125]

We know that this suggestion of Luther's was never put into effect, and that he finally dropped the idea of a gathered confessional church (*Bekenntniskirche*) and accepted the existence of a national church (*Volkskirche*). It is more difficult to ascertain why. Did the extremism of Karlstadt at Wittenberg during his absence and the events of the Peasants' War and the intervention of Müntzer turn Luther in a more conservative direction? Or was it, as some of the Free Church persuasion have suggested, evidence of a loss of nerve, a failure to follow through on his original aims? [126]

The only direct clue which Luther gives is in the remark which immediately follows his original suggestion about the third kind of service. "As yet," he declares, "I neither can nor desire to begin such a congregation or assembly or to make rules for it. For I have not yet the people or persons for it, nor do I see many who want it." [127] Here it appears to be basically a personnel problem. The evangelical order is intended for the truly earnest Christians who could be ruled by the Gospel, and Luther remained highly pessimistic in his expectations of finding such people. His sober opinion was that Christians generally could not be ruled by the Gospel alone, and therefore the need remained for the Mass to retain its place as the basic order of service.

In any case, it is anachronistic to see a modern, free-church type of organization as a live possibility for Luther. He lived in a culture where Christianity was self-evident and did not have the options open to a church in a secularized, pluralistic society. The only possibilities for him were a withdrawal from society in the manner of the Anabaptists or some kind of responsible association with society and its centers of power.

This situation naturally posed some difficult problems, since Luther's doctrine of the two kingdoms ruled out as a notion of the Devil any arrangement by which the Church became a function of government. The evidence suggests, however, that Luther was able to take the necessary steps without violating the doctrine of the two kingdoms. For example, because of the function of religion in society, it was clear that false worship and heresy could not be tolerated. Luther's acceptance of the government's duty to crush the rebellious Anabaptists was not an endorsement of a religious operation by a state-church but of a civic act in the worldly realm for the sake of public order. Nor is Luther's use of the prince as an auxiliary bishop in the inspection and reform of churches to be interpreted as a case of the use of the sword in the spiritual realm. For Luther made clear that he used them not in their capacity as worldly rulers but in their position as eminent churchmen. The prince, like every other Christian, was called to use his gifts for the benefit of all, and his gift was that of ruling. Since he alone had the means and the authority to carry out these reforms, it was his duty to do so, not as a prince but as a humble Christian exercising his gifts in the service of his neighbor. "Is it not unnatural," Luther wrote, "not to say unchristian, that one member does not help another and prevent its destruction?" [128]

These fine theoretical distinctions which Luther made tended to break down in practice. Since the Anabaptist disturbance was religiously motivated, it was difficult to see how its suppression could be regarded as a purely civic act. Moreover, though Luther may have seen the prince's role in the Church as nonpolitical in character, the princes themselves rarely accepted that limited understanding of their function, and as early as 1526 the Diet of Speyer gave the princes rights of religious determination. But the difficulties of maintaining

these principles in practice does not invalidate the genuine-
ness of Luther's attempt to come to terms with political
realities without surrendering the integrity and independence
of either church or state.

Luther's understanding of the Church, based on Word and
faith, contained within it the seeds of the eventual collapse
of the *corpus Christianum* by breaking through the conception
of the church as a universal society into which one could auto-
matically be born; and the kind of suggestion which he
offered in the *German Mass* is, in a sense, far more in keeping
with his understanding of the "communion of saints" than was
the idea of the national church. The fact that he did not insist on such a radical change, but felt free to operate within
the structure of a national church, certainly does not imply
an uncritical endorsement of the latter as the necessary or
desirable form of the Church but only a recognition of the
possibility of using it to serve the purposes of the Gospel.

To put the matter another way, the real key to understanding Luther's abandonment of the idea of the gathered confessional church lies not so much in discerning particular
historical circumstances and reasons as in recognizing that the
whole question is a secondary one for him. His characteristic
attitude to the question of the Church's institutional forms is
a consequence of his understanding of the Church as con-
stituted by faith rather than by external form and organization. The fact that his suggestions about a new, evangelical
order for the Church did not materialize can hardly have
been for him a major disappointment. For in the matter of
ecclesiastical forms, the operative word was freedom, born of
faith. Luther had as little patience with those who demanded
the obliteration of old forms as with those who insisted on
their retention. He defended against the papalists the freedom to use new forms and against the sects the freedom to
continue with the old forms. Since the Church was not con-

stituted by forms but by faith, it was a matter of Christian freedom to employ whatever was possible and most desirable in
the given circumstances, for the sake of the Gospel.

The same criterion of freedom is also evident in his attitude
to the forms and rites of worship. He is conscious of the
educational value of such things for those who are learning
to grow in faith. For such people, he notes, "one must read,
sing, preach, write and compose. And, if it would help matters
along, I would have all the bells pealing and all the organs
playing, and have everything ring that can make a sound." [129]
The trouble with the papal Church, according to Luther, was
not its use of forms and rites as such, but the fact that

*men made laws, works and merits out of them—to the detri-
ment of faith—and did not use them to train the youth and
common people in the Scriptures and in the Word of God, but
became so engrossed in them as to regard them as inherently
useful and necessary for salvation. That is the work of the very
Devil.* [130]

Luther's freedom in the matter of ecclesiastical forms and
rites was qualified by two central criteria—truth to the Gospel, and the best interests of the neighbor. The former reflects
his conservatism, the latter, his pastoral concern. That is to
say, the forms initially come under critical judgment according
to whether and how accurately they reflect and proclaim the
Gospel. But, once that criterion has been satisfied, there remains a large area of flexibility and freedom, within which
decisions about details of form and ritual can be made according to their appropriateness in the circumstances. Luther's
overriding concern was that these details should not be
confused with the issue of salvation, so that a man might
consider himself to be justified by either having or not having
them. The Christian man, liberated by faith from dependence
on such outward details, is free to use them or to dispense
with them in the best interests of his neighbor. Luther sums

up his position very succinctly in the preface to the *German Mass,* where he counsels his readers:

Do not make it a rigid law to bind and entangle anyone's conscience, but use it in Christian liberty as long, when, where and how you find it to be practical and useful. . . . the exercise of this freedom is up to everybody's conscience, and must not be cramped or forbidden; nevertheless, we must make sure that freedom shall be and remain a servant of love and of our fellowman.[131]

In Luther's approach to institutional concerns, therefore, theological criticism is always balanced by a very practical pastoral concern for the neighbor, and the result is an unusual degree of openness and flexibility in the visible institution. Luther is able to affirm the necessity for the Church to be concretely embodied in the world without falling into the trap of attributing to institutional questions any ultimate significance.

SPIRIT AND FLESH. The relationship between the inward reality of the Church and its outward form is made more explicit by Luther in a number of parallel dialectical images—soul and body, faith and works, and, most significantly, spirit and flesh.

In his treatise of 1520, entitled *The Papacy at Rome,* he employs the image of **soul and body** to speak of two Churches,

the first, which is the natural, essential, real and true one, let us call the spiritual, inner Christendom. The other, which is man-made and external, let us call a bodily, external Christendom: not as if we would part them asunder, but just as when I speak of a man and call him, according to the soul, a spiritual, according to the body, a physical man; or as the Apostle is wont to speak of the inner and of the outward man.[132]

While the terminology here employed is open to a Platonic interpretation as if the relationship of soul and body were that of opposites, it is clear from the passage that Luther conceives of it rather in dialectical terms. Soul and body are inseparable, and there is no attempt to deny the significance of the bodily Church. The Church necessarily possesses the same twofold nature as man, and the important thing is to recognize that membership is a spiritual reality; that is to say, it is by faith alone.[133]

The mutual relationship of these two realities is stated with more precision in the tract against Ambrosius Catherinus, where Luther declares that "without place and body there is no Church, and yet body and place are not the Church nor do they belong to it." [134] We may paraphrase Luther by saying that the Church inevitably has institutional form and structure but does not define itself by them. This was no theological abstraction, for the very quality of Christian discipleship was at stake. If the Church were to define itself by its institutional forms, then

we would not be strengthened or trained by it to desire or put our trust in the things that are unseen and eternal (2 Cor. 4:18). Instead, we would be trained to put our trust only in things that are transient and seen, and would become so accustomed to them as to be unwilling to let them go; . . . we would thereby be prevented from ever coming to God.[135]

The fundamental theological issue to which Luther is pointing here is that of faith itself, and the soul-body distinction is employed chiefly to insist that membership of the Church is an inward reality of faith and not a matter of external qualities or possessions. "For one who is not a Christian may have all those other things and they will never make him a Christian without true faith, which alone makes Christians." [136] While membership is by faith alone, the bodily form of the Church is never rejected or ignored. It is indispensable to the life of faith, but it must be understood as a mask (*larva*) of the Church's inward reality.[137]

The same approach to the Church's institutional form is articulated also in a dialectic of *faith and works.* In his exposition of Psalm 110.3, for example, he launches into an attack on the

abominable presumptuousness and boasting of those among us who want to produce Christians and children of God by means of their doctrine of works; who make Christianity an external matter, the invention of men, and bind the Christian Church to such external laws, ordinances, customs and behavior. Claiming to be the successors of the apostles, they quote and lay claim to the holy fathers and councils in order to fortify their position. But they say nothing of the faith in Christ which those holy fathers believed and taught. Instead, they direct people to the ordinances of men alone, as though we were under obligation to keep them. They pretend that those who do not obey the See of Rome and its bishops and agree with their ordinances cannot be Christians—in spite of the fact that they believe in Christ and live as Christians.[138]

In the light of Luther's firm position against the Papacy, it is instructive to observe that he clearly distinguishes between the Papacy and its idolatrous self-understanding. In the 1535 Galatians commentary, he even allows that he could acknowledge the Pope and honor him if only he would correctly understand his own place.

Thus I shall honor the Pope and love his position, provided that he leaves my conscience free and does not require me to offend against God. But he wants to be adored and feared in a way that must offend the Divine Majesty, wound the conscience and return me to the bondage of sin. Since we have to give up one or the other here, let us give up the social position and cling to God. . . . if Paul refused to yield to the false apostles, who boastfully cited the authority of the true apostles against him, much less should we yield to the wicked papists, who brag about the authority of their idol, the Pope. . . . All we aim for is that the glory of God be preserved, and that the righteousness of faith remain pure and sound. Once this has been established, namely that God alone justifies us solely by his grace through Christ, we are willing not only to bear the

Pope aloft on our hands but also to kiss his feet. But since we cannot obtain such a concession, we, in turn, become immensely proud in God.[139]

What is fundamentally at stake in Luther's dialectical interpretation of the institutional Church, therefore, is the theological issue of idolatry—worship apart from God's Word, which deflects man from faith in Christ toward reliance on his own works and righteousness.[140] The Papacy was seen by Luther as idolatrous because it made the outward succession in the chair of Peter the basis of the Church, allowing it to usurp the place which rightfully belonged to the Word.

If you ask the Pope why he is the people of God he answers: "Because I am sitting in the seat of the apostles Peter and Paul and am their successor. . . ." Even a dog or a swine, however, can sit in the place of St. Peter; but to have the call—that is, the Word which you believe over and above that succession— that, of course, establishes the Church and the children of God. This the Pope does not have, but he persecutes it in a hostile manner. Therefore, he is not a son of God, but is God's enemy and an adversary of Christ. . . . The true Church is the one that holds fast to the Word and faith and does not rely on works but hears and follows God when he calls.[141]

Luther's most significant statement of the problem of the institution, finally, was through his use of the Pauline dialectic of **spirit and flesh.** It was part of Paul's polemic against the Jews to draw the distinction between Israel after the flesh and Israel after the Spirit, the former resting on natural descent, the latter on spiritual rebirth. In his commentary on Genesis 25:21, Luther contrasts spirit and flesh in terms of two kinds of birth; he points, by way of illustration, to the dualism running through Genesis between the pairs of brothers, Cain and Abel, Ishmael and Isaac, Esau and Jacob, in which the crucial point of distinction was not the natural birth but the second birth by the call and promise of God.[142]

The distinction becomes important to ecclesiology at the

point where he takes over the twofold pattern and applies it
to the distinction between the "Church of God" and the
"Church of the Devil." As the Jews boasted in the flesh, so
now did the Papacy. It judged everything on external appearance, trusting in its laws, customs, and temporal possessions, and thereby making Christian communion into an outward and material matter. It did so, according to Luther, with
even less justification than the Jews, who at least had laws and
regulations of divine origin.

*But these papists can make no claims of birth or of a divine
command or ordinance for their practices, because they are
nothing but the trifles and vanities which they have chosen for
themselves. . . . If the glory and honor of natural birth and
descent from the holy patriarchs, the Law, the priesthood and
the worship which God ordained for them did not entitle the
Jews to become children of God on this account; if the Jews
were utterly rejected, together with all they boasted about,
because they would not accept this Christ in faith, but defied
him instead on the basis of their physical birth as the children
of Abraham; and if Christ has his people and his children
nevertheless—it is certain that the Papists, with their self-
chosen trifles and boasts, will amount to much less, so that,
despite their proud claims and their arrogation to themselves
of the name "church," he can let them err and fall.*[143]

Luther insisted that the message of Scripture, both against
the Jews and against the Romanists, is that "neither birth,
sonship or descent from Abraham, or belonging to this race
or line nor anything at all that is born of flesh and blood—
none of this is of any account in the kingdom of God." [144] The
only thing which counts in the true Church is the Word of
God, his call and promise which effectuates the second birth.
The Roman Church lives by the first birth because it has
neglected this call and promise, because it has concentrated on
the outward and not the inward reality of the Church, the shell
and not the kernel.[145] To Luther, the Roman Church repre-

sented "Israel after the flesh" not because it had outward form
and body, or even laws and ceremonies, but because it
trusted in these institutional structures and possessions and
therefore ceased to be "Israel after the Spirit," living by
faith in God's promise alone.

The true Church, on the other hand, is the one which neither
trusts in its outward institutional forms nor retreats into a
purely spiritual world, but rather cultivates a life "in the
flesh . . . not according to the flesh" (*in carne . . . non
secundum carnem*).[146] That is to say, it is free to adopt whatever outward forms are necessary and desirable, as long as its
faith is placed not in those forms, but in the Word alone,
which all valid forms must convey. Once again, the crucial
question is not the presence, absence, or nature of the forms
but the issue of faith and the rejection of idolatry.

In his commentary on Psalm 110:3, Luther found in the
image of the morning dew a picture of the true Church, which
is not man's creation but God's. The Church, he noted, is

*not something that can be understood or measured by external
categories or on the basis of rules and regulations, or by pretending to know the people who belong to it and saying,
"Christians, or the Christian Church, consists of all those born
of this line or race," or "they are those who live according to
such and such rules and regulations." In short, nothing men
can do out of their own resolution or capacity produces Christians, and, therefore, creates the Christian Church. Instead we
read, "Thy children will be born to Thee like the dew at
dawn." No one can say how this happens, nor can any man
contribute anything to this event. No, it is entirely God's work.
Without any thought or care on our part, dew appears every
morning.*[147]

While the idolatry of Rome was uppermost in Luther's
thoughts, it is implicit in his position that any Church can
become idolatrous if it makes its outward forms and institu-

tions into objects of faith and sets them in the place of God's Word.

IDOLATRY AND TRANSCENDENCE. Luther's development of the theme of the institutional church on a dialectical pattern gave to his ecclesiology a richness and profundity of content without any sacrifice of clarity and simplicity. Essentially, his stance is that of the prophet pointing to the issue of idolatry as the negation of true faith. It is precisely on this issue that the lines of his eschatological and his Christological thought come jointly into focus.

His eschatology, as we have noted, involves a dialectical understanding of the world as, on the one hand, an order marked for destruction and, on the other hand, the creation of God to be used and enjoyed. Because the world is rapidly passing away, it is denied any redemptive significance, any destiny of radical renewal. But precisely by being stripped of any sacral significance, the world comes into its own as a human sphere, God's gift to man, where he may exercise his vocation to the glory of God and in service to his fellowman. The significance of this position for the understanding of the institutional Church is clear. Everything in the world is God's good creation, but nothing is sacred. Therefore, any worldly form may be used if it directs man away from itself to Christ the Word, but no form may be regarded as essential or indispensable, for that would be to tranform a creature into an idol, and to accord to it the allegiance which belongs to the Word alone.

The Christological analogy which Luther develops in his ecclesiology points in the same direction. As the Word of God was an Incarnate Word, so the Church has to assume concrete and particular form in the world. But the Church can no more be understood by its outward form than can Christ be understood by his earthly appearance. The Church, therefore, is not an institution in its essence, but it has institutional forms.

Some of these forms—such as preaching and sacraments—are integral to the Gospel. But as for the rest—the details of organizational structure and liturgical practice—these are relative, human matters, determined by practical necessity and utility and valid only as long as they convey the reality of the Gospel and serve the needs of the neighbor.

Both eschatology and Christology, therefore, point on the one hand to the necessity of the Church taking outward form, and on the other hand to the relativity and ambiguity of all such forms. To absolutize any form, whether papal or evangelical, is to make an idol out of it, and to transform the Church from a work of God into a work of man.

The institutional form and the personal reality of the Church, therefore, are not in basic conflict but stand in a dialectical relationship in which the former is both posited and judged by the latter. The institution is an ongoing attempt to embody the Church's reality as a communion of saints outwardly in the world, but it stands always under radical judgment. In recognizing and living under that judgment, the Church is delivered from absolutizing or idolatrizing the institution as the immanent embodiment of the kingdom of God and is therefore freed to acknowledge its own relativity and humanity. It is enabled to live a life which is both worldly and yet marked by a quality of transcendence—that is to say, a life in the world but not dependent on the world, using everything freely but avoiding all idolatry, subject in all things to Christ, the living Word.

III · JOHN CALVIN

As a SECOND-GENERATION reformer, John Calvin played a very different role from Luther in the development of the Reformation, yet history has justly accorded him an equally significant and crucial place in the formation of the Protestant tradition. If he lacked Luther's passionate genius and personal dynamism which inspired the Reformation in its early stages, his own special gifts of calm and careful scholarship, a powerful intellect, and steadiness of purpose were ideally suited to the second generation of the Reform, when consolidation and systematic organization had become matters of the highest priority.

Calvin maintained throughout his life an attitude of great admiration and deference toward Luther, yet he was in almost every respect a man of vastly different personal and intellectual characteristics.[1] Although his family were *petit-bourgeois*, his early education in the home of a local patrician family and the deep personal friendships which he formed there combined to foster in him a distinctly aristocratic temper and outlook which remained with him throughout his life, and which contrasts sharply with the rough "earthiness" of Luther.

The precocious intellectual gifts which the young Calvin
showed in these early years were given ample opportunity to
develop in his later education, which took him to a number of
the great centers of learning in France. At Paris he perfected
his Latin under the teaching of the great Mathurin Cordier
and began his theological studies under the noted Nominalist
theologian John Major, concentrating on the study of the
fourteenth- and fifteenth-century schoolmen but becoming
acquainted to some extent also with the Church Fathers,
especially Augustine.

Although he probably became aware at this time of Luther's
views, through his teachers' refutations of them, he was in no
way drawn toward the Reform. He did, however, come increasingly under the spell of the new humanist learning, and
this fresh intellectual interest blossomed when he left Paris to
study law in Orleans under Pierre de L'Estoile and in Bourges
under the Milanese humanist Alciat. During his stay at Orleans, he learned Greek from the German Lutheran Wolmar,
but there was still no evidence of change in his religious
outlook. If his humanism at this time revealed no trace of the
sensuousness of Italian humanism, it showed also no particular
preoccupation with the question of religious reform, but remained chiefly a concern for free inquiry and good scholarship.

When the death of his father left Calvin free to follow his
own scholarly inclinations, he proceeded to take out his degree
in law, yet the law became at this time a matter of secondary
importance to the pursuit of his literary interests. His first
publication—the commentary on Seneca's *De Clementia*—
showed evidence not only of his achievement of high
scholarly status but also of considerable personal interest in
the ethical philosophy of the Stoics. Here already in Calvin
is a clear recognition of natural law, and a conception of
supernatural providence which foreshadows in outline (though
not in content) the grand doctrine of Providence which was to

achieve such central importance in the theology of the *Institutes of the Christian Religion.*

Although Calvin's conversion to the cause of the Reform came when he was only twenty-seven years old, his mind was by that time thoroughly mature, and his patterns of learning and scholarship were firmly established. There is, accordingly, a clear and unmistakable continuity between Calvin the humanist scholar and Calvin the Christian theologian. Humanism, which remained to Luther a thoroughly alien philosophy despite his use of its linguistic and exegetical tools, had in Calvin's case exercised too profound and formative an influence on his whole intellectual development to be lightly shaken off. Yet, by the same token, his humanism was necessarily qualified and limited by his conversion, for while he continued to admire the classics for their truth and beauty, they now took second place in his concerns to the Scriptures, and while he never repudiated humanism as such, his reading of the Scriptures inevitably led him to deny key humanist assumptions about human nature, sin, and free will. His scholarship had not changed in its basic characteristics, but it had acquired a new focus.

Although he would gladly have devoted the rest of his life to the pursuit of his scholarly work for the cause of the Reformed faith, Calvin was thrust instead into the unwelcome role of active prosecutor of reform, not in his native country of France but in the city of Geneva, in French-speaking Switzerland. Geneva had been in recent times a troubled and restless city, subject to the uncertainty which usually accompanies declining prosperity, threatened by the dominance of the dukes of Savoy on the one hand and the aggressive city of Berne on the other, yet striving for freedom and independence from both.

Calvin took no part in the decisive religious struggle in Geneva, in which Catholicism was soundly defeated, but he arrived at a time when the future of the Reform was uncertain

and precarious, and it was his task to lay secure foundations
on which it could grow and flourish. Our concern within these
pages, however, is not the new society which he helped to
construct in Geneva but rather that vision of the institutional
Church and of its role in human history which informed and
inspired all his labors there.

1

THEOLOGICAL FOUNDATIONS: THE PATTERN
OF SALVATION-HISTORY

Calvin's theology shows, in relation to Luther's, both a
recognizable dependence and a distinct originality. There
is a large measure of common understanding on the question
of the nature and purpose of the Church and a considerable
measure of common statement. Yet the independence and
originality of his ecclesiology is ultimately more striking, because it emerges on the basis of a radically different theological
structure. Eschatology and Christology exercise an equally
crucial role in Calvin's ecclesiology as in Luther's—but the
dialectical pattern which we found to be determinative for
Luther is no longer evident. Calvin's doctrine of the Church
emerges rather on the basis of a total vision of salvation-
history unfolding steadily from Creation to the Last Judgment under the providence of God.

CHRISTOLOGY: THE HEART OF SALVATION-HISTORY. The heart of
Calvin's theology of history is his Christology. Indeed his
theology, despite certain critics, may be acknowledged as
"Christocentric," though not, let it be admitted, in the sense
that all his thinking begins with Christ. Within the total
exposition of his theology, Christology is dealt with in due
course after consideration of God's work in creation and
providence. Yet Calvin's theology is Christocentric, never-

theless, in the sense that all his thinking points toward and reaches its climax in the figure of Christ. Christology is the source of the intrinsic unity and wholeness of Calvin's theology. Creation, Providence, and Covenant are preparatory for the emergence of Christ into the center of the stage of human history.

Calvin never tired of insisting that the ultimate purpose of *creation*, as of all the works of God, was the showing forth of his glory. The world is the "theater of his glory," and every created thing, every living creature, whether destined for salvation or perdition, lives to manifest that glory.[2] Yet we would seriously misrepresent Calvin if we interpreted this to mean that man is somehow incidental to the divine purpose. For it is equally true to say that, for Calvin, man is the immediate goal of God's creative purpose, since God's glory is manifest most clearly precisely in man, the "noblest and most remarkable example" of his work.[3] The story of Creation teaches us, says Calvin,

that God by the power of His Word and Spirit created heaven and earth out of nothing; that thereupon He brought forth living things and inanimate things of every kind, that in a wonderful series he distinguished an innumerable variety of things, that he endowed each kind with its own nature. . . . Finally, we shall learn that in forming man and in adorning him with such goodly beauty, and with such great and numerous gifts, he put him forth as the most excellent example of his works.[4]

God as revealed in Creation, therefore, is no distant and detached being who is later shown to have the character of fatherhood. Rather, the creative process itself establishes the relation between God and man as that of a father and his children, "whom he has received into his faithful protection to nourish and educate." [5] The measured process of six days by which the world came into being is a testimony to his fatherly solicitude in preparing everything useful and salutary for man.[6]

Creation, therefore, is the first, if not the chief, evidence of faith in the order of nature, and it is fitting for man not only to derive spiritual lessons from it but to "take pious delight in the works of God open and manifest in this most beautiful theater." [7] If Calvin lacks something of Luther's joyful exuberance concerning the world of nature, it is to be ascribed to a more sober and restrained temperament rather than a fundamentally different outlook.

From the start, therefore, the doctrine of Creation is cast in a personal framework, and the God who reveals Himself to man as Creator shows Himself at the same time to be Father. Accordingly, when Calvin turns, in the last three chapters of Book I of the *Institutes,* to a direct discussion of the *providence* of God, he is not so much moving to a new topic as drawing out further some of the implications of the doctrine of Creation. That is to say, the doctrine of providence does not enlarge the understanding of God's character but points to the continuance of the same fatherly purpose throughout human history.

To make God a momentary Creator, who once for all finished his work, would be cold and barren. . . . Faith ought to penetrate more deeply, namely, having found him Creator of all, forthwith to conclude that he is also everlasting Governor and Preserver—not only in that he drives the celestial frame as well as its several parts by a universal motion, but also in that he sustains, nourishes and cares for everything he has made, even to the last sparrow.[8]

Providence, thus understood, is a dynamic reality in the life of the world, which puts the lie to the idea that the world is governed by chance. God does not sit idly in heaven watching the world he has made; he is actually involved in the world, governing with his own hand the course of events.

Calvin's articulation of the content of the doctrine of providence is similar to that of Luther. The doctrine includes a

firm belief in the Devil as leader of an "empire of wickedness" set up in opposition to God's kingdom of righteousness;
and Calvin, as clearly as Luther, avoids any ultimate dualism
by making clear that the Devil is God's Devil who exercises
his sway by God's will alone.[9] Temporal authority has, for
Calvin, a basically similar purpose and rationale, as an instrument of God's providence in the time before the fulfillment
of all things. The principle of subjection is regarded as a
temporary instrument of God which has no validity within
his kingdom but a necessary and salutary purpose on earth
"without which the earth could not subsist." It is established by
God and reflects his glory; and the magistrate, therefore, acts
with a divine mandate as God's vice-regent on earth.[10]

While Calvin insisted, like Luther, on maintaining a proper
distinction between the Kingdom of Christ and earthly government, he brought the two into closer relationship than Luther
was willing to do. Spiritual government, he declared,

*is already initiating in us upon earth certain beginnings of the
heavenly kingdom, and in this mortal and fleeting life affords a
certain forecast of an immortal and incorruptible blessedness.
Yet civil government has as its appointed end, so long as we
live among men, to cherish and protect the outward worship
of God, to defend sound doctrine of piety and the position of
the Church, to adjust our life to the society of men, to form our
social behavior to civil righteousness, to reconcile us with one
another, and to promote general peace and tranquility.*[11]

Behind this variation is an important underlying difference
between the two Reformers which will become increasingly
evident in the later exposition. The dialectical balance which
Luther maintained between spiritual and worldly government, each having its own independent role, tends in Calvin
to be broken down, to the point where the world practically
loses its integrity and independent status and becomes an ad-
junct of the Church. Indeed, Calvin insists on more than one
occasion that the world was created for the Church, and

derives thence its only significance. While all Creation is under God's providence, it is the Church which is his real dwelling place.[12]

A corollary of this Church-centered perspective, and one of immense significance for our study here, is that the Church assumes in Calvin's theology a high status as the instrument of God's universal purposes and the focus of the movement of history. Without the proper functioning of the Church, Calvin insists, "the whole order of nature will be thrown into confusion and creation will be annihilated." [13]

The centrality of the Church in the providential movement of history is a theme which Calvin develops to its fullest extent in his discussion of the Church in Book IV of the *Institutes,* yet the basic foundations of this perspective are laid in his development in Book II of the theme of the *covenant.* The bearer of God's historical purposes is the covenant community which stretches back in unbroken continuity to the patriarchs of Israel.

Calvin's deep sense of the continuity and order of God's purposes in history leads him to assert the close identity of Old and New Covenants. The covenant with Israel is "so like ours in substance and reality that the two are actually the same." Its basis is grace and not merit, its goal immortality and not merely carnal prosperity, and its mediator and sole foundation is none other than Jesus Christ.[14] So close is this identification in Calvin's theology between Old and New Covenant that he has frequently been accused of failing to maintain a proper distinction between them, and attributing equal authority to both, with the result that his understanding of revelation is unhistorical, and his view of history fundamentally static.[15] This criticism is clearly an important one in view of the contradictory contention made in this chapter that Calvin's thought is dominated by a highly dynamic vision of history as the steady unfolding of God's providential purposes for the Church and the whole created order. It seems clear at the start that Calvin does attempt to make a clear distinction between old and new convenants. In Chapter XI of Book II of the *Institutes,* he lists several significant differences, and here and elsewhere he defines the difference by employing the distinction betwen identical substance and differing form. A good example of this distinction is his comment on the Passover ceremony in Exodus 12:14, where he explains the command that the feast be kept forever in the following way:

I admit that by this expression perpetuity is meant, but only such as would exist until the renovation of the Church, and the same explanation will apply to circumcision, as well as to the whole ceremonial of the law; for although by Christ's coming it was abolished as concerns its use, yet it did only then attain its true solidity; and therefore the difference between ourselves and the ancient people detracts nothing from this perpetual statute; just in the same way as the new covenant does not destroy the old in substance but only in form.[16]

Elsewhere, Calvin compares the two in terms of shadow and substance, foretaste and full meal,[17] and he uses the image of the patriarchs as the "swaddling clothes" of the Church, and Israel as a child heir, appointed to the same inheritance but

not yet old enough to be able to enter upon it and manage it. The same Church existed among them, but as yet in its childhood. Therefore, keeping them under this tutelage the Lord gave, not spiritual promises unadorned and open, but ones foreshadowed, in a measure, by earthly promises. When, therefore, he adopted Abraham, Isaac, Jacob and their descendants into the hope of immortality, he promised them the land of Canaan as an inheritance. It was not to be the final goal of their hopes, but was to exercise and confirm them, as they contemplated it, in hope of their true inheritance not yet manifested to them.[18]

The identity of substance of the two covenants, therefore, is not inimical to a recognition of diversity and progression in God's dealings with his covenant people.

Even more important, however, in understanding Calvin's view of the covenant is his conception of "suspended grace." [19] The Old Covenant is not only continuous with the New but also, in another way, contingent upon it. Without the appearance of the Son of God in the flesh, without his death and resurrection, it would all have been vain and empty. The kingdom begun in David was a prelude or "shadowy representation" of a greater one, for grace was held in suspense until the advent of the Messiah.[20] The identity and distinction between the two convenants is summed up in terms of the idea of "suspended grace" in Calvin's commentary on Acts 13:32.

But the question is asked if those who lived under the Law were not also sharers of the promises. I reply that the fellowship between us of the same grace is such that it does not, however, prevent there being a great difference between us. But Paul here means this one thing, that their faith was, so to speak, in a state of suspense, until Christ appeared, in whom all the promises of God are Yea and Amen, as he teaches in II Cor. 1:19–20. Therefore, we are heirs of the same heavenly kingdom, and sharers of the spiritual blessings with which God provides his sons; and God also gave them the taste of his love in this present life, just as we now enjoy it. But Christ, who is the substance of eternal life and of all blessings, was only promised to them, while he has been given to us.[21]

It is clear from passages such as this that Calvin's understanding of the covenant does not imply a static, monistic view of history. Since the content of the covenant is nothing but the living Christ who was present in creation, who mediated the covenant, who later appeared in the flesh, and who will finally return to fulfill all things—the theme of the covenant is precisely the means by which Calvin expresses his comprehensive understanding of salvation-history as a process with meaningful stages, by which God's creative and providential purposes are carried forward.

In Calvin's development of the themes of creation, providence, and covenant, a number of the distinctive features of his ecclesiology are already present implicitly—the conception of history as a meaningful divine drama, and of the covenant community as the instrument of God's purposes; and the recognition of Christ as sole foundation of the covenant and source of the community's life. These features become more explicit when Calvin turns his attention in due course directly to the Church.

Like Luther, Calvin makes Christology the basis of his understanding of the Church, though he does so in a very different way. For Luther, as we noted, the Church's basis lies in the dynamic and personal relationship between God and man created by the Word and answered by faith—for Calvin, it is most adequately comprehended under the image of *"union with Christ."* This image is a complex one in Calvin's thought, and its meaning must be explicated with some care. While there are many shades of meaning in the image, its fundamental purpose is to relate the life of the believer in faith to the pattern of God's purposes of salvation. The believer becomes a part of salvation-history by election; he becomes conformed to Christ's sufferings, death, and resurrection; and he grows up into Christ through sanctification. This pattern may now be explicated in more detail.

Recent critical study of Calvin's thought has done much to correct some long-standing misconceptions concerning the meaning of his doctrine of election and to permit a more sober evaluation of the significance of this doctrine within his theological work as a whole.[22] A careful examination of Calvin's writings makes it clear that, while he showed an increasing preoccupation with the doctrine, neither its scope nor its placement in the *Institutes* justifies the opinion that it is the central fulcrum around which his theology revolves. Moreover, it is apparent that the doctrine is practical rather than speculative in orientation. Calvin is insistent in his warnings against speculation into the "sacred precincts of divine wisdom." "To seek any other knowledge of predestination than what the Word of God discloses is not less insane than if one should purpose to walk in a pathless waste or to see in darkness." [23] He declares that those who would seek for salvation in the "labyrinth of predestination" thereby turn away from faith which is the one true witness to election.[24] Clearly, this is not the language of one whose thought is dominated by a rigid concept of double predestination.

Our best avenue to a positive understanding of the significance of this doctrine is to trace the way in which it developed through the various editions of the *Institutes*. In the 1536 edition, the doctrine of election has no specific locus and finds expression only in Calvin's definition of the Church as the "number of the elect." [25] In the *Geneva Catechism* of the following year, where Calvin first gives specific attention to the doctrine, he does so not out of abstract theological considerations but as an attempt to come to terms theologically with the practical reality that the Gospel is not equally effective with all.[26] Since the attribution of this ineffectiveness to the weakness of the Gospel or the powerlessness of Christ would have been unthinkable, it must be understood as God's will. The double decree, therefore, is above all a safeguard for the glory of God and the majesty of the Gospel. In the 1539 *Institutes*, the doctrine of election is directly linked with the doctrine of providence, with the same motive of safeguarding the truth that nothing happens except by the will of God.[27] Finally, in the 1559 *Institutes*, the doctrine of election and the doctrine of providence are separated again but, as Wendel correctly notes,[28] the link is still maintained because, while they are no longer directly conjoined in the exposition, they exercise parallel functions at the close of Books I and III respectively. As the doctrine of providence rounds off the doctrine of God by pointing to the ongoing relationship established by God with his creation, so the doctrine of election completes the doctrine of redemption by pointing to the eternal bond between Christ and his people.

Election, therefore, is grounded in Christology, and it points not to an abstract and impersonal decree, but to the filial relationship of man to God by adoption, known only through the Word. If the Christological foundation of this doctrine was not always evident in Calvin's polemical writings,[29] it is certainly consistently clear in the *Institutes*. In Book III, for example, he offers this comment on the Pauline understanding of adoption:

. . . *those whom God has adopted as his sons are said to have been chosen not in themselves but in his Christ (Eph. 1:4); for unless he could love them in him, he could not honor them with the inheritance of his kingdom if they had not previously become partakers of him. But if we have been chosen in him, we shall not find assurance of our election in ourselves; and not even in God the Father, if we conceive him as served from his Son. Christ, then, is the mirror wherein we must, and without self-deception may, contemplate our own election. For since it is into his body the Father has destined those to be engrafted whom he has willed from eternity to be his own, that he may hold as sons all whom he acknowledges to be among his members, we have a sufficiently clear and firm testimony that we have been inscribed in the book of life (cf. Rev. 21:27) if we are in communion with Christ.*[30]

It is no coincidence, therefore, that the doctrine of election at the end of Book III ushers in Calvin's treatment of the Church in Book IV,[31] since there is, implicitly, an intimate relationship between the two. While the notion that the double decree is the keystone of Calvin's theology is to be rejected, and while the direct treatment of election in the *Institutes* is very limited, it is true, nevertheless, that election understood in Christological terms has an important and far-reaching significance for his whole theology and especially for his ecclesiology. For if the reality of the Church is life in union with

Christ, then election is the precondition and foundation of that life. It points to the fact that the community of faith is not a product of chance or a human work but a community grounded in God's call—not a transient creature of time but a reality embedded in the divine plan from the foundation of the world.

Election in Christ is the ground on which the Christian life may be characterized as a real participation in Christ. Calvin's major presentation of this theme is located in Book III of the *Institutes,* in the context of his discussion of the work of the Spirit in faith, regeneration, justification, and sanctification. A close look at Calvin's treatment of this theme indicates that it represents the real basis of his ecclesiology. Such an assertion, however, is not self-evidently true and cannot be made without coming to terms with some serious questions about Calvin's theology raised by Emil Brunner.

Brunner opens his book, *The Misunderstanding of the Church,* with a strong attack on what he describes as the "fundamentally individualistic outlook which determines Calvin's concept of the Church." [32] He asserts that Calvin comes to a discussion of the Church in Book IV of the *Institutes* only after an independent treatment of justification and the Christian life in Book III, and that the *Institutes,* therefore, is both a cause and an expression of the individualism which has since plagued Protestantism. Brunner's position on this question had only solidified further when he wrote of Calvin's ecclesiology in the final volume of his *Dogmatics:*

Between faith and the Church, there is no inner necessary relation, but only an accidental, subsidiary one, in which faith is essentially regarded as something individual, the fellowship of faith being added to it as something which does not belong to its nature. That is to say that although Calvin in practical matters was in the highest degree a Churchman and a founder of Churches, he makes an individualistic separation of faith from the Church. Believers indeed require the Church, but they are believers even apart from it.[33]

While such statements from one who sees himself in many respects as a follower of Calvin are to be taken with great seriousness, it is most difficult to regard this comment as anything other than a gross misunderstanding, approaching superficiality. For a start, the fourfold organization of the *Institutes* corresponds roughly to that of the classical Creeds, and there is little doubt that Calvin meant it that way.[34] The four parts are no more separable from each other than the articles of the Creed. Any dogmatic structure requires some order for treating the various aspects of its subject matter, and if a subject is not specifically and comprehensively treated until the last part, it does not necessarily signify that it has not informed the previous discussion.

Clearly, however, Brunner means to imply also that the Church is absent even from implicit consideration in the earlier parts of the *Institutes,* and it is here that he makes his greatest error in judgment. Certainly, we do not find the word "Church" to any extent in the earlier books. Nevertheless, in Calvin's exposition of the theme of the covenant in Book II, and his picture of the covenant community as the agent of God's plan of salvation, we have a theme which is no less definitely ecclesiological because it does not happen to mention specifically the *ecclesia.* Moreover, in Book III, which is our present concern, the theme of union with Christ in his death, resurrection, and ascension is anything but individualistic in nature. When Calvin speaks of the Christian as being "engrafted into Christ," he frequently employs the Pauline image of the Church as the body of Christ and this image functions as his most characteristic description of the Church.[35] While we are at liberty to wish that Calvin had been more explicit on this point, a careful consideration of the evidence suggests that Brunner's charge is sadly astray. Calvin's conviction that the Church is the mother of believers and the sole way to salvation is not an afterthought introduced in Book IV—it both grows out of and informs his understanding of the Christian life in Book III. When he speaks of the Christian as being "in Christ," he is not leaving ecclesiology in suspense but pointing to its most profound dimension. The truth of this contention must now be shown in greater detail.

Calvin regarded the phrase "in Christ" as the only term which could adequately express the depth of the relation between the believer and his Lord.[36] Its meaning becomes clear in the context of the doctrine of redemption, which Calvin interprets in a twofold way. On the one hand, Christ has acted effectively in man's place and on man's behalf, and the sacrifice is complete. His purpose in consecrating himself to the Father was precisely "that everything that was his should be ours"[37]; and his victory, therefore, is something which is "for us" from start to finish. On the other hand, that victory "for us," though real, is hidden and therefore in a sense still "outside of us."

We must understand that as long as Christ remains outside of us and we are separated from him, all that he has suffered and done for the salvation of the human race remains useless and of no value for us. Therefore to share with us what he has received from the Father, he had to become ours and to dwell within us. For this reason he is called our "Head" (Eph. 4:15) and "the first-born among many brethren" (Rom. 8:29). We also, in turn, are said to be "engrafted into him" (Rom. 11:17) and to "put on Christ" (Gal. 3:27); for, as I have said, all that he possesses is nothing to us until we grow into one body with him.[38]

Therefore, man requires not only the once-for-all sacrifice of Christ but also the gift of the Holy Spirit who creates in man the faith which seals the bonds of union. For faith "does not look at Christ merely from afar, but embraces him, that he may become ours and dwell in us. It causes us to be united in his Body, to have life in common with him and, in short, to be one with him."[39] The work of the Holy Spirit, therefore, is understood as the actualization and fruition of this union between

Christ and the faithful, as the title of Book III of the *Institutes* makes clear.

But what is the nature of this union which takes place between Christ and the believer? Clearly, Calvin intended to describe more than an ethical relationship, and he states so explicitly in his commentary on Rom. 6:5, where he indicates that the image of engrafting into Christ signifies "not only our conformity to the example of Christ, but also the secret union by which we grow together with him in such a way that he revives us by his Spirit, and transfers his power to us." [40]

Nor is participation in Christ to be interpreted primarily in a sacramental sense. Calvin's interpretation of the Supper is certainly informed by his understanding of union with Christ, and he describes the sacrament in terms of being "united in one life and substance with Christ." [41] The Supper, in conveying the real, spiritual presence of Christ, in some sense augments and deepens the union with Christ. It does so, however, because it is a showing forth or re-presentation of what is at its deepest level a personal union of participation in the redemptive drama enacted in Christ—a union with Christ in his death, resurrection, and ascension. Conformity with Christ's death means both identification with him in reproaches and troubles and an inward crucifixion of the old nature.[42] Conformity to Christ in his death brings about a resurrection to new life in him, and the believer partakes of the holiness of Christ, not merely by imputation, but by a real sanctification and renewal.[43]

The crucial point to recognize here is that this is not, as Brunner claims, an individualistic understanding of faith but is profoundly ecclesiological in orientation. While it would be a misrepresentation of Calvin to imply that the meaning of the concept of union with Christ is exhausted by the ecclesiological reference, or that the image of the "body of Christ" in Calvin always denotes the Church, it is an equally serious error to fail to recognize the ecclesiological dimensions of these terms,

which Calvin develops at times quite explicitly. Notwithstanding the preoccupation of interpreters of Calvin with his
description of the Church as "mother of the faithful" and the
number of the elect, the Pauline image of the "body of Christ"
is the dominant ecclesiological image in both Book III and
Book IV of the *Institutes*. Both in the *Institutes* and in the
New Testament Commentaries, Calvin uses phrases like "in
Christ" and "in the Body of Christ" interchangeably.[44] Generally, the wording is such that an ecclesiological reference is
unmistakable. When Calvin describes the work of the Holy
Spirit, for example, in these words—"that he should insert us
into His Body, and communicate His benefits to us"[45]—it
seems to be stretching a point not to see an implicit reference
to the Church.

If there is any further need of evidence that Calvin's understanding of the life of faith is far removed from individualism,
it may be found in the way in which he conceives of the
mutual relations of the members of the body of Christ to each
other and to their common Lord. Negatively, it is clear that
Calvin cannot conceive of reconciliation to God in Christ apart
from the closest bonds of human fellowship within the body.
"For if we are split into different bodies we also break away
from Him. To glory in His name in the midst of disagreements
and parties is to tear him in pieces. . . . For he reigns in
our midst only when He is the means of binding us together
in an inviolable union."[46] Positively, the possession of a common faith and reconciliation demands and effects such a close
bond of union between the faithful that their life can only be
described in terms of complete mutual sharing, embracing one
another in brotherly love, and sharing one another's burdens.[47]
Christians, therefore, participate in the death and resurrection
of Christ not as isolated individuals but as a new community
in which the members share mutually with each other all the
gifts and graces which they have received.

We may conclude, therefore, that Calvin's understanding of the Christian life as participation in Christ is not only the core of his doctrine of the Spirit but also the fundamental root of his doctrine of the Church. The image of the Body of Christ as the community which binds together all believers by their common participation in Christ represents the heart of his ecclesiology, and what he deals with in Book IV of the *Institutes* is to be understood as a spelling out of this foundation.

Participation in Christ is never for Calvin a finished possession, but remains an eschatological reality which points beyond death and resurrection to ascension with Christ at the last day. The blessedness of the faithful is

always in progress up to that day which shall conclude and terminate all progress, and . . . thus, the glory of the elect, and complete consummation of hope, look forward to that day for their fulfillment. For it is admitted by all, that perfection of blessedness or glory nowhere exists except in perfect union with God. Hither we all tend, hither we hasten, hither all the Scriptures and the divine promises send us.[48]

The same position is written into the very structure of the *Institutes*. Book III, where Calvin discusses the whole issue of participation in Christ, is concluded by chapters on Election and on the Last Resurrection. The meaning of the pattern is clear—participation in Christ is placed in its eschatological context by looking backwards and forwards, to its origin (election) and its goal (final resurrection). Christ rose from the dead, Calvin declared,

not just to linger on earth, but that He might enter into the heavenly life and draw believers with Him. In short, with this word, He forbids the apostles to stop at his resurrection itself, and bids them come further until they come to the spiritual kingdom, to the heavenly glory, even to God himself. There is a strong emphasis on the word "ascend," for Christ stretches out His hand to His own that they may seek their happiness

nowhere else than in heaven. . . . Christ states that he as-
cends on high. Therefore we must ascend unless we want to
be separated from Him.[49]

Calvin's understanding of the Christian life, therefore, is as
much marked by tension as Luther's, but the tension is of a
somewhat different character. Luther expressed the tension in
terms of the dialectic between the two kingdoms in which the
Christian lives until the last day. Calvin's view is characterized
rather by the image of growth into the fullness of what is already possessed in foretaste. While the goal is similar, there
is a recognizable difference of emphasis. Luther is preoccupied
with the continual stance of man as a justified sinner before
God, and he says little about the growth of the sinner into the
likeness of Christ. Calvin stresses the power of the resurrection
life to effect a real sanctification, to transform the sinner into
a growing conformity with Christ. For "not only does he
cleave to us by an indivisible bond of fellowship but with a
wonderful communion, day by day, he grows more and more
into one body with us until he becomes completely one with
us." [50] Faith, Calvin declared, casts its anchor in heaven, so
that even now the Church is sitting in the heavenly places, not
entertaining a mere hope of heaven, but possessing it in Christ
already.[51] The full enjoyment of this victory is deferred until
the end of the warfare, but what is promised is real even
now.[52] Calvin, therefore, expresses a note of triumphant
optimism not easily detected in Luther, and clearly he
expects more by way of real transformation here and now.
These variations do not represent serious differences of
content, but they are significant differences of emphasis which
carry important implications for the understanding of the
Church. We shall have occasion to return to these implications
later.

Much of the commentary on Calvin's doctrine of the Church
has shown a preoccupation with the question of the visible
Church—its nature, structure, and relationship to the invisible

Church.[53] Certainly, this is a matter of considerable importance for Calvin, as a glance at the scope and content of Book IV of the *Institutes* readily makes clear. But if our exposition of Calvin's Christology as it relates to the Church is sound—if Calvin's long discussion of the Christian life as participation in Christ's death, resurrection, and ascension is already ecclesiological in character—then it is apparent that all such approaches by-pass the most profound dimensions of Calvin's ecclesiological thought.

While Calvin develops his Christology along lines different from Luther's, its ultimate effect on the doctrine of the Church is very similar. His exposition of the theme of union with Christ in his Body performs the same ecclesiological function as Luther's polarity of Word and faith, for it constitutes the Church as a community of persons in relationship to their transcendent Lord. Institutional concerns are properly understood only on the basis of this personal center. If the Christological theme indicates a measure of close agreement between Luther and Calvin, the eschatological theme is a point of profound contrast. The core of Calvin's eschatology lies in his vision of the coming of God's Kingdom and the destiny of the whole created order. It is this vision which shapes most clearly Calvin's distinctive approach to the question of the institutional Church.

ESCHATOLOGY: THE GOAL OF SALVATION-HISTORY. Calvin is as strongly motivated as Luther by eschatological hope and conceives of the Church as living already in **the last days.** He describes the expectation of the resurrection from the dead and the life eternal as "the greatest mysteries of heavenly wisdom, and the goal of all our religion, to which we ought to strive through our lives." [54]

No one has made progress in the school of Christ who does not joyfully await the day of death and final resurrection. . . . Let us not hesitate to await the Lord's coming, not only with long-

ing, but also with groaning and sighs, as the happiest thing of
all. He will come to us as Redeemer and, rescuing us from this
boundless abyss of all evils and miseries, he will lead us into
that blessed inheritance of his life and glory.[55]

The hiddenness of the Last Day in no way lessens its importance for the Christian but increases it, for it means that he must constantly await it with eager expectation. While this note of expectation is as strong in Calvin as in Luther, its flavor is different. The abrupt apocalypticism which we found be important in the formation of Luther's eschatology is almost entirely absent from Calvin. While he affirmed that the return of Christ would be sudden, he denounced any attempt to name the day and time as fantastic, destructive, and inspired by Satan, a "curious and unprofitable pursuit for the Christian." [56] Calvin's eschatological perspective differs from Luther's in that the Last Day takes its sequential place in his vision of history as an unfolding and ordered divine plan. Accordingly, it is not so much the dissolution of the present order as the culmination or climax to which history steadily moves under the guiding hand of God.

This radical rejection of apocalypticism is expressed very clearly in the way in which Calvin characteristically applies the terms "last hour" or "last days" to the time beginning with the historical advent of Christ, God's final testimony in whom all things are brought to completion. All future expectation is solidly grounded on what is already achieved in Christ's coming. The last day is the "approbation of the teaching of the Gospel." [57] It will come not as an abrupt, cataclysmic event bringing everything to nought, but rather like the final chords of a grand symphony, in which the themes which were given their definitive statement in the coming of Christ and have run their course through history are brought to a final and glorious resolution.

The culmination of history brings the full *revelation of the kingdom.* We have noted the pervasive significance in

Luther's theology of the dialectical tension between the earthly and spiritual kingdoms as two realities in sharp disjunction. In Calvin, this kind of distinction enters only in relation to politics and ethics, and his thought is dominated rather by the eschatological tension between the present and future states of the one kingdom of Christ. When Calvin speaks of the kingdom of Christ in this context, he more or less equates it with the Church (in a noninstitutional sense) and at times he uses the two terms interchangeably. What he says in this regard, therefore, is a kind of transposition from the inward descriptions of faith and the life in Christ on to the broader canvas where he depicts the progress of the kingdom in the world.

Much of this exposition of the eschatological tension between present and future is simply repetition of New Testament, and especially Pauline, theology. The kingdom is already a reality, based on the redemption of man from sin and death by Christ, who sits at the right hand of God and holds in his hands the government of heaven and earth.[58] But what the Church possesses now of this victory is only a foretaste of its final glory.

The nature of the kingdom of Christ is that it every day grows and improves, but perfection is not yet attained, nor will be until the final day of judgement. Thus both are true—that all things are now subject to Christ, and yet that this subjection will not be complete until the day of the resurrection, because that which is now only begun will then be completed.[59]

The most interesting aspect of Calvin's description is the way in which he conceives of the transition to full possession of the kingdom. The major image which he uses here is the contrast between the kingdom hidden and revealed. Christ's glorious victory is now hidden and the fullness of the kingdom will be brought not by a cataclysmic event but by the fuller revelation of what is even now a reality, by the open display of his now hidden majesty.[60] The coming of the kingdom will

be by a "fuller advance and increase of regeneration." [61] While
the Church remains in the shadow of the Cross, assigned to a
period of warfare before the final victory, it already in a sense
sits with Christ in glory, having a vivid image of good things
to come.[62] The mood throughout is one of triumphant hope,
for what is completed in the Head "must of necessity be
brought to completion in the members," and there is a real
participation now in the victory of Christ as he "regenerates his
people to the heavenly life, forms them again to the image
of God, and associates them with the angels." [63]

Here, therefore, the same difference is to be observed between Luther and Calvin as in their respective understandings
of the coming of the last day. While both understand the
present as a foretaste of the future, Calvin sees the coming of
the Kingdom not so much in terms of the hard and terrible
judgment of God as in terms of the growth to full fruition of
a victory already secure, the gradual unveiling of the glory
which is now hidden.

The contrast with Luther is seen even more clearly, however,
in the way in which Calvin relates the coming of the kingdom
to the destiny of the world. For Luther, the new heaven and
earth, the fulfillment of the kingdom, and the resurrection of
the Church come through the radical dissolution and collapse
of the present world. For Calvin, the fulfillment of the kingdom
includes within it the *renovation of the world*—the renewal
and restoration of the whole created order. Calvin's tendency
to deny any autonomous status to the world and to derive all
its significance from the Church does not lead to a rejection of
the world but rather to its inclusion within the destiny of the
Church. So powerful and triumphant is the grace of Christ
that the renewing power which he sheds abroad among the
redeemed who are brought into union with him is dispersesd
also through the world, so that the whole world, in a sense,
participates in him.

Calvin saw the world as having been undergoing renewal

ever since the Incarnation. In the first coming of Christ "the world began to be renewed and arose out of the darkness of death into the light of life." The glory of God shines forth at its brightest in the Cross, which brings with it the renewal of the whole world. The triumph is sealed by the Resurrection, and the second coming represents both the fulfillment of the kingdom of God and the completion of the world's renovation.[64] The present life of the Church is a time of real renewal and of eager expectation, for "we now begin to be formed anew by the Spirit after the image of God, in order that our entire renovation, and that of the whole world, may afterwards follow in due time." [65]

Such a positive and hopeful affirmation appears at first in strange contrast to the motif of world rejection which is prominent in Calvin's theology. In the *Institutes*, he devotes a full chapter to the theme of "Meditation on the Future Life," and he commends to the reader a stance of "contempt" in relation to the present world.

Let the aim of believers in judging mortal life, then, be that while they understand it to be of itself nothing but misery, they may with greater eagerness and dispatch betake themselves wholly to meditate upon that eternal life to come. When it comes to a comparison with the life to come, the present life can not only be safely neglected but, compared to the former, must be utterly despised and loathed. For, if heaven is our homeland, what else is the earth but our place of exile? If departure from the world is entry into life, what else is the world but a sepulcher? And what else is it for us to remain in life but to be immersed in death? If to be freed from the body is to be released into perfect freedom what else is the body but a prison? . . . Therefore if the earthly life be compared with the heavenly, it is doubtless to be at once despised and trampled underfoot.[66]

Yet this stance which Calvin advocates is not adequately described by the phrase "world rejection." For Calvin makes very clear that the *contemptio mundi* must be such that it "engenders no hatred of it or ingratitude against God." [67] Fundamentally, it signifies on the part of the believer the recognition that his salvation is not to be expected from the world but from what God holds in store for him. He is therefore freed from dependence on the world, but not from life in the world. For, while the world has no intrinsic significance, it is the Christian's sentry post, the place of pilgrimage to which God has called him.[68]

Accordingly, meditation on the future life is always conjoined in Calvin's thought with the call to increased earthly activity. Whereas Luther's eschatology is overshadowed by the judgment of the Cross, Calvin's is dominated by the resurrection hope which enfolds even this world of "infinite miseries," returns to the Christian man that dominion over the earth which he lost in Adam, and calls him to joyful and victorious obedience within it.[69] Nowhere is this outlook more clearly demonstrated than in Calvin's comment on John 12:31, the statement of Jesus, "Now is the judgement of this world." The context in the Gospel is the discourse of Jesus concerning his impending death, and the atmosphere is one of grim foreboding. Yet Calvin's interpretation of the word judgment (*krisis*) breathes the spirit of a triumphant hope which embraces the whole creation.

The word judgment is taken as "reformation" by some and "condemnation" by others. I agree rather with the former who expound it that the world must be restored to due order. For the Hebrew word משפט *which is translated as judgment means a well-ordered constitution* (rectam constitutionem). *Now we know that outside Christ there is nothing but confusion in the world. And although Christ had already begun to set up the kingdom of God, it was His death that was the true beginning of a properly ordered state and the complete restoration of the world.*[70]

2

THE INSTITUTION IN THE WORLD

Our analysis of the theological foundations of Calvin's ecclesiology has shown that for Calvin, as much as for Luther, Christology and eschatology provide the context within which the understanding of the Church emerges. Moreover, because of important variations from Luther in his exposition of the Christological and eschatological motifs, a significantly different approach to the institutional Church is already indicated. For, whereas Luther interprets faith in Christ primarily in terms of hearing and responding to the Word, Calvin's emphasis is rather on participation in Christ's body; and while Luther is preoccupied in his eschatology with the radical judgment of God on the present order, Calvin's thought is dominated by the triumphant resurrection hope which embraces the whole creation and promises transformation of the present order. In each case, therefore, Luther's position clearly implies for the institution a secondary status, as necessary for worldly life but essentially impermanent and always under radical judgment. By contrast, Calvin's outlook in both cases directs him toward the institution as God's instrument for transforming man and the world according to his purposes.

It is therefore no cause for surprise that almost all of Book IV of the *Institutes* is a close description of the nature and character of the institutional Church, its structure, offices and powers. Indeed, these matters are given such prominence and attention that it is legitimate to ask whether Calvin is ultimately defining the Church by its institutional forms and substituting a new legalism for the old one. Such a judgment, however, would indicate a very superficial understanding of what Church order implies for Calvin. The notion of order has

great significance throughout Calvin's theological exposition—
so much, in fact, that it may even be legitimately described
as the inner meaning of the history of salvation. God's creation
is described as a work of order, for it is "so arranged and regu-
lated that nothing deviates from its appointed course." [71] Creation is the image of God, but the destruction of this image in
the Fall represents the introduction of disorder into Creation.[72]
Jesus Christ is the perfect image of God, because he originates
a restoration of creation to its original integrity, bringing a
new creation out of the ruin of the first, restoring affairs from
confusion and disorder to "true and complete integrity." [73]

The way in which Calvin relates this general conception of
order to the more precise question of Church order is shown
very clearly in the Commentary on Ephesians where he writes
that

*Paul wants to teach that outside Christ all things were upset,
but that through Him they have been reduced to order. And
truly, outside Christ, what can we perceive in the world but
mere ruins? We are alienated from God by sin, and how can
we but be wandering and shattered? The proper state of
creatures is to cleave to God. Such an ἀνακεφαλαίωσις as would
bring us back to regular order, the apostle tells us, has been
made in Christ. Formed into one body, we are united to God,
and mutually conjoined with one another. But without Christ,
the whole world is as it were a shapeless chaos and frightful
confusion. He alone gathers us into true unity.*[74]

The Church, then, is that sphere where God's work of re-
ordering his creation, begun in Christ, is extended until the
time when Christ will come again to establish his kingdom, the
state of perfect order.

Church order, therefore, is not fundamentally a structure,
a code, or a system, but rather a ceaseless activity which has
its rationale in God's work of bringing order out of confusion.
Because God uses it as his instrument, order is the essence of
the Church's present task. Because the Church will never

transcribe on earth the perfect form of the kingdom of God, it remains always an eschatological goal.[75] The tension between order as a present task and order as a final goal provides the most useful approach to Calvin's understanding of the institution, and a significant perspective on the so-called dichotomy between the Church visible and the Church invisible.

ORDER AS A PRESENT TASK. Despite the amount of attention which Calvin lavishes on the description of the visible, institutional Church, its position in his theology appears at first to be equivocal. For while he insists on the utter necessity of the visible Church for salvation, this necessity seems to be not so much inherent in the nature of faith as derivative of human sloth and ignorance. The visible Church is described as the "external means" by which God accommodates himself to human weakness.[76]

In view of this terminology, it is not surprising that Brunner chided Calvin for failing to give the Church its due significance in the economy of salvation.[77] Yet the difficulty here is primarily one of terminology. While the phrase "external means" inevitably suggests something incidental or at least secondary, this impression is dispelled when it is recalled that in Calvin's theology the Incarnation itself has a similar kind of necessity. Just as God could have acted directly and immediately, yet chose to become incarnate as a man among men, so he shows a parallel accommodation to man in using the Church as an "external means." That is to say, while the institutional Church was not a necessity for God, it is most certainly for man the only way to forgiveness and salvation. "For there is no other way to enter life, unless this mother conceive us in her womb, give us birth, nourish us at her breast, and . . . keep us under her care and guidance until putting off mortal flesh, we become like the angels." [78]

Nor is the significance of this visible institution confined to the function of nurturing the believer's faith. Our analysis of

Calvin's understanding of order and of the history of salvation indicates a more fundamental significance. The institutional Church is the place where that restoration of order in creation, initiated by Christ and destined to be completed at the last day, is realized in the present. When Calvin states that the purpose of Christ's saving work is the creation of the Church, this universal perspective must be kept in mind.

That Calvin understands Church order in the way here defined is confirmed, first, by an analysis of how he speaks of the *marks of the true Church*. Much of what he says at this point is so close to Luther's position that we need spend no time dwelling on the issue. It will suffice to indicate these areas of agreement briefly before considering those aspects of Calvin's position which are distinctively his.

The Church is said to exist "wherever we see the Word of God purely preached and heard, and the sacraments administered according to Christ's institution." [79] Calvin, like Luther, emphasizes the primacy of the Word as the "abiding mark with which our Lord has sealed his own" and of which all other marks are derivative.[80] The Word is closely, but not completely, identified with Scripture, which remains the touchstone of faith and judge over the Church, and is never delivered into the Church's control.[81] There is in Calvin, to be sure, a far greater tendency to equate the Word with "pure doctrine," [82] but it is no more fair to him than to Luther to interpret this in the sense which the phrase acquired in seventeenth-century orthodoxy. In the commentary on Acts 2:42, for example, it is clear that the phrase "pure doctrine" is equated with the living apostolic witness to Christ.[83] Moreover, Calvin stresses continually the inseparability of Word, Spirit, and faith. The Word is the touchstone of true doctrine but, without the inward, secret power of the Spirit to enlighten the mind and seal the witness on the heart, the Word is powerless; and unless this Word is received in faith and followed by a growth in grace, it has no effect.[84] The similarity with Luther is apparent not only in these details but in the underlying pattern, by which Word, Scripture, and doctrine are regarded as expressions of the Lordship of Christ, which is the one true mark of the Church and the only bond of unity.[85]

Notwithstanding this basic similarity with Luther, Calvin went beyond him in some respects, specifically in his emphasis on the ministry and in the growing significance which he established for discipline within the institutional Church. While he accepted the universality of the Christian call to priesthood, he placed an important emphasis on the mediating role of the Church's ecclesiastical ministry and regarded it as a distinct order set up by Christ as part of the Church's constitution.

Among the many excellent gifts with which God has adorned the human race, it is a singular privilege that he deigns to consecrate to himself the mouths and tongues of men in order that his voice may resound in them. . . . For although God's power is not bound by outward means, he has nonetheless bound us to this ordinary manner of teaching.[86]

The power of the keys, which Luther clearly committed to the whole congregation, is bound by Calvin to the Word preached, and therefore its exercise is reserved to the ministry. For the ministry is the means by which God cleanses the Church, and in exercising its function of preaching the Word it may even be described as the very mouth of God.[87]

While he assigns the ministry this distinct status and crucial role, however, Calvin consistently sees their ministry as exercised in relationship to the whole community. The task of the ministry is understood in terms of servanthood, since it consists of "ruling the people committed to them according to the Word of God so that Jesus Christ may ever remain supreme pastor and sole Lord of the Church." [88] Their position of leadership not only expresses the rule of Christ's Word but assures the achievement of the secondary goal that "everything be done decently and in order." [89]

The motive of establishing "order" is also behind Calvin's growing stress on discipline within the institutional Church. At times, he couples discipline very closely with Word and Sacrament, and if he never formally made it a third mark of the Church like Bucer or later Calvinism, perhaps it was because he saw it as an enduring characteristic of the entire life of the Church. "The body of the Church," he wrote to Sadolet, "must be bound together by discipline as with sinews." [90] The purpose of discipline is identical with the purpose of the ministry—namely, that the Christian be properly subject, not to the ministry or even to the Church, but to the royal and priestly imperium of Christ. Discipline is the way in which God's work of bringing order is effected and guaranteed within the Church. The Church's task is to make visible "the order approved by the Lord," thereby reflecting in its life the restoration of God's image.[91]

It is in the light of this urgent demand for a truly disciplined community that we must interpret Calvin's strong emphasis on separation from the worldly. "There is more distance," he said, "between the children of God and the unbelievers than between heaven and earth." [92] The Christian's baptism means a death to the world as radical as Noah's entry into the ark, and salvation is possible only through such separation from the world. By such a separation, the Church becomes a community truly disciplined for service to its Lord, and its rectitude is evidenced by persecution at the hands of the world.[93]

Calvin's perspective on the signs or marks of the Church, therefore, is substantially similar to Luther's, though with a greater stress on the ordained ministry and on the function of discipline. On the issue of the institutional *form of the Church,* however, the difference between the two Reformers is marked. We have noted that Luther approached the matter of the specific details of Church order and organization in a spirit of radical Christian freedom, in the context of serving and upbuilding the neighbor. The issue emerges for Calvin

within the context of God's work of re-ordering the world, and
accordingly there develops in his thought a stress on the insti-
tuting and keeping of "the Church order established by
God." [94] He declared that he would accept in the Church "only
those institutions which are founded on God's authority drawn
from Scripture, and therefore wholly divine." [95] In a letter to a
French priest in 1543, he explained his position in this way:

*The order which our Lord has once delivered to us ought to
be for ever inviolable. Thus, when it has been forsaken for
a season, it ought to be renewed and set up again, even should
heaven and earth commingle. There is no antiquity, no custom which can be set up or pleaded in prejudice of this doctrine, that the government of the Church established by the
authority of God should be perpetual even to the end of the
world, since he has willed and determined that it should
be so.*[96]

Accordingly, whereas Luther used old and new forms freely
according to their appropriateness in the present, Calvin
stressed very strongly the restoration of the true and ancient
order of the Church. He maintained against his Roman op-
ponents that he was not introducing disorder and schism into
the Church, but rather overcoming the Babel and confusion
which characterized the Roman Church by renovating it according to its true and ancient basis. He argued for the Reformed order against Rome on the basis of antiquity and
described the task of the Reformed Churches as being "to renew the ancient form of the Church which, at first distorted
and stained by illiterate men of indifferent character, was after-
ward criminally mangled and almost destroyed by the Roman
pontiff and his faction." [97]

Calvin, therefore, clearly saw himself not as an innovator but
as a renovator, calling for the restoration of the Church's form
"to the exact standard of the Word of God"; [98] and much of
Book IV of the *Institutes* is taken up with Calvin's attempt to
apply the standards of Scripture and antiquity to determine the

true and ancient form of the Church and to facilitate its adoption in Geneva, in terms of structure, ministry, and worship.

Nevertheless, while his approach to Church order is recognizably different from Luther's, it would be a mistake to see them as vastly different in actual practice. For Luther also saw his reform as a purging of later accretions from the true and ancient faith, while Calvin, on the other hand, is far from a servile and legalistic imitation of the primitive Church. His desire to restore the ancient order of the Church was broadly conceived, and he was willing, indeed insistent, that with the broad outlines properly laid down, it was sufficient in details to adhere to the spirit of Paul's instruction that "all things be done decently and in order."

The Lord has in his sacred oracles faithfully embraced and clearly expressed both the whole sum of true righteousness, and all aspects of the worship of his majesty, and whatever was necessary for salvation; therefore in these the Master alone is to be heard. But because he did not will in outward discipline and ceremonies to prescribe in detail what we ought to do (because he foresaw that this depended on the state of the time, and he did not deem one form suitable for all ages), here we must take refuge in those general rules which he has given, that whatever the necessity of the Church will require for order and decorum should be tested against these. Lastly, because he has taught nothing specifically, and because these things are not necessary to salvation, and for the upbuilding of the Church ought to be variously accommodated to the customs of each nation and age, it will be fitting (as the advantage of the church will require) to change and abrogate traditional practices and to establish new ones. Indeed, I admit that we ought not to charge into innovation rashly, suddenly, for insufficient cause. But love will be best judge of what may hurt and edify; and if we let love be our guide, all will be safe.[99]

This passage comes from a section on the *Institutes* headed "Bondage and Freedom of Church Constitutions," and its spirit is very close indeed to Luther's concern for Christian freedom. Although the two Reformers approached the matter of Church order in a different way, their final positions are not very different. It is true that Calvin accepts a greater degree of prescribed order than does Luther, and that the scope of Christian freedom in his understanding of order is somewhat less broad by comparison. However, he never expected that an institution would emerge which would be in complete conformity to God's will.[100] While the making visible of the ordering work of God is the Church's present task of obedience, this task is never complete but remains an eschatological goal.

ORDER AS A FINAL GOAL. Wherever order is re-created and things are brought into subjection to Christ, the *kingdom of God* comes to expression. But this kingdom remains an incomplete and partial reality, both within the Church and within the world.

The visible Church as a practical reality is not the glorious and unspotted bride of Christ but a mixed body in which hypocrites who have nothing of Christ but the name and appearance mingle freely with the elect.[101] The visible Church is like a net in which all kinds of fish are gathered unsorted or a field of wheat and tares which remain mingled together until the threshing floor of the day of judgment, and no mattter how hard the Church labors to purge itself of this pollution, it will never achieve a state of purity in this world.[102] Called to conjugal fidelity, the bride of Christ remains polluted by base seducers. The Church is holy, therefore, only "in the sense that it is daily advancing and is not yet perfect: It makes progress from day to day, but has not yet reached its goal of holiness." [103]

The fact that the Church is a mixed body, however, gives

no one the right to forsake its fellowship. There is no excuse for abandoning the outward fellowship of the Church and thus forsaking the Word and Sacraments, and he who does so acts in pride and arrogance and breaks the lawful order of the Church as much as the wicked.[104] For the sinful body is still the body of Christ which day by day is advancing toward the state of perfection in which God's kingdom will be fully realized among men.

That kingdom will not be complete until its reality fills the whole created order. Calvin's concern to purify and discipline the Church and to maintain separation from the evil world is not an end in itself but a means to the end of preparing the Church to claim the whole world for Christ. As the instrument of God's new order, the Church has a universal mission to carry the "shining clarity of the light of the Gospel" into the world and to bring all men's hearts and minds into obedience to it. Christ came not to reconcile the few but to "extend his grace over all the world." The light which has been shed upon Christians is not to be hidden under a bushel but shown forth to all mankind.[105]

The final goal of Calvin's vision, therefore, is not restricted to the Church but embraces the whole creation and sees it as filled with the kingdom of Christ. The new order of God must be made visible not only in the ecclesiastical community but also in society as a whole. That is to say, the Church must extend its sway over the whole social order. Calvin's organization of the city of Geneva is an outgrowth of this drive, and there is no doubt that he saw his purpose there in the same terms as he once used to describe the growth of the reform movement in Poland—namely, to "establish the heavenly reign of God upon earth." [106] As the Gospel moves out to claim all nations, the kingdom of Christ comes into full splendor. The structures of the world which oppose his rule are destroyed, as the structures of grace become manifest, and the whole creation is transfigured into conformity with Christ.[107] The fact that this goal will always remain ahead for the Church in no way lessens the urgency of its present task of being the agent of the restoration of order throughout the world.

ORDER AND TRANSCENDENCE. Our exposition to this point has carefully avoided any reference to the distinction between the Church visible and the Church invisible, which more often than not is the starting point of discussions about Calvin's ecclesiology. This decision was taken deliberately in the conviction that the distinction between visible and invisible Church is misleading unless it is seen in the context of Calvin's pattern of salvation-history, and especially of his profound understanding of order as the inner meaning of that history. In the proper context, however, the polarity of visible and invisible Church provides an important final perspective on Calvin's understanding of the institutional Church.

The Church visible is defined as the multitude "who profess to worship one God and Christ," and therefore adhere to the community of Word and sacraments, under the ministry instituted by Christ.[108] The invisible Church is defined, by contrast, as "that which is actually within God's presence, into which no persons are received but those who are children of God by grace and adoption and true members of Christ by sanctification of the Holy Spirit." [109] It includes, therefore, not only the true saints on earth but all the elect from the beginning of the world.

If we were to begin and end with this description, we would inevitably be led to see the polarity as a dichotomy, since the Church visible and the Church invisible are defined by radically different principles—the former by institutional adherence, the latter by eternal election. On this level, there is no hint of the subtlety and profundity of Luther's conception of the hiddenness and visibility of the Church. It is quite clear, however, that Calvin did not intend to speak of two churches in dichotomy. If we see the distinction in terms of the pattern of salvation-history, and his conception of order as a present task and a final goal, it becomes clear that what is implied in this distinction between the invisible and the visible Church is not an abstract ontology but an eschatological polarity. The invisible Church is not an abstraction but as essential a part of Calvin's scheme of salvation-history as the visible Church. The latter is Calvin's way of describing God's work of bringing order out of chaos. The former is his testimony to the fact that this work is never complete. That is to say, the invisible Church functions in Calvin's theology in relation to the visible institution in an analogous fashion to Luther's concept of the Word, as a transcendent norm of judgment over the institutional Church. It ensures that the institution, for all its importance in the ongoing drama of salvation, can never be regarded as the immanent realization of the kingdom of God but stands under the judgment of its own incompleteness and imperfection. The doctrine of the invisible Church is Calvin's way of pointing to the fact that the Church, in the final analysis, is created by God and remains known only to him.[110] The final goal of perfect order lies in the future, and though the Church daily strives toward that goal, it will never be attained in this life.

This consistently eschatological pattern ensures that Calvin, for all his stress on the setting up of true order in the Church, never lapses into a new legalism, in which the present institution is absolutized or divinized. The Church is called to make visible in its institutional character God's work of reordering his creation and bringing his kingdom to fruition. But it can never claim to represent that kingdom in an unqualified way. It is always in a state of "becoming" and stands under the transcendent judgment of God.

IV · MENNO SIMONS

THE SIGNIFICANCE of Menno Simons in the history of Christian thought does not approach that of Luther or Calvin, and his writings reveal neither the profound insight of the former nor the formidable intellectual power of the latter. Although the moderate Anabaptist tradition as it endured in the subsequent history of Europe and America has come to bear his name, he was not its founder, and his work is only one of several important contributions to the formation of that tradition.[1]

Yet, for a number of reasons, Menno Simons deserves special attention here. Historians cannot afford to limit their attention to the towering giants of history whose writings have fashioned whole new societies; they must be responsible also for that host of other historical figures of lesser stature who, nevertheless, exercised in their own way an important influence both in and beyond their time. Menno Simons was such a man. Although he was not the founder of Anabaptism, or even of Dutch Anabaptism, it is not without some justice that this tradition has come to bear his name, for none contributed to it in such a substantial way as he or did more to preserve it from disin-

tegration. He was both close enough to the urgent struggle of
the Anabaptist movement for survival in a hostile world to reflect its authentic spirit and at the same time sufficiently detached from its immediate birth pangs to write with a balance,
a perspective, and a wholeness not characteristic of most of
the key figures of the movement. Moreover, while the radical
impulse frequently dissipated itself in individualism, Menno
reflects that segment of radical thought which found expression
in a distinct and enduring ecclesiological tradition.

It is this latter point in particular which has prompted the
detailed treatment here of Menno's thought and the omission
of other Reformation figures of greater personal theological
stature. The Anabaptist tradition, as represented by Menno
Simons, has a distinctive theological outlook, and one of its
most crucial concerns is precisely the question of the Church
and its institutional embodiment in the world. The study of
Menno's thought unveils an important new perspective on the
problem under discussion and may provide, therefore, a fuller
and more balanced picture of Reformation thought concerning
the institutional Church.

Anabaptism in the Low Countries was a complex movement,
and its origins remain to this day rather obscure. Undoubtedly,
it owed something indirectly to the influence of the Lutheran
Reformation and of early Swiss Anabaptism, yet it seems to
have been, fundamentally, a native Dutch development. Its
religious roots lay most deeply in the Sacramentarian movement, though it may have been influenced to some extent also
by the piety and spirituality of the Brethren of the Common
Life. Socially, it was primarily a lower-class urban movement,
and the severe economic conditions of the time certainly
played a large part in the formation of its protest and particularly in the development of its strongly apocalyptic outlook.

The movement soon became a significant factor in the religious life of Holland, but it exercised no influence whatever in

the early religious and intellectual development of Menno Simons. The son of a Dutch peasant family, Menno was consecrated early in life by his parents to the service of the Church, and he followed an entirely orthodox path toward his priestly vocation. In due time, he entered a Franciscan monastery, and his training there was in every way quite conventional. He acquired a facility in Latin and Greek, made some acquaintance with the writings of the Church fathers, but remained almost entirely ignorant of the Bible. There is no evidence to suggest that he was in any way affected either by humanist reforming ideas or by the spirituality of the "new devotion." On the contrary, his priesthood was marked, according to his own report, by a perfunctory performance of his duties and a thoroughly frivolous and worldly attitude.[2]

Nevertheless, though he was to remain in the Catholic priesthood for about ten years, he was troubled by nagging doubts and uncertainty almost from the start. He came to question and to reject in turn both the dogma of transubstantiation and the practice of infant baptism, basing his rejection on his reading of the New Testament, which became increasingly from this time the standard of his theological judgment. It was not these developing theological convictions, however, which caused him to break with Rome and throw in his lot with the Anabaptists, but rather the fanatical activities of the Münsterite revolutionaries, who had swept away many of his own flock with their apocalyptic dreams and revolutionary programs. The struggle against the Münsterite aberrations not only clarified his own convictions further but finally brought home to him his hypocrisy and cowardice. Renouncing the priesthood, he became an open and fearless supporter of the Anabaptist cause and eventually its most distinguished leader. It was due in large measure to his leadership that the scattered and discouraged Anabaptist groups were preserved from either fanaticism or disintegration.

1

THEOLOGICAL FOUNDATIONS: THE PATTERN
OF RADICAL DUALISM

During his twenty-five years as an Anabaptist leader, Menno produced a body of writings which, if dwarfed by the literary output of Luther and Calvin, represents nevertheless the most substantial body of sixteenth-century Anabaptist literature, and the most important source for our understanding of moderate Anabaptist thought. Throughout these writings, the question of the institutional Church and its embodiment in the world remains one of Menno's most crucial concerns. His perspective on the issue is, understandably, radically different from those of the other Reformers, and the difference is rooted in the fundamental structure of his theology. For, whereas Luther's thought is characterized by a balanced dialectic of Church and world, and Calvin's by a pattern of salvation-history enfolding both Church and world in God's universal purposes, Menno's is notable for its radical and thoroughgoing dualism between Church and world.[3] This fundamentally different pattern of theological understanding is clearly articulated in both his Christology and his eschatology, and determines the basic character of his understanding of the institutional Church.

CHRISTOLOGICAL DUALISM:[4] THE TWO BIRTHS. The contemporary revival of scholarly interest in the radical religious movements of the sixteenth century, and the consequent recognition of Anabaptism as a movement deserving consideration in its own right, has issued in a continuing attempt to discern the core idea which gave some unity to the scattered and diverse radical groups which emerged at the time of the Reformation. Harold S. Bender found the concept of Christianity as discipleship to be the most fundamental element of what he called the

"Anabaptist vision," and he defined it as "the transformation of the entire way of life of the individual believer and of society so that it should be fashioned after the teaching and example of Christ." [5] On the other hand, the suggestion that the distinctiveness of Anabaptism lies in its ecclesiology has found a ready endorsement from a number of scholars. Cornelius Krahn, for example, observes that, although Menno was not a theoretical systematic theologian, he did have a theology, and that the core of that theology was his unique concept of the Church.[6]

It would be a mistake to attribute too much importance to these differences of opinion, for in Menno's thought, as in most Anabaptist theology, the concepts of discipleship and the Church are really dependent on each other. What has not always been recognized, however, is that they are closely related to each other because both have their origin in another concept more fundamental than either—namely, Menno's understanding of *regeneration through Christ.* Discipleship is a living out of the demand and promise of the new birth, and the Church is the body of the regenerate. To claim regeneration in this way as a more basic concept in Menno's thought than either discipleship or the Church does not imply a fundamental difference of interpretation, but neither is it merely a matter of splitting hairs. It does indicate a subtle shift of emphasis which more clearly safeguards the *sola gratia* character of salvation. Discipleship and the Church are derivative in the sense that they include the human response. The charge often leveled at the Anabaptists—that they instituted a new legalism and works righteousness—would be far less plausible if it were more clearly recognized that behind Menno's understanding of discipleship in the Christian community is his understanding of regeneration as a sheer act of God's grace.

Menno employed the doctrine of regeneration through Christ in parallel fashion to Luther's use of the polarity of Word and faith and Calvin's use of the concept of union with Christ. That is to say, it is the point at which his Christology becomes the basis of his interpretation of the Church and his understanding of the life of man within the Church.

It is important to recognize that Menno's doctrine is Christologically based and has none of that subjectivism about it which characterized later Pietism. Regeneration is no decision of man but an act of God in Christ through his Word and Spirit. "We cannot be led to this godly gift of faith and of regeneration," Menno writes, "otherwise than by the Word of God through His Holy Spirit." [7] The Word is the living seed by which man is nourished and renewed, by whom alone children are born into the Church, and without whom there is nothing but blindness, error, disobedience, and eternal death.[8] Accordingly, Menno counseled his followers: "Let Christ Jesus with His Spirit and Word be your teacher and example, your way and your mirror. . . . In your life you must be so converted and changed that you become new men in Christ, so that Christ is in you and you are in Christ." [9]

Regeneration, therefore, effects a radical change in the believer, but it happens only because Christ has acted to become one with him. The outward baptism with water is significant only as man's obedient response to the inward baptism of God's grace.[10] The Church, accordingly, is to be understood as the body of the regenerate. "You must learn and know from the Word of God," Menno declared,

that the holy Christian Church is no assembly of unbelievers, carnal or brazen sinners, even if they falsely appropriate the name of Christ Jesus and think themselves to be the true Christian Church. No, kind readers, no. They are not all Abraham's seed who are born of Abraham. Only the children of promise are counted for the seed (Rom. 9:8). So, also, the holy Christian Church must be a spiritual seed, an assembly of the righteous, and a community of the saints; which church is begotten of God, of the living seed of the divine Word, and not of the teachings, institutions and fictions of man. Yes, they are those who are regenerated, renewed and converted; who

hear, believe and keep all the commandments and will of God;
who have crucified the flesh with the affections and lusts (Gal.
5:24); who have put on Christ Jesus, and reflect Him, and be-
come like unto Him (Rom. 8:17).[11]

Menno's doctrine is rich and profound, and it breathes the
spirit of Pauline theology. Regeneration implies on the part of
God an act of sheer grace and on the part of man a response
which includes not only sincere belief but a transformation of
life. Moreover, as the Christian community can only be understood on the basis of regeneration, so regeneration is inescap-
ably communal in character. The Church is a community of
brothers tied to each other by bonds closer than those of any
human family. Nowhere is this more tellingly expressed than
in Menno's discussion of the Lord's Supper where he writes in
terms very similar to those of the ancient *Didache:*

Just as natural bread is made of many grains, pulverized by
the mill, kneaded with water, and baked by the heat of the
fire, so is the Church of Christ made up of true believers,
broken in their hearts with the mill of the divine Word, bap-
tized with the water of the Holy Ghost, and with the fire of
pure, unfeigned love made into one body. Just as there is
harmony and peace in the body and all its members, and just
as each member naturally performs its function to promote the
benefit of the whole body, so it also becomes the true and liv-
ing members of the body of Christ to be one: one heart, one
mind, one soul. Not contentious, not spiteful and envious,
not cruel and hateful, not quarrelsome and disputatious, one
toward another, long-suffering, friendly, peaceable, ever ready
in true Christian love to serve one's neighbour in all things
possible.[12]

Such an emphasis as this, however, was present also in Luther
and Calvin, and it is more important for our purposes to note
an important contrast between Menno and the other two Reformers. In Menno's doctrine of regeneration, there is an emphasis very different from Luther's understanding of man as

simul justus et peccator, or indeed from Calvin's conception of growth into Christ. Menno clearly conceives of this new birth as effecting a transformation far more immediate and radical than either Luther or Calvin thought possible. He speaks of the regenerate as living "unblamably," as being "one with the Father, of one mind and disposition, having the divine nature of their Father," "the same aptitude for good that He has of whom they are born and begotten." [13]

It is clear, nevertheless, that Menno never intended to imply that the regenerate had reached a state of perfection beyond which no progress was possible. The regenerate, he insisted, "daily sigh and lament over their poor, unsatisfied, evil flesh, over the manifest errors and faults of their lives. Their inward and outward war is without ceasing." [14] Sin is not entirely destroyed in baptism, and works remain mixed with imperfection, so that the regenerate never attain wholly to the righteousness required by the commandments. The Christian can never comfort himself with the thought of his good works but only with the grace of God in Christ. [15]

On the strength of such clear affirmations as these, Franklin Littell has maintained that Menno clearly avoids perfectionism and consistently pictures the Church as the *ecclesia viatorum,* or "pilgrim Church." [16] On closer analysis, however, it appears that those passages which Littell advances in support of his position are inadequate for the purpose. What remains in the regenerate is "weakness," which Menno elsewhere explicitly differentiates from willful and intentional sin. In the *Reply to False Accusations,* for example, Menno distinguishes four kinds of sin—first, original sin, inherited by birth from Adam; secondly, actual sin, the fruit of original sin, being gross sins such as adultery, hatred, and murder, which bring man to corruption and death; thirdly, the human frailties and errors still found among the regenerate but being neither willful nor intentional; and, finally, the willful renunciation of the grace of God on the part of those who have tasted salvation. [17] The clear implication is that what remains in the regenerate is not a real battle against a sinful will and against actual sin but minor and unintentional infractions and weaknesses. One could maintain, of course, that inasmuch as even weakness and frailty indicate a state short of perfection, Menno is strictly speaking not "perfectionist," but such a position amounts to playing with words. The real point is that, despite Menno's obvious intention of preserving the eschatological nature of Christian holiness, his restriction of continuing sin to such minor and unintentional shortcomings resolves the eschatological tension of the Christian life too easily and projects an understanding of Christian existence considerably removed from Paul's anguished testimony concerning the continuing struggle with his sinful will. Menno's motive, of course, was never pride in the human achievement of holiness, but rather a desire to give full weight to the transforming power of regeneration, but we must take into account not only motive but also achievement, and it is hard to escape the conclusion that he was not able to maintain a properly eschatological understanding of Christian holiness.

Nowhere is this tendency to imply perfection in the regenerate clearer than in Menno's use of the Pauline image of the Church as *the spotless bride* of Christ, an image which is as important in Menno's thought as is the "communion of saints" in Luther's and the "body of Christ" in Calvin's. The image of the spotless bride not only suggested a close and intimate relationship between the believers and their Lord but provided an obvious link with the ideas of newness and purity in his doctrine of regeneration.

The Church is "the new Eve, the pure chaste bride. . . . flesh of Christ's flesh and bone of His bone, the spiritual house of Israel, the spiritual city Jerusalem, the spiritual Temple and Mount Zion. . . ." [18] Significantly, in passages like this, Menno turns for his image of the Church on the one hand to the state of paradise in Genesis, and on the other to the vision of the

holy city at the end of history, and he blends the two together
to describe the nature of the Church in the present age. That is
to say, the Church is lifted above the corruption and sin of the
present age. The scriptural dialectic between the unchaste
harlot and the spotless bride she is destined to become is
not consistently maintained. Although Menno recognizes that
God has chosen a "poor, despised, unesteemed, yes, unchaste
servant," the implication seems to be that the transformation
has already occurred, and that the Church has already become
the "fairest, purest and noblest among women." [19] Christ's
bride, the Church, is

*flesh of His flesh and bone of His bone: she conforms to Him;
is made after His image; partakes of His nature; seeks nothing
but heavenly things where Christ Jesus is sitting at the right
hand of His Father. Yes, in God's Church nothing is heard,
seen or found but the true doctrine of our beloved Lord
Jesus Christ and His holy apostles, according to the holy
Scripture.*[20]

Clearly, there is a strong tension at this point in Menno's
thought, and it will not do either to attribute to him an unqualified perfectionist stance or, on the other hand, to deny
that this tendency finds expression in his thought. The ambiguity exists because, while his reading of the Scriptures and
his own theological instincts told him to avoid a perfectionist
standpoint, he is driven inexorably toward that position by the
radically dualistic structure of his thought, which merits, at
this point, a closer and more detailed examination.

The doctrine of regeneration, which we have already identified as the fundamental key to Menno's ecclesiology, is articulated in terms of the Biblical dualism of **the two births.** The
contrast between those of the first birth and those of the second
birth becomes one of his central themes and is expressed with
unusual radicalism. The sharply dualistic character of this
doctrine is indicated very clearly in his tract on the New Birth,
where he notes that

*The first birth of man is out of the first and earthly Adam,
and therefore its nature is earthly and Adam-like, that is,
carnally-minded, unbelieving, disobedient and blind to divine
things; deaf and foolish; whose end, if not renewed by the
Word, will be damnation and eternal death. . . . The regenerate, therefore, lead a penitent and new life for they are
renewed in Christ and have received a new heart and spirit.
Once they were earthly-minded, now heavenly; once they were
carnal, now spiritual; once they were unrighteous, now righteous; once they were evil, now good, and they live no longer
after the old corrupted nature of the first earthly Adam, but
after the new upright nature of the new and heavenly Adam,
Christ Jesus. . . . Their minds are like the mind of Christ,
they gladly walk as he walked.*[21]

While Menno does acknowledge that this new birth is all
of God's grace, there is nothing in his thought corresponding
to Luther's understanding of righteousness as an alien reality
imputed to unrighteous man. Man is not *simul justus et peccator*—he is one or the other, either unrighteous or righteous,
unregenerate or regenerate. The separation between those of
the old birth and those of the new birth is clear and unqualified. Menno thus appropriates a dualistic concept which
is certainly Biblical, but he pushes it beyond Biblical limits.
Specifically, he applies it with such radicalism that he places
in jeopardy the doctrine of creation. The image of fallen man
which emerges from Menno's writings is not the image of a
glorious creature corrupted, but rather the image of a being
who is—with no apparent qualification—"unclean slime and
dust of the earth." [22] Apart from isolated and incidental references to God's love in the creation and preservation of the
world,[23] one searches in vain in Menno's writings for any positive content to the understanding of creation. The distinction
between creation and fall seems to have disappeared entirely.
In creating the new Adam, Christ, by implication, does not
restore and renew the first Adam, but rather destroys him.
There is no hint at all of Luther's delight in the goodness of

creation, or of Calvin's sense of the universality of God's creative purpose.

The distinctiveness of Menno's position here is important to note. All of the Reformers found it necessary to define "Church" over against "world" in some sense, but Luther and Calvin did so in such a way as to imply some positive relationship between the two entities. The impact of Menno's doctrine of the two births, however, is to introduce a radical and total disjunction between Church and world into the heart of his theology so that the relationship between them becomes one of total opposition. Such a pattern of thought has clear consequences for the understanding of the Church, one of which is the tendency which we have already noted to attribute perfection now to the Church of the regenerate. We shall be in a better position to evaluate its broader significance, however, when we have taken note of a parallel development within Menno's eschatology, in which the radical dualism between Church and world implied in Menno's doctrine of the two births is reinforced by a doctrine of "two worlds."

ESCHATOLOGICAL DUALISM: THE TWO WORLDS. There is much in Menno's eschatological thought which is strongly reminiscent of Luther. Like the Saxon reformer, he believed that *the last day* would come suddenly and without warning, that it was already imminent, and that the signs of its appearing were already to be discerned in the corrupt state of the world and the bright shining light of the Gospel.

The prophecy of Christ concerning the last days, as well as that of Daniel and of the apostles, are being fulfilled in force. The flesh-consuming sword of the Lord glistens everywhere; and his bloody darts wing their way through every land. Kingdom is pitted against kingdom, realm against realm, neighbor against neighbor, and friend against friend. Some of your subjects are murdered by the sword, some are imprisoned; cities and citadels are laid waste and destroyed. . . .

One grave pestilence and epidemic succeeds another; one infla-
tion drives the other forward. On the sea as well as on the
land, we hear of storms, distress and trouble. In a word, the
persistent and hard chastisement testifies that the Lord is
offended, yet the wicked world does not turn over a new
leaf, but grows worse and worse daily. . . .

Since then everything is so corrupt on every hand that it has
become a second Sodom, yes, a confused Babel or a pitch-
dark Egypt, under the pretense and name of Christian
Churches, and since the merciful and great God has, in these
last days of unrighteousness, once more allowed the noble and
worthy Word of His divine grace to be known again to some
in pure, Christian understanding, and since He has placed it
as a pure light in the midst of darkness, the means whereby
He in everlasting love will assemble unto Himself for the great
and dark day an obedient and willing Church . . . therefore
all the gates of hell bestir themselves and rave, so that, alas,
a true Christian can find but little rest upon earth, it seems.[24]

Menno believed that the return of Christ would bring all his
enemies to punishment, and that all those who had undergone
in this life the washing of regeneration, the first resurrection,
would take part in the final resurrection to eternal life.[25]

There is, furthermore, a related eschatological theme in
Luther which Menno takes much further—the theme of the
persecution of the faithful. This concept was implicit in
Luther's treatment of Pope and Turk in terms of the eschatological symbols of the Antichrist and the Beast who make
war on the saints during the last days. In Menno, this concept
blossoms into a full-blown doctrine of *the martyr-Church.*
That he should have taken this concept further than Luther is
hardly surprising for, while Luther had powerful friends in
the world as well as enemies, Menno's people, more often than
not, were faced with the combined fury of Rome, the reformers, and the secular power.

It was a strong conviction of Menno's that the Gospel had always been hated and persecuted. This was so in the time when

the purity of faith was still intact in the early Church, and the
advent of the last days had brought an intensification of persecution, as Satan pressed forward his work knowing that his
time was short. The Word could not be taught and lived without the Cross—it has to be "declared with much suffering and
sealed with blood." [26] There was no other path possible for the
true disciple than the path which his Lord had trodden before,
the path of suffering, revilement, and persecution. "If the Head
had to suffer such torture, anguish, misery and pain, how shall
His servants, children and members expect peace and freedom
as to their flesh." [27] Suffering and martyrdom, therefore, is an
integral part of the life of discipleship, and the practice of true
discipleship within the world inevitably invites persecution.
The very faithfulness of God's people to His Word has called
down on them the wrath of the world; but to those who tread
faithfully the "winepress of sorrow," the day of release is already at hand,

*the day in which you shall stand with great constancy against
those who have afflicted you and taken away your sweat and
your toil, yes, your blood and your life. Then shall all those
who pursue us be as ashes under the [soles]* [28] *of our feet,
and they shall acknowledge too late that emperor, king, duke,
prince, crown, scepter, majesty, sword and mandate, were
nothing but earth, dust, wind and smoke. With this day in
view, all afflicted and oppressed Christians who now labor under the Cross of Christ are comforted in the firm hope of the
life to come.*[29]

While these similarities with the thought of Luther cannot
be denied, the fact remains that Menno's eschatological
thought as a whole differs radically from Luther's, and the
difference can be seen most clearly in a concept which was
equally crucial to both, but which each interpreted in a fundamentally different way—the doctrine of the two kingdoms. In
the case of Menno, this is more accurately described as the

doctrine of *the two worlds,* and it represents a clear and definite parallel to his doctrine of the two births.

In the *Reply to False Accusations,* Menno describes the two kingdoms in this way:

The Scriptures teach us that there are two opposing princes and two opposing kingdoms: the one is the Prince of peace, the other is the prince of strife. Each of these princes has his particular kingdom and as the prince is, so is also the king-dom. The prince of peace is Christ Jesus; His kingdom is the kingdom of peace; His messengers are the messengers of peace; His Word is the word of peace; His body is the body of peace; His children are the seed of peace; and His inheritance and reward are the inheritance and reward of peace.[30]

The difference from Luther is not always evident on the surface, but it is a fundamental one. For Luther, as we have observed, regards the two kingdoms as interwoven in the present age and dialectically related in the existence of the Christian, who lives within both. Both are finally under the one rule of God who will separate them only at the last day. Menno, on the other hand, clearly identifies the kingdom of Christ with the visible brotherhood of the regenerate and the kingdom of Satan with the unregenerate world including the churches of Rome and of the Reformation. For him, it is apparent that the separation between the two kingdoms is entirely clear and, while they coexist, they are related not by the subtle dialectic which Luther employed, but like two armies facing each other across a battleline. One cannot live in both kingdoms—the separation is total, and the boundaries entirely clear.

Accordingly, Menno is able to spell out in terms of doctrine and life a clear contrast between the true and the false Church:

Here is faith, there unbelief; here truth, there falsehood; here obedience, there disobedience; here believers' baptism, accord-ing to God's Word, there infant baptism without Scriptural warrant; here brotherly love, there hatred, envy, tyranny, cruelty and plentiful bloodshed; here a delightful service of others, there much wrangling, legal action, gossip, cheating, and in some cases, also theft, robbery and murder. Here we see instruction, admonition, consolation, reproof in righteousness; there we hear only hurt, accusation, of heresies, vituperation and slander; here is blessing, praise and thanksgiving. . . . In fine, here is Christ and God, and there is Antichrist and the devil. Yes, dearly beloved brethren, the pure, chaste and spotless bride of our Lord Jesus Christ (judge for yourselves) is quite different from this carnal, unclean, adulterous and shameful affair.[31]

The one is the body of Christ, the other the body of Antichrist; the one the chaste bride, the other a carnal harlot. The one owes allegiance to Christ and His Word, the other to the evil traditions of Antichrist. So clear and unambiguous is the distinction between the two that it can be discerned with "half an eye." It is a comparison of "truth with falsehood, light with darkness, and white with black." [32]

There are a few places in Menno's writings where he recognizes the universality of God's power as "creator of all things, who holds heaven and earth in His hand, who rules all things by the Word of His power," and where he acknowledges the unity of the whole human race.[33] But this perspective is absent from the bulk of his writings and exercises little or no practical influence. The world is for Menno a "narrow, shameful, and bloody way of all miseries, crosses and sufferings." [34] So much Luther and Calvin had said before him. But there is in Menno no emphasis corresponding to Luther's understanding of the world and the common life as the place where man may joyfully exercise his vocation, or to Calvin's understanding of the world as renewed by the power of Christ. For Menno, "world" seems to have no other meaning than the constellation of demonic forces ranged against the faithful, ruled by the Antichrist, and operating through his followers, the unregenerate "Church of the world," the persecutors of the faithful. In order to avoid confusion with Luther's doctrine of the two kingdoms, therefore, it is in every way more appropriate to speak, as Robert Friedmann does, of a doctrine of the "two worlds," [35] for the contrast which he draws is between two utterly separate and contradictory entities, locked in deadly battle as the last day approaches.

2

THE INSTITUTION IN THE WORLD

The question has been raised in scholarly circles whether it is appropriate to use the term "institution" at all in relation to Menno's thought. Bender and Littell, for example, both speak of Anabaptism as being essentially "non-institutional" in character.[36] The intent of such assertions, however, is chiefly to indicate that the Anabaptists see the Church fundamentally not in terms of form and structure but as a personal community of brothers. This may readily be acknowledged as true, and it is true also of both Luther and Calvin. The word "institution," however, may legitimately be used without the specific connotations which it assumed in medieval Catholicism, and it is important to use it, or some equivalent word, if we are to comprehend the full dimensions of Menno's doctrine of the Church. Its purpose is simply to point to the character of the regenerate community as a visible community in the world.

The radical disjunction between Church and world implied in Menno's doctrine of the two births and underlined in his understanding of the two worlds is the key to his distinctive understanding of the Church's institutional life. Negatively, it entails the total separation of the institution from the world, its communities, and its values. Positively, it places upon this separated people the obligation of realizing without qualification or compromise that perfection of doctrine and life which belonged to the apostolic Church.

THE NEGATIVE PRINCIPLE: SEPARATION. The entire Scriptures
teach, Menno declared,

that the Church of Christ was and is, in doctrine, life and wor-
ship, a people separated from the world. Acts 2:42. It was that
also in the Old Testament. And since the Church always was
and must be a separate people, as has been heard, and since it
is as clear as the noonday sun that for many centuries no dif-
ference has been visible between the Church and the world,
but that they have without differentiation run together in
baptism, life and worship. . . . we are constrained to gather
them under the cross of misery in spite of all the violence and
gates of hell . . . and to separate them from the world, as the
Scriptures teach.[37]

Such separation Menno regarded as more than a desirable and
convenient matter. It was utterly essential, because those forces
who were not of the true Church were by definition "sent by
Antichrist and ordained in his employment and service." [38] The
doctrine of the two worlds implies that there is no neutrality,
no middle ground, no area of doubtful allegiance. Whatever is
not definitely of Christ is of the Antichrist, and the inevitable
consequence is total separation. The faithful bride must not
listen to the voice of the stranger.

The distinctiveness of Menno's position may be seen also in
his interpretation of the parable of the wheat and the tares,
which the other Reformers had used before him. They had
employed it generally, as we have already seen, to maintain
that the institutional Church remained a mixed body, that the
believer and the unbeliever would live beside each other in the
present age, and that God alone would know the true believer's
identity. Menno insisted that they had misinterpreted the
parable of the wheat and tares in seeing the field as the
Church, whereas Jesus had identified it as the world. For him,
the conjunction of wheat and tares meant that the body of
Christ and the body of Antichrist continued to coexist in the
world, but not in the sense of being in any way intermingled

or confused, and discernible only to God. On the contrary they
are clearly distinct according to whether or not they follow
God's Word. The distinction is possible because regeneration
is known by its fruits, which prove manifestly whether one
belongs to Christ or to Antichrist.[39]

In describing this separation from the world as Menno's
"negative principle," we need to protect ourselves from misunderstanding. It is negative in the sense that Menno's radical
"no" to the world is the necessary prelude to an equally radical
"yes" in affirming the possibility of the Church really becoming the spotless bride of Christ. Moreover, this very principle
of separation can be seen as a highly positive phenomenon, for
it meant anything but passive withdrawal. It was an aggressive
stance, signifying warfare on the world of Antichrist and all
that it stands for.[40]

Separation, therefore, did not mean that the regenerate no
longer had anything to do with the world though Menno's
language at times seems to imply this—for example, in his picture of the Church as Noah's Ark, riding out the destruction of
the world, with Christ, its spiritual Noah.[41] For the most part,
however, he implies an ongoing relationship which can be seen
in two areas: secular government and the missionary task.
The regenerate are enjoined to be obedient to secular rulers in
all matters not contrary to God's Word,[42] and it is an integral
part of their discipleship that they let their light shine before
men, testify to their faith in life and death, and assume the task
of rebuking and admonishing the world out of a godly love.[43]
What is terminated is not the relationship to the world as such,
but any relationship conceived in terms of belonging or common citizenship. The Christian obeys rulers but he cannot hold
office. The Church has a mission to the world, but the faithful
are not witnesses to their own people but emissaries from a
foreign kingdom. The Church is like the city set on the hill
rather than the leaven in the lump.

Separation from the world of Antichrist is ensured by a

rigorous use of *the ban.* When there are tares found to be growing among the wheat, the community must purge itself of them in order to retain its purity, for a congregation without the Ban is like "a city without walls, a field without trenches or fences, or a home without walls and doors." [44] The Church's Ban is

a valid declaration of the eternal death of our soul, announced by the faithful servants of Christ on the basis of the Scripture against all offensive, carnal sinners and confirmed schismatics. It is a delivering over to Satan, yes, a public expulsion, excommunication or separation from the congregation, church body and kingdom of Christ, and that in the name of Christ, with the binding power of His Holy Ghost and powerful Word. [45]

The exercise of the power of the keys through the Ban delivers over the apostate to the world of Antichrist to which he already belongs, by his despising of the Word and his open disobedience and rebellion. It is no arbitrary act but the Church's confirmation of God's own act of judgment or, from another point of view, of the sinner's own act of self-expulsion by false doctrine or improper conduct. [46] Nonetheless, the aim of the Ban is not merely to maintain the purity of the Church but to win back the sinner to repentance. "For we do not want to expel any, but rather to receive; not to amputate but rather to heal; not to discard but rather to win back; not to grieve but rather to comfort; not to condemn but rather to save. . . . In this way the ban is a great work of love, notwithstanding it is looked upon by the foolish as an act of hatred." [47]

For the Ban to be effective it must be accompanied by outward *shunning,* without which it remains "as powerless as a mill without a millstone, and as a knife without a blade." [48] Menno explicitly rejects the notion that shunning extends only to false doctrine and not to those who hold it, and the idea that it applies only to evangelical transactions and not to the ordinary contacts of life. [49] Only with a stern policy, he believed, would there be any guarantee that the Church would truly forsake the Babel of this world and remain the chaste bride of Christ.[50]

The regenerate must, therefore, "loathe the apostate and impenitent brother" as the Jews in the time of Christ shunned Gentiles and sinners. In this analogy with the Jews, Menno makes a curious departure from his usually careful use of the Bible. His own standards of New Testament precedent, applied here, clearly contradict the notion of shunning as he has expressed it. Jesus in his words and actions was highly critical of Jewish leaders precisely because they hated the apostate and impenitent brother, and he chose to associate directly with sinners, eating and conversing with them. Menno deals with this point, but very unsatisfactorily, since he rests his position on the fact that sinners like Matthew and Zaccheus turned away from sin after confronting Jesus.[51] Even assuming that all such sinners with whom Jesus associated showed repentance— which is by no means necessarily the case—it still does not justify the application of shunning until repentance is evident. If anything, it suggests the opposite, for the penitence of those who met Jesus was the result and not the precondition of his association with them. Menno's urgent desire to draw the line of separation clearly, and justify the practice of shunning, causes him to lapse from his usual care in employing scriptural evidence.

Nevertheless, his position is clearly consistent with the dualistic premises from which he operates. The Ban and the outward shunning represent the radical implementation of that separation from the world which is inherent in the nature of the Church, as he understands it. Internally, Menno's thought is quite consistent here. The question which will have to be asked later is the fundamental one of whether his radically dualistic structure of thought is an adequate vehicle for articulating Christian theology.

Meanwhile, it is important to see the Ban and shunning within its proper context. The defense of the community against corruption and defilement is for Menno not an end in itself; rather, it is instrumental to the Church's chief task of conforming its institutional life in every respect to the standard of the Gospel.

THE POSITIVE PRINCIPLE: RESTITUTION. It has become commonplace now to refer to the importance of the theme of "restitution" among the Anabaptist writers of the sixteenth century.[52] While no systematic doctrine of restitution as such is spelled out in Menno's writings, it is clearly the basic principle which governs his approach to the institutional Church. He declared that he had no other purpose in life than "to reclaim this adulterous bride, this erring Church, from her adulterous actions and to return her to her first husband to whom she was so unfaithful." [53]

Yet it cannot be too clearly emphasized, in the light of the common misunderstanding of Menno as a legalist who did not understand the proper relation of faith and works, that the restoration of the true Church to its pristine purity was consistently regarded by him as a work of God's grace. Only God could rebuild the holy city and repair the Temple, and man's role could only be that of prayerful cooperation.[54] The covenant with the regenerate is based solely on grace, and accordingly, the Church is not saved by the correctness of its doctrine and ordinances. Rather, being saved by grace, it seeks to be obedient in all respects to the commands and intentions of Christ, and to cooperate in the divine work of restitution, "so that the fallen city, which is the Church, may be built again on its former foundation, namely on the firm basis of the apostles and the unadulterated doctrine of Christ, and then give witness to it in a godly and penitent life before the whole world according to the Scriptures." [55]

The exacting and detailed task of restitution is carried out according to the criterion of *apostolicity*. In determining every question of belief and practice, the Church seeks to be ruled by "Christ's plain Word and the salutary doctrine and open practice of the apostles." [56] The characteristic formula of "Christ and the apostles" is not a twofold but a single standard of measure, for Menno firmly believed that the early apostolic Church was an "unfalsified representation of the will and intent of Christ." [57] To conform to the apostolic Church was to conform to Christ, and therefore the fashioning of the true Church in the last days was essentially a restitution of the most ancient apostolic Church established by Christ.

In his *Reply to Gellius Faber,* Menno lists six signs of the true Church:

1 . . . *the salutary and unadulterated doctrine of His holy and divine Word. . . .*
2 . . . *the right and Scriptural use of the Sacraments of Christ. . . .*
3 . . . *obedience to the holy Word, or the pious Christian life which is of God. . . .*
4 . . . *the sincere and unfeigned love of one's neighbor.*
5 . . . *that the name, will, Word and ordinance of Christ are confidently confessed in the face of all cruelty, tyranny, tumult, fire, sword and violence in the world.*
6 . . . *the pressing Cross of Christ, which is borne for the sake of His testimony and Word. . . .* [58]

The pervasive dualism of his thought is indicated in his adjacent listing of six exactly opposite signs for the false Church of Antichrist. [59] Moreover, a key difference from Luther and Calvin, to which we shall have occasion to return, is that these signs are visible not only to faith but also to sight. [60]

The enumeration of the signs of the Church, however, did not have the same importance for Menno as it did for the other Reformers, and he concerned himself far more frequently with two more general criteria—*doctrine and life*—based on his principle of apostolicity. Apostolic doctrine signified above all a true understanding of Word and sacraments, while apostolic life included true discipleship, open confession of faith, and

persecution for the sake of the Word. The way in which
Menno employed this dual principle is shown very clearly in
the *Foundation of Christian Doctrine,* where he declares:

*Examine this our faithful exposition and judge by Christ's own
Spirit and Word as much as in you is. Compare it with the
doctrine and lives of the apostles; with the piety, love, customs, deeds, misery, cross and sufferings of the primitive
Church; and I hope by the grace of God that you may see
plainly that our doctrine is the infallible doctrine and position of the Scriptures. . . . the pure Gospel which the Lord
taught by his own mouth and which his holy apostles
preached through the whole world, and in the power of the
Spirit testified to with life and death. Ours is no new doctrine,
as the preachers without truth assert and would have you
believe. It is the old doctrine which was preached and prac-
ticed in the Church for more than 1,500 years, the doctrine
by which the Church was begotten, is being begotten, and
will be begotten to the end.*[61]

Menno rests very heavily here on the authority of the Scriptures, but it is notable that he avoids any slavish and legalistic
following of the letter. The Scripture is seen in a dynamic
sense as the expression of the Spirit and Word of Christ, whose
truth stands confirmed in the doctrine and lives of the apostles
who preached it and sealed the testimony with their lives and
deaths.[62]

It is by this broad principle of apostolic life and doctrine
that Menno evaluates every matter of Church order. For example, infant baptism is excluded on the grounds that Christ
intended baptism only for those who experience the new birth,
that the apostolic Church never used it, and that it makes the
hearing of the Word and the response of faith of no importance.[63] Similarly, the attitude toward secular government is
derived from the teaching of Christ, and seen from the point
of view of the concrete testimony of the early martyr-Church.[64]
The standard is not the bare letter of Scripture, but the

Scripture as breathing the Spirit of Christ, and as lived out in the Church's experience.

That same combination of true doctrine and a life of obedient discipleship which prevailed in the "first, unfalsified Church" is the single goal of the true Church being restored in the last days. The task is arduous, but no sacrifice is too great for the attainment of the prize.

THE QUESTION OF TRANSCENDENCE. In Luther and Calvin we discerned two radically different approaches to the question of the Church and its institutional form. Luther defined the Church in terms of the dynamic polarity of Word and faith, Calvin in terms of participation in the redemptive drama of Christ. Luther saw the Church's forms as a necessary expression of her inward nature but believed that very little was prescribed in detail; Calvin sought to restore the ancient face of the Church according to the pattern of Scripture. Luther worked with a dialectic of the two kingdoms and looked for the final triumph of the Church amidst the dissolution of the world; Calvin had a vision of the Church as God's instrument in the total renewal of creation, according to the divine plan.

Despite these differences, however, a consensus emerged between them in opposition to the medieval tradition on three basic issues. First, both redefined the Church on the basis of Christology as a community of persons gathered around Christ, and thereby shifted the basis of ecclesiology away from the impersonal and ontological categories characteristic of the medieval tradition. Secondly, while this redefinition shifted the focus of concern away from the institution to the Church's inward nature, it was in no sense anti-institutional; rather it implied the need for an institutional form which expressed that inward nature. Thirdly, the institution was seen in a thoroughly eschatological context, in the realm of becoming, and was therefore regarded as never complete, never perfect or absolute, but always under transcendent judgment.

Menno's exposition of ecclesiology is sharply different again from that of either Luther or Calvin, and we may now clarify how he stands in relation to these three issues. His understanding of the Christian Church as a community of the regenerate points him initially in the same direction as Luther and Calvin. The fundamental reality of the Church is not structure or form, but the personal communion of the regenerate with their Lord and with each other. Moreover, while the Church is not in its essence an institution, Menno is as clear as Luther and Calvin that it must seek institutional expression according to its inward nature. The visible Church for Menno, therefore, is the way in which regeneration becomes visible in discipleship. Menno bears more resemblance here to Calvin, since he is impelled to structure the Church according to the pattern of the ancient Church, and though he understood that pattern somewhat differently, he was as insistent as Calvin that this was not a legalistic work of man but an obedient response to God's gracious work of restoration.

It is on the third point, however, that Menno is finally equivocal. At times, the eschatological tension is maintained in his thought, and he clearly asserts that the visible institution is the true Church in the process of being realized, rather than the final, perfect reality. But at other times, as we have noted, he tends to attribute a finished perfection to the institution in the present and to speak of it as if it already transcribed on earth the kingdom of God.

This cannot be accounted for by the fact that Menno recognized no meaningful distinction between the hidden or invisible Church and the visible institution. It is true that these distinctions helped Luther and Calvin to maintain the eschatological distinction between the true Church and the institution, and that the whole terminology was alien to the thought of Menno, for whom faith was inseparable from its visibility in the regenerate life. But the visible-invisible terminology has its own problems, and the maintenance of the eschatological distinction does not depend on such terminology.

Nor can this tendency to dissolve the eschatological tension be attributed to Menno's heterodox Christology. There is, perhaps, a superficial plausibility in suggesting that Menno's Eutychean tendency to eliminate the human nature of Christ [65] is responsible for his ecclesiological tendency to eliminate the sinful human element in the Church and to treat the Church as a perfect, divine reality. But while this Christology was undoubtedly congenial to a perfectionist view of the Church, there are no adequate grounds for suggesting a causal relationship between them. Menno rarely connects the two themes in his writings, and it is clear that other Anabaptist writers whose Christological orthodoxy was in no way suspect showed a similar ecclesiological tendency to identify completely the visible institution and the true Church.

The explanation seems to lie, rather, in the kind of eschatological pattern which Menno adopted as the framework for his understanding of the Church. This pattern of a clear and total disjunction between Church and world—that is, between the true Church and the Church of Antichrist—and the consequent polarization of the human race, the clear separation of the redeemed and the unredeemed, leads him inexorably in the direction of identifying without qualification the visible institution and the true Church. His dualism, though originating in New Testament themes, is ultimately made too absolute and undialectical to stand his own test of Scriptural validity. The final separation, which Luther and Calvin, along with the New Testament, see at the end of time appears essentially to have taken place. Accordingly, while Menno establishes the Church as surely as Luther and Calvin on a Christological base as a community of persons, he finally fails to maintain a sense of transcendent judgment over the Church's present institutional expression.

V · THE REFORMATION HERITAGE

The protestant Reformation has been hailed by some historians as the herald of the modern age, yet regarded by others as the movement which delayed the dissolution of the medieval Christian culture, and made possible its partial survival for two centuries more.[1] That historiography should reflect such diversity of interpretation is no cause for surprise for, like most periods of historical transition, the Reformation was a bewildering and complex blend of the old and the new, and it is both arbitrary and unhistorical to try to make it exclusively one or the other.

Even in the most apparently abrupt historical upheavals, there is a thread of continuity with the past, and the Reformation, at least from the perspective from which we have chosen to examine it, may be seen as a fresh attempt to come to terms with a problem which had taken on special importance in the medieval period (though it was, at the same time, a problem as old as Christianity itself).

If the Reformers were dependent on the medieval theologians for the problems and questions which exercised their attention, and for some of their basic terminology, they were not necessarily dependent on them for their responses and solutions, and an element of newness in the Reformers' thought compared with the medieval tradition cannot be denied. Yet we must be careful to see in what this newness lay. The Reformers broke from the tradition not so much by a step forward as by a large stride backward, behind their immediate tradition to the earlier traditions of the Bible and the primitive Church. Their appeal was not to new ideas, but to elements in the tradition which, they believed, had been neglected or forgotten. It was a return to the sources, not to read off a detailed blueprint which they might reproduce, but to recapture the living tradition of early—and especially Pauline—Christianity, and to apply it in a fresh and creative way to the Church in their own time. The newness evident in the Reformers' work lies, therefore, not in innovation, but in the derivation of new meaning from the tradition.

To speak collectively in this way of "the Reformers," however, is a problem in itself. If there is one thing which emerges very clearly from this study of Luther, Calvin, and Menno, it is the extraordinary diversity of their approaches to the issue of the institutional Church, a diversity which inheres, as we have seen, in basically different approaches to the theological task. A clear recognition of this diversity is a warning that to search for any neat formula which will sum up their common achievement will be to end with no result whatever, or with a lowest common denominator which is empty of meaning and unjust to the richness of the Reformers' thought. In any case, such an attempt would be a clear misunderstanding of the historical process, for the heritage which one age passes on to the next is more like an open letter than a sealed package. It is a dynamic reality which defies simple classification and neat summation. When we search for the heritage of the Reformers, therefore, we are not looking for clearcut "achievements" or unified systems of thought, but for dominant themes and tendencies which emerged from their work and bore fruit during the succeeding generations.

Five such themes—by no means an exhaustive list—appear worthy of note. Some of these themes which we shall examine find clear expression in all three of the Reformers and testify to close agreement. Others are not present in all, or present in varying degrees, and indicate strong tension or disagreement. Some are clearly stated and their implications are followed through. Others emerge tentatively, hesitantly, at times warring with contrary tendencies, and their significance can be seen only with the hindsight of history.

1

THE PERSONAL CENTER

One element common to all three of the Reformers, and one in which they appear in strong contrast to the central tradition of the Middle Ages, is their reinterpretation of the Church on the basis of a dynamic understanding of Christology. Thomas Aquinas, to be sure, had based his understanding of the Church on the doctrine of Christ, but it is the static, ontological categories of divinity and humanity, nature and supernature, which inform his ecclesiology. The Reformers have no quarrel with the ancient creedal formulations of the doctrine of Christ, and reaffirm them clearly and enthusiastically. Even Menno's tendency toward Eutycheanism is an argument which takes place within an acceptance of the classical Christological categories, and he believed himself to be safeguarding the intent of the classical formulae.

Yet, while the classical descriptions are affirmed, in each case the vital center of Christological reflection has shifted to a more dynamic, Biblical emphasis, in which Christology is explicated not by abstract categories of divine and human nature but by a dynamic description of Christ in relationship to his people. Luther employs the Biblical understanding of the Word as God's address to man in Christ, calling forth the response of faith. Calvin stresses union with Christ, understood as the believer's participation in his death, resurrection, and ascension. Menno directs attention to the new birth by which the believer becomes united with Christ. This dynamic, relational emphasis coexists harmoniously with the affirmations of classical Christology, yet it is the former and not the latter which in each case informs the understanding of the Church.

The change has the character not of innovation but of reappropriation of a forgotten element of the Biblical tradition. Accordingly, in searching for ways of describing the Church, the Reformers had no need to forge a new terminology, but used the traditional Biblical terms and purged them, where necessary, of what they regarded as false associations. Luther's concept of the communion of saints, Calvin's understanding of the body of Christ, and Menno's picture of the Church as the regenerate bride of Christ are all built on this Christology conceived in terms of personal relationship.

This represents not a mere qualification of characteristic medieval understandings of the Church or a minor change in emphasis but a radical reshaping of ecclesiology. The adoption of personal categories in place of impersonal ones shifts the center of attention from the Church understood in terms of ontology, substance, structure, and organization to the Church understood as a personal community in which the members are bound together by a common faith in Christ and a common love toward each other.

As the place where salvation becomes a reality for man, the visible Church is as crucial as in medieval theology, but its self-understanding has undergone an important change. It is no longer seen as an hierarchical structure dispensing divine substance to man through the sacramental system, but—in terms which clearly reflect Pauline thought—as a living community in which man's humanity is restored and fulfilled in Christ.

The change does not represent a denial or rejection of the visible, institutional Church, but it does ensure that matters of order, structure, and form, no matter how important, remain secondary and derivative, related instrumentally to the Church's nature as the community of Christ, and her task of expressing the life of faith and love in the world.

2

THE HISTORICAL FOCUS

We have noted how each of the Reformers reappropriates the Biblical-Augustinian eschatological theme and applies it to his understanding of the Church in the world. There are, of course, substantial differences between the apocalyptic note evident, in different ways, in both Luther and Menno, and Calvin's vision of the transformation of the whole creation through the visible Church, and these differences ought not to be underestimated.

At the same time, however, there is, at least potentially, a common element. When the institutional Church is placed in the framework of eschatology, it can no longer be regarded as the perfect, earthly image of a heavenly reality, but is seen instead as an historical reality. That is to say, it is delivered clearly into the realm of historical ambiguity and imperfection. The institution no longer *is* the Church, *simpliciter*. It is the Church which is coming to be, the communion of saints who, though justified, remain sinners, the body of Christ growing up into the Head, the impure bride destined to appear spotless before the Bridegroom.

The differences between the Reformers emerge within this common framework and are attributable to different emphases within their eschatological perspectives. That is why Menno, despite his own intentions, does not realize the potential of this eschatological outlook in reference to the

visible Church and ultimately tends to attribute perfection
to the institution as much as did medieval Catholicism, not
because there is no eschatological scheme of thought, but
because he tends to bring the goal of perfection into the
present and to identify it with the visible Church. Luther
and Calvin, by contrast, consistently maintain the eschatological perspective over the institution. Luther employs
a dialectical pattern of contrast between the inward, personal reality of the Church and its outward, institutional
form, so that the latter is both posited and judged by the
former. Calvin's comprehensive vision of salvation-history
leads him to attribute a more significant role to the institutional Church as the bearer of God's purposes in history,
but because the final goal of God's purposes always remains
ahead and is never attained, the institution remains imperfect and incomplete.

If the Christological theme ensured that institutional
questions be regarded as secondary and derivative, the
eschatological theme clearly marked the institution itself as
an ambiguous, historical reality. Therefore, while the static,
ontological ecclesiology of the medieval period placed the
institution beyond basic theological criticism, the dynamic,
eschatological pattern which came to expression through the
Reformers demanded such criticism. Parenthetically, it may
be noted that this transformation paved the way for an understanding of the Church in terms of an "event." [2] Since the
Church is not identifiable with any given institution, it has
no resting place, but only a constant pilgrimage. It is not so
much something which *is* as something which happens as
the pattern of history unfolds, and as man attends to the
Word of God.

While this understanding of the institutional Church as an
historical reality has been described here as characteristic of
Protestantism in distinction from the medieval tradition, it is
worth remembering that recent Catholic thought has modified

to some extent the traditional Catholic position. While the Dogmatic Constitution of Vatican II, *De Ecclesia,* officially changes nothing in Catholic doctrine, the final adoption of historical rather than ontological categories in the text of the decree implies a reorientation of ecclesiology in the direction of recognizing the relativity and ambiguity of the Church's institutional expression.

3
THE SECULAR AFFIRMATION

The work of the Reformers implied, thirdly, a new and positive understanding of the secular order. The word "implied" is used advisedly, for it must be admitted that in the Reformation period this emphasis is often latent rather than apparent. Moreover, it is not present in the three Reformers in the same way. In Menno Simons, it is not present at all, since the world outside the Church of the regenerate is nothing but evil and corruption and is, therefore, in no sense a positive value for Christian faith.

Both Luther and Calvin, however, responded very positively to the secular order, though in different ways. In Luther, the apocalyptic vision of a world bound for collapse and destruction became, paradoxically, the key to a positive evaluation of secular reality. He depopulated the world of its gods and its demons and allowed it to stand as a neutral sphere of human activity and enterprise, with its own integrity. He let the world be the world. In adopting such a stance, he broke sharply with a sacral conception of the world, in which earthly things are seen as impregnated with divine substance. But this was not to espouse its opposite— a secularism, in which the world itself becomes an object of allegiance and devotion. For though the world is not seen as a sacral reality, it is nevertheless, precisely in its secular character, a manifestation of the glory of God. And if human society is regarded as a sphere for creative and rational human activity, it nevertheless runs its course within the limits of a divinely appointed destiny. That is to say, the autonomy and independence which Luther accords to the secular order is real, but not absolute. Indeed, it is real precisely because it is not absolute, for if it were absolutized, it would no longer be a free and open sphere of human activity but a religious reality, an idol. Luther's unequivocal acknowledgment of the transcendence of God and the thoroughly relative character of the secular order is, therefore, iconoclastic in intent—it frees secular life both from a heteronomous sacral framework of understanding and from the incipient idolatry of naked secularism.

The origins of this stance lie in certain basic but long-obscured theological perspectives which Luther reappropriated and restored to prominence—especially the Old Testament doctrine of creation, with its insistence on the utter transcendence of God and the relativity of the created order; and the Mosaic-prophetic prohibition against idolatry, with its denial of religious meaning to anything worldly. The finitude and relativity of the created order become the charter and guarantee of its character as a secular sphere, neither divine nor demonic, given over to the responsible care and dominion of man.

Calvin shares with Luther this basic theological perspective on creation, and he too directs man to secular life as the sphere where his vocation is to be lived out. But, unlike Luther, his eschatological vision includes within it the goal of restoration and renovation of the whole created order. He is not content with letting the world be the world, but marks it as a field for Christian conquest. Accordingly, the goal of Christian discipleship is not merely responsible obedience within secular life but participation in God's work of renovating the entire world. He affirms the secular as the

sphere of discipleship; but, unlike Luther, he would have it
become something other than it now is.

The positive affirmation of secular life, derived from the
doctrine of creation, remains muted in both Reformers, because it appears in conjunction with another interpretation
of the world wherein "world" is understood as that which
stands in opposition to God. The source of this interpretation
is equally Biblical and finds its clearest expression in the
letters of Paul, who counsels nonconformity and even crucifixion to the world.[3] There is no essential opposition here, for
the world in this sense is the world understood as a religious
reality, an object of allegiance or a source of meaning, that is
to say, the world as an idol. It is in this context that the
Church is counseled to be in but not of the world. If there
is no essential opposition here, the fact remains that the Reformers did not always spell out clearly the relationship
between the world as God's creation and the world as the
Devil's instrument, with the result that this note of world-
rejection is often emphasized in such a way as to dim rather
than enhance their positive understanding of the secular
order.

This is seen very clearly in the way in which the Reformers tried to deal with the problem of being in but
not of the world. Each of them, Luther and Calvin as well
as Menno, saw the issue in terms of maintaining a concrete separation or distinction as a community over against
the community at large. They regarded it as a necessity to
draw some definite line of separation, even if they then went
on to affirm the necessity of crossing the line. Menno
drew the line in an absolute way, Luther and Calvin in a
less definite way by their elaboration of the signs or marks
of the Church; but all of them drew the line. That is to say,
they were not able to distinguish between separation from
the world in Paul's sense (as a center of values and commitment) and actual separation from the world in Genesis'

sense (the neutral, secular order). Consequently, their positive affirmation of the world was unnecessarily qualified and muted.

There is an alternative way of articulating this issue which does justice both to Biblical faith and to the Reformers' essential insights, and that is to define the Church's rejection of the world (in the negative, Pauline sense) precisely by its solidarity with the world (in the positive sense of Genesis). For if the world in the sense of creation is intended as a community of men bound closely to each other by their common humanity and common creaturehood under God; and if the world in the fallen sense is marked by the disruption of the human community; then the Christian community most surely rejects the values of the fallen world when it most clearly commits itself to unconditional solidarity with man in the world. That is to say, utter rejection of the world as a value system may be joined to unqualified acceptance of the world as a sphere of action. The paradigm for this is Jesus, who most clearly demonstrated his nonconformity to the world by placing himself without qualification alongside the outcast and the despised.

Perhaps when one bears in mind the situation of Luther and Calvin within a modified "Christendom," where a substantial identity prevailed between the civil and the religious community, one can understand the necessity of clearly distinguishing the true Church from the community of the nominally Christian. But those who see themselves as heirs of the Reformers may legitimately be less concerned to define their distinctness from the world and more concerned to undertake a radical commitment to the world. Such a commitment does not represent an acceptance of the values of the fallen world but an identification with the original purpose and destiny of creation. Radical commitment to God and radical involvement in the world are, therefore, inextricably joined. The one implies the other. "From the starting-point of Biblical religion, the antithesis to faith is not involvement in secular responsibilities or obligations, but idolatrous concern about secular matters."[4]

The perspective of the Reformers pointed toward a strong affirmation of the secular order, but their inability to distinguish between the two Biblical senses of "world" meant that their positive affirmation remained unnecessarily muted, and that the potentialities of their understanding of vocation, discipleship, and servanthood are not fully realized.

4
THE ICONOCLASTIC POSTURE

The radical distinction which the Reformers made between God and his creation is essentially equivalent to what H. Richard Niebuhr meant by the term "radical monotheism," and the intent of the Reformers is very well conveyed in a passage of Niebuhr's from *Radical Monotheism and Western Culture,* where he says:

When the principle of being is God, then He alone is holy and ultimate sacredness must be denied to any special being. No special places, times, persons or communities are more representative of the One than any others are. No sacred groves or temples, no hallowed kings or priests, no festival days, no chosen communities are particularly representative of Him in whom all things live and move and have their being.[5]

To put it another way, the posture which the Reformers adopted was one of radical, Biblical iconoclasm. Iconoclasm in this sense must be clearly distinguished from the superficial attack on religious objects which is a common phenomenon in the history of religious reform movements. Biblical iconoclasm may be defined, in the words of Gabriel Vahanian, as the "deflation of man's natural inclination to deify himself, or his society or the State, or his culture . . . radical opposition to all divinization of symbolic events and institutions as well as of man himself." [6] The classical formulation of Biblical iconoclasm is in the first two of the Ten Commandments, and its essential spirit is carried through in the Old Testament prophetic tradition, and finds echoes also in Paul. The prophets relentlessly expose man's proclivity for engaging in idolatry by worshipping the creature instead of the Creator, while Paul's counsel to the Church to use everything "as if not" ($\dot{\omega}s\ \mu\dot{\eta}$) is clearly in the same tradition.

The iconoclastic issue is raised in relation to the institutional Church whenever there is a tendency to attribute infinitude, permanence, and ultimacy to what is finite, ephemeral, and transitory, and it was just such a tendency which the Reformers saw in the Roman understanding of the institutional Church. The prophetic tradition, as Vahanian notes, "does not deny the world and its traditions and organizations. It even makes use of them. But it does not wed itself to them. Nor does it enslave them." [7] The crucial issue, therefore, was not the existence of the institution with its Pope, its laws, ceremonies, and traditions, but the attitude which these engendered. The central criticism was that these had ceased to be aids and servants to faith and had come to be regarded as necessary for salvation—a clear case of idolatry, of raising the creature to the status of divinity.[8] By shifting the focus of ecclesiology away from the institution to the personal center, and by assigning the institution to the relativity of history, the Reformers indicated that the only commitment of faith was the radical commitment to God, and that all else was instrumental to that end.

It is a sad confirmation of man's idolatrous nature that the Protestant Churches since the Reformation have shown the same potentiality for idolatry as the Roman Church, abandoning the old idolatries only to raise their own golden calves, such as the Bible, or a particular conception of order and ministry. Such a situation, however, increases rather than diminishes the significance of the Reformers' recovery of the Biblical iconoclastic tradition, for it points to this posture as an essential and continuing aspect of the institutional life of the Church.

5

THE TRANSCENDENT ORIENTATION

The point at which all the foregoing themes converge, and which represents the key to the significance of the Reformers on the issue of the institutional Church, is their achievement in overcoming the tendency of medieval ecclesiology to absolutize the institution, and in reorienting the latter toward the transcendent. Luther expressed this sense of transcendence in terms of the judgment of the Word of God over all human actions and institutions, Calvin by his vision of the Church's transcendent goal. Menno might have preserved this same sense with his goal of restitution, but his failure to maintain consistently the eschatological perspective over the institution led to the loss of this transcendent reference.

Transcendence, in this case, indicates the awareness of a reality over against the institution, by which it is placed under radical judgment. The contrast between medieval theology and the Reformers is at this point very clear. The central ecclesiological tradition of the Middle Ages pointed, as we have observed, to the institution as a divine reality, a timeless reflection of the eternal world within this world. The Reformers, by contrast, affirmed the institution's humanness by understanding it not as a timeless reality but as an eschatological community subject to the ambiguities of history. The implication of the medieval position, therefore (whether papal or conciliarist), was that the holy was immanent in the visible institution as a possession; and the implication of the Reformers' position, by contrast, was that the holy is not an immanent possession but a transcendent norm over against the institution, holding it up to judgment. The institution's awareness of transcendence, therefore, depends on the firm maintenance of the iconoclastic posture, and the consequent recognition of its own humanity. Conversely, the loss of this sense of transcendence represents a lapse into self-idolatry.

It is most interesting to reflect at this point on the issue from a contemporary perspective. Gabriel Vahanian has analyzed the transformation which has come about in modern man's self-understanding in terms of the radical change from a transcendent to an immanental world view. Whereas man used to understand himself and his worldly involvement in a transcendental frame of reference, today

only the reality of the world, in all its immediacy and its immanence, provides man with a context for possible self-understanding. This self-understanding is amputated from any necessity of a fundamental knowledge of God. It is easier to understand oneself without God than with God. Modern man lives in a world of immanence. If he is the prey of anxiety, it is not because he feels guilty before a just God. Nor is it because he fails to explain the justice and love of God in the obvious presence of evil and injustice. God is no longer responsible for the world—since he is dead. But man is. He cannot avoid assuming full responsibility for a world of immanence, in terms of which he understands himself, or seeks to do so. The dilemma of Christianity is that it has taught man how to be responsible for his actions in this world and for this world itself. Now man has declared God not responsible and not relevant to human self-knowledge. The existence of God, no longer questioned, has become useless to man's predicament and its resolution.[9]

The immanence of which Vahanian speaks here is, of course, sharply distinct from what we have described as the immanence of medieval ecclesiology. The latter represented a domestication of the transcendent within the world. Vahanian, however, speaks of a perspective in which the world is seen as an autonomous reality from which the transcendent perspective has entirely disappeared.

Whatever qualifications might need to be made to Vahanian's analysis, it is difficult to dispute the central point. Accordingly, it would appear that the essential outlook of the Reformers is as sharply opposed to modern man's self-understanding as was medieval theology. The scandal of faith involved here is unavoidable and ought not to be minimized. It is never incumbent on theology to capitulate to a world view, for to do so is to fashion that world view into an idol. In any case, the notion of transcendence cannot be yielded without abandoning everything distinctive about faith. Moreover, it is precisely on this issue that the Reformers' uncompromising perspective of transcendence has most to contribute to the contemporary situation.

The emancipation of the modern world from heteronomous religious self-understandings, often accomplished in the name of human freedom, has brought in its stead a sinister caricature of freedom, a hideous series of secular idolatries—national, cultural, and ideological—which have enslaved man as surely as the abandoned religious idolatries. The perspective of the Reformers sheds important light on this point, not only in pointing to the human spirit's endless propensity for idolatry, but in indicating the issue of transcendence as the key to the whole position. For, far from representing a curtailment of human freedom, the notion of transcendence is the only path to real freedom, because it effects a radical judgment over all the idolatries to which man enslaves himself—the old religious ones as well as the newer, secular ones—and thereby liberates man for the free exercise of his humanity. This liberation is not absolute, but dialectical and analogous to Luther's understanding of the Christian as *simul justus et peccator.* That is to say, man's idolatrous nature is not over come, but it is no longer the most important thing about his existence. Faith enables him to recognize his idolatry for what it is, and thereby to achieve a real measure of freedom from it.

If theology must avoid capitulation to modern world views, it must also reject the equally idolatrous error of binding itself to past world views, whether medieval or even Biblical. In maintaining that the issue of transcendence which the Reformers raised in relation to the Church is crucial and cannot be abandoned, we are not thereby limiting ourselves to a mere repetition of their formulation of the issue. It is apparent on analysis that their understanding of transcendence is associated with certain other perspectives which are neither necessary nor helpful to the task of articulating this concept in the present. To be specific, the Reformers' development of the theme of transcendence is associated not only with the motif of world-rejection to which attention has already been drawn, but also with an otherworldly metaphysic, with the result that the transcendent is seen as encountering man from outside his world rather than from within the very fabric of history. Such an outlook, however, is by no means an essential part of a theology which seeks to be true to the Reformers' intentions and to the perspectives of Biblical faith.

The Bible is highly reticent about inquiry into a world beyond, and focuses clearly on the encounter with transcendence in time and space, within man's historical life. The faith of the Hebrews rested not on an otherworldly metaphysic, but on the conviction that they had encountered the transcendent through their history. Transcendence, therefore, was not a metaphysical postulate but an event, not an abstraction but a relationship in which man found himself.

The same possibility of interpreting transcendence in terms of historical encounter is inherent in the way in which the Reformers establish the Church on the basis of a dynamic

Christology—that is, an understanding of Christ in terms of relationship. The metaphysical otherworldliness which is evident in their thought is not essential to this transcendent perspective.

It is in this context that we can best interpret the significance of Dietrich Bonhoeffer's search for a "this-worldly transcendence." Unlike many of those who have based their thought on his, Bonhoeffer was convinced that the notion of transcendence was crucial to Christian theology and could not be surrendered; but he was equally insistent that it must not be enslaved to an otherworldly metaphysic. In his well-known "Outline for a Book," he stated the problem in terms of the meaning of God-language.

Who is God? Not in the first place an abstract belief in God, in his omnipotence, etc. That is not a genuine experience of God, but a partial extension of the world. Encounter with Jesus Christ. The experience that a transformation of all human life is given in the fact that "Jesus is there only for others." His "being there for others" is the experience of transcendence. It is only this "being there for others," maintained till death, that is the ground of his omnipotence, omniscience and omnipresence. Faith is participation in this being of Jesus (incarnation, cross, and resurrection). Our relation to God is not a "religious" relationship to the highest, most powerful, and best Being imaginable—that is not authentic transcendence—but our relation to God is a new life in "existence for others," through participation in the being of Jesus. The transcendental is not infinite and unattainable tasks but the neighbour who is within reach in any given situation. God in human form—not, as in oriental religions, in animal form, monstrous, chaotic, remote and terrifying, nor in the conceptual forms of the absolute, metaphysical, infinite, etc., nor yet in the Greek divine-human form of "man in himself," but "the man for others," and therefore the Crucified, the man who lives out of the transcendent.[10]

Bonhoeffer gave no more than a few hints of what he meant, and his cryptic statements have become the playground of theologians of many shades of opinion. Ronald Gregor-Smith perhaps came closest to what Bonhoeffer intended when he defined "this worldly transcendence" as "a temporal and historical experience of an actual encounter, in which the self is continually overcome, both judged and forgiven, and then renewed in being for others." [11]

We cannot here explore all the theological and ecclesiological implications of the interpretation of transcendence in historical terms. Let it suffice to say that it is along these lines that the insights of the Reformers may best be appropriated by those who see themselves as heirs of the Reformation. For, while the presence of an otherworldly metaphysic in the thought of the Reformers cannot be denied, the search for an understanding of transcendence in historical, this-worldly terms is essentially closer to the heart of their understanding of the Church. In beginning all their reflection on the Church with Christology, the Reformers were acknowledging the appearance of transcendence within history as the key to the Church's self-understanding. The Christ separated in lofty distance yielded to the Christ whose being was understood in terms of relationship to his people. In this relationship in the Church, man found himself taken up and fulfilled, so that his whole life became oriented toward the transcendent.

To be oriented toward the transcendent, understood in historical terms, does not mean preoccupation with a world beyond, but rather the continual acknowledgment of a claim upon man in this world, and a continual openness to judgment and renewal. The acknowledgment of this transcendent claim confers upon man a new freedom—freedom from the tyranny of all those penultimate concerns which would exercise their idolatrous sway over him, and freedom, therefore, for nonidolatrous participation in the world.

Since this transcendent norm of judgment is Christ, the claim which man encounters is given concrete form in the historical being of Christ, so that the latter becomes the pattern which the Church is called to express in the world. It is the pattern of solidarity with man, of self-giving and of crucifixion. Accordingly, the Church's primary concern can never be the preservation of its institutional life, but rather participation in the work of restoring a broken and divided humanity. The depth of its commitment to man is therefore the measure of its acknowledgment of Christ as transcendent Lord.

NOTES

INTRODUCTION

1. Edward Schweizer, in *Church Order in the New Testament* (London, SCM Press, 1961), has drawn attention to a specific debate which emerges in the New Testament. He contrasts the institution-centered view of the Pastoral Epistles (the Church as preserver of tradition) with the radical institutional criticism of the Johannine tradition (the Church as governed directly by the Spirit). See especially pp. 77 ff., 117 ff., and 163 ff.

I. THE MEDIEVAL HERITAGE

1. On the background of this concept and its usage in the early Church, see Christopher Dawson, "Augustine and His Age," in M. C. D'Arcy, ed., *St. Augustine: His Age, Life and Thought* (New York, Macmillan, 1957).

2. *De Civitate Dei*, Book X, Ch. 25. English translation by Marcus Dods, *The City of God* (New York, Random House, 1950), pp. 329–31. Hereafter cited as *C.D.* and Dods.

3. *Ibid.*, XV. 1; Dods, p. 478.

4. On this point see E. Stakemeier, *Civitas Dei: Die Geschichtstheologie des heiligen Augustinus als Apologie der Kirche* (Paderborn, Schöningh, 1955), p. 34.

5. *C.D.* XX. 4; Dods, pp. 714 ff.; *Enchiridion* XXX; *De Genesi ad Litteram* XI. 15.

6. *C.D.* XIX. 5; Dods, p. 680.

7. Cf. H. Hoffmann, "Platonism in Augustine's Philosophy of History," in R. Klibansky, ed., *Philosophy and History* (New York, Harper & Row, 1963), p. 175; and K. Löwith, *Meaning in History* (Chicago, University of Chicago Press, 1949).

8. *C.D.* XX. 9; Dods, p. 726.

9. Ernst Benz, *Evolution and Christian Hope* (New York, Doubleday, 1966), p. 26.

10. *C.D.* XXII. 30; Dods, p. 867.

11. Benz, *Evolution*, p. 34.

12. *C.D.* XX. 9; Dods, p. 726.

13. Benz, *Evolution*, p. 34.

14. *Summa Theologica* 3a. viii. 1. English Translation in T. Gilby, ed., *St. Thomas Aquinas: Theological Texts* (London, Oxford University Press, 1955), p. 338.

15. *Commentary on St. John*, Ch. 2; Gilby, p. 339.

16. *Summa Theologica*, 2a–2ae, 1–10; Gilby, pp. 345–46.

17. Marsilius of Padua, *Defensor Pacis,* Discourse I, Ch. I, 8. English translation by A. Gewirth, *The Defender of Peace*, 2 vols. (New York, Columbia University Press, 1951, 1956), II, 7. Hereafter cited as Gewirth.

18. *Ibid.,* I. ii. 3; Gewirth II, 9.

19. Gewirth, I, 51–52.

20. *Defensor Pacis* I. v. 10–11; Gewirth, II, 18–19.

21. *Ibid.,* II. ii. 3; Gewirth, II, 103.

22. Thomas Aquinas, *Compendium Theologiae*, Ch. 147, *Opera Omnia,* Vol. 27 (Paris, 1871–1880). English translation by Vollert, *Compendium of Theology* (London, Herder, 1948), p. 157.

23. *Defensor Pacis* II. xx. 2 ff.; Gewirth, II, 280 ff.

24. *Ibid.,* II. xi. 3; Gewirth, II, 183.

25. *Ibid.,* I. vi. 4; Gewirth, II, 22–23.

26. *Ibid.,* I. vi. 1; Gewirth, II, 21.

27. On this point, see especially Brian Tierney, *Foundations of the Conciliar Theory* (Cambridge, Cambridge University Press, 1955).

28. English translation by James Kerr Cameron, *Ways of Uniting and Reforming the Church*, in M. Spinka, ed., *Advocates of Reform*, Library of Christian Classics, Vol. XIV (Philadelphia, Westminster, 1953), pp. 149 ff.

29. *Ibid.,* pp. 150–51.

30. *Ibid.,* pp. 151–52.

31. *Ibid.,* pp. 160, 165.

32. See, on this point, the contemporary accounts of the Council

translated by L. R. Loomis, in *The Council of Constance,* ed. by
J. H. Mundy and K. M. Woody (New York, Columbia University
Press, 1961), especially pp. 129–35, 247–48, and 283–84; also, the
account of Peter of Mladoňovice, in M. Spinka, ed., *John Hus at the
Council of Constance* (New York, Columbia University Press,
1965), pp. 89 ff.

33. See Löwith, *Meaning in History,* pp. 145–59 and 208–13;
M. W. Bloomfield, "Joachim of Flora: A Critical Survey of his
Canon, Teaching, Sources, Biography and Influence," in *Traditio,*
13 (1957), pp. 249 ff.; E. Benz, *Ecclesia Spiritualis* (Stuttgart,
1934); and *Evolution and Christian Hope,* Ch. III.

34. *Concordia* 5. 48; 5. 84, cited in Bloomfield, pp. 265–66.

35. John Wyclif, *Tractatus De Ecclesia,* ed. by J. Loserth (London, Wyclif Society, 1886); *The Church and Her Members,* ed.
by T. Arnold in *English Works of John Wyclif,* 3 vols. (Oxford,
Clarendon Press, 1871), III, 338 ff.

36. I.e., tonsures, a reference to monks.

37. *English Works,* III, 447.

38. *Tractatus De Ecclesia,* p. 37.

39. *Ibid.,* pp. 5–8.

40. *Ibid.,* p. 102.

41. *Ibid.,* p. 75.

42. *Ibid.,* pp. 22, 124.

43. *Ibid.,* pp. 76, 132–33; *English Works,* III, 213. See also on
this point Martin Schmidt, "John Wiclifs Kirchenbegriff: Der Christus
humilis Augustins bei Wiclif," in F. Hübner, ed., *Gedenkschrift für
D. Werner Elert* (Berlin, 1955), pp. 72–108.

44. *English Works,* III, 447.

45. Cf. J. T. McNeill, "Some Emphases in Wyclif's Teaching,"
Journal of Religion, 7 (1927), pp. 460 ff.

46. J. Loserth, *Wiclif and Hus* (London, Hodder and Stoughton,
1884), and Introduction to Wyclif's *Tractatus De Ecclesia,* pp. xxvii
ff.

47. See the discussion in M. Spinka, *John Hus' Doctrine of the
Church*(Princeton, Princeton University Press, 1966), pp. 4, 253–
54.

48. John Hus, *Tractatus de Ecclesia,* ed. by S. H. Thompson
(Boulder, Colo., University of Colorado Press, 1956), English trans-
lation (from an earlier edition) by D. Schaff, *The Church* (New
York, Scribners, 1915). For Hus's use of Augustine, see especially
Schaff, pp. 1–5, 23–32.

49. Schaff, p. 18. Cf. p. 14.

50. *Ibid.*, pp. 27–28.

51. *Ibid.*, pp. 13–14.

52. *Ibid.*, p. 71. Cf. pp. 131 ff., 161 ff. Scripture as the criterion of judgment is often linked in Hus's thought with "reason." This, however, is not to imply two standards of judgment, or any qualification over the authority of Scripture, any more than does Luther's demand at the Diet of Worms that he be convinced by "Scripture and plain reason." Rather, since Scripture is regarded as being eminently reasonable, it cannot be conceived of as opposing plain reason. It is opposed only to that kind of reason which blurs the message of Scripture with scholastic subtleties.

53. This is increasingly recognized in contemporary scholarship. See, e.g., G. A. Lindbeck, "A Protestant View of the Ecclesiological Status of the Roman Catholic Church," and H. Fries, "The Ecclesiological Status of the Protestant Churches from a Catholic Viewpoint," in the *Journal of Ecumenical Studies,* I (2), Spring, 1964, pp. 243 ff. and 195 ff. respectively. Fries states the situation as follows: "In the theological reflection on the event of the Reformation, it constantly becomes clearer that the difference between Protestant and Catholic lies in this different ecclesiological view, in the material and relevant differences in what is called *Credo ecclesiam.* The function of the Church as mediator and bearer of revelation and of faith, as being authoritative and regulative, is defined differently." (p. 202).

II. MARTIN LUTHER

1. Gerhard Ritter, *Die Neugestaltung Europas im 16 Jahrhundert* (Berlin, Propyläen Verlag, 1950), Ch. 8. Translation by G. H. Nadel, "Why the Reformation Occurred in Germany," *Church History,* XXVII, June, 1958, 99–106.

2. J. Huizinga, *Erasmus and the Age of the Reformation* (New York, Harper & Bros., 1957), p. 103.

3. In 1485, for example, the Franciscan John Hilten calculated that the Papacy would collapse in about 1514 or 1516, and that Rome would be destroyed in 1524. See J. Lortz, *The Reformation in Germany* (London, Darton, Longmans and Todd, 1968), I, 118.

4. N. Cohn, *The Pursuit of the Millennium* (London, Secker and Warburg, 1957).

5. Gerhard Ebeling, in "Luther: Theologie," *Die Religion in Geschichte und Gegenwart,* IV, 510, and in "The Necessity of the Doctrine of the Two Kingdoms," *Word and Faith* (London, SCM

Press, 1963), pp. 386 ff., makes the case that the doctrine of the two kingdoms is a hermeneutical key of immense significance for Luther's whole theological enterprise. He rejects any attempt to narrow down the significance of the term to the ethical sphere, shows its close relationship to the distinction between Law and Gospel, and makes a persuasive case for the fundamental importance of the concept to Luther.

6. *LW* 45, 88–92 and *WA* 11. 249. 24–252. 14.

7. Exposition of Psalm 101 (1534–35), *LW* 13, 194 and *WA* 51. 239. 24.

8. *Open Letter Concerning the Hard Book against the Peasants,* *LW* 46, 69–70 and *WA* 18. 389. 19.

9. *LW* 13, 197 and *WA* 51. 241. 39.

10. *LW* 46, 99–100 and *WA* 19. 629. 17 ff.

11. *LW* 45, 89 and *WA* 11. 249. 36–250. 20.

12. *Ibid.,* 90–91 and *WA* 11. 251. 2–35.

13. *Ibid.,* 90 and *WA* 11. 250. 26.

14. *WA* 56. 347. 8 ff. Cf. *Unbekannte Fragmente aus Luthers zweiter Psalmenvorlesung* (1518) (Berlin, 1940), 85.1, cited in Gordon Rupp, *The Righteousness of God* (London, Hodder and Stoughton, 1953), p. 225; cf. also the sermon "Two Kinds of Righteousness," where Luther explains alien righteousness in this way: "Through faith in Christ, therefore, Christ's righteousness becomes our righteousness and all that he has becomes ours; rather, he himself becomes ours. . . . this alien righteousness, instilled in us without our works by grace alone—while the Father, to be sure, inwardly draws us to Christ—is set opposite original sin, which we acquire without our works, by birth alone. Christ daily drives out the old Adam more and more in accordance with the extent to which faith and knowledge of Christ grow. For alien righteousness is not instilled all at once, but it begins, makes progress, and is finally perfected at the end through death." (*LW* 31, 298–99 and *WA* 2. 146. 8.)

15. *LW* 26, 340–43 and *WA* 40(I). 523. 31–527. 24; cf. Preface to the Apocalypse, *LW* 35, 411 and *WA DB* 7. 421. 10.

16. Sermon on Luke 21: 25–36 (Advent 2, Dec. 9, 1537), *WA* 45. 336. 18; cf. *WA* 11. 61 ff (an earlier version of the same sermon); Sermon for Christmas, 1522, *WA* 10 (I), 93 ff.; Exposition of Ps. 6:2, *WA* 5. 204. 5. The closest Luther ever came to predicting when the end would come was in a sermon of 1540 on the text Mt. 24, 32–33, where he declared, "I fully expect him not to

delay long. The world has now stood for some 5500 years. Now, in the course of the sixth period of a thousand years the end should come and this last thousand will not be completed; for God customarily acts as he did in the resurrection of Christ; in the middle of the third day, Christ rises from the dead." (*WA* 47. 621. 16.) More characteristically, however, he contented himself with declaring that the world would not endure "over a hundred years." (*WA TR* 6. 306 [No. 6985].)

17. *LW* 45, 352–53 and *WA* 15. 32. 1.

18. Sermon on Luke 21. 25–36(Dec. 10, 1531), *WA* 34(II). 461. 27; cf. *WA* 45. 336 ff.

19. *WA Br* 4. 122. 8(No. 1042); cf. *WA* 51. 214. 29.

20. *WA TR* 5. 184 (No. 5488).

21. *WA TR* 6. 306–307(No. 6985). The increase of falsehood and wickedness which he detected in the world was therefore a source of great comfort to him, for it heralded the Lord's coming. See *Commentary on Galatians* 3:20, *LW* 26, 326 and *WA* 40(I). 505. 15; *WA* 47. 623.

22. *WA Br* 5. 247.

23. This is evident, for example, in the 1518 proceedings at Augsburg. See *LW* 31, 263 and *WA* 2. 8. 27.

24. *LW* 48, 114 and *WA Br* 1. 359. 29 (No. 161).

25. Letter to Spalatin, Feb. 14, 1520; *WA Br* 2. 48. 27; cf. *Why the Books of the Pope and His Disciples Were Burned by Doctor Martin Luther* (1520); *LW* 31, 392 and *WA* 7. 176. 1, 16; Letter to John Lang (Aug. 18, 1520); *WA Br* 2. 167(No. 327).

26. John Wyclif, *English Works,* III, 276, and *De Eucharistia,* ed. by J. Loserth (London, 1892), pp. 30–31; John Hus, *The Church,* p. 128. "As for Antichrist occupying the Papal chair, it is evident that a Pope living contrary to Christ, like any other perverted person, is called by common consent Antichrist. In accordance with John 2.22, many are become Antichrists. And the faithful will not dare to deny persistently that it is possible for the man of sin to sit in the holy place." (Cf. p. 107.) Note how, in this passage, the term is broad enough to be applied to any number of people leading wicked lives. Note also Hus's tendency to use the term frequently in reference to wicked clergy (e.g., pp. 159, 177, 184, 253, 284, 291). Luther's use of the term was far more precise and restricted, and focused always on the theological rather than the moral issue.

27. *LW* 26, 180 and *WA* 40(I). 301. 17; *Smalcald Articles,*

Art. IV, in T. Tappert, ed., *The Book of Concord* (Philadelphia, Fortress, 1959), pp. 300–301; *WA* 50. 217. 23–219. 17; Preface to Ricardus' Refutation of the Koran, *WA* 53. 395. 10; Sermon for Advent 2, *WA* 10(I.2). 96. 19.

28. *Commentary on Galatians* 1:2, *LW* 26, 25 and *WA* 40 (I). 71; cf. *WA TR* 3. 318. 21(No. 3443); *LW* 31, 393 and *WA* 7. 178. 13.

29. Luther is not entirely consistent at this point. He does on occasion use the term Antichrist to include the Turk. He describes the Turk as a part of the Antichrist (*WA* 52. 549. 31) and the "flesh of Antichrist" (*WA TR* 1. 135. 15) (No. 330). Nevertheless, the identification of the Turk with the beast from the pit is more characteristic.

30. *On War against the Turk*, *LW* 46, 199–200 and *WA* 30(II). 144. 1.

31. *WA TR* 1. 135. 15(No. 330); cf. *WA TR* 3. 158. 32(No. 3055); *On the Misuse of the Mass* (1521), *LW* 36, 219 and *WA* 8. 554. 28.

32. Sermon on Matthew 24: 8–13(Nov. 2, 1539), *WA* 47. 561. 12; cf. *WA* 34(II). 466, 53. 401. 35, 52. 170; *WA Br* 2. 561 (No. 509), 9. 175(No. 3512); *WA TR* 5, 349. 18(No. 5775).

33. Preface to the *Church Postils*, *WA* 21. 203. 18; *WA* 39(II). 237. 25; *WA* 52. 20. 12; *WA* 47. 102 ff.

34. Sermon on Luke 21:25–33(1544), *WA* 52. 20. 18; cf. *LW* 35, 407 and *WA DB* 7. 415. 32.

35. "On the last day there will be great destruction, when all the elements will be reduced to ashes, and the whole world will return to its original chaos. Then a new heaven and a new earth, and we shall be changed." (*WA TR* 3. 665. 10 [No. 3861].)

36. *LW* 13, 221 and *WA* 51. 261. 20.

37. *WA* 14. 70. 27.

38. *WA* 12. 556. 9.

39. *WA* 12. 557. 1; cf. *WA* 10(III). 140. 17.

40. *WA* 21. 387. 23.

41. *WA* 10(III). 140. 17.

42. *That These Words of Christ, "This Is My Body," etc., Still Stand Firm against the Fanatics*, *LW* 37, 57–58 and *WA* 23. 132. 30.

43. *Ibid.*, *LW* 37, 59 and *WA* 23. 136. 18; cf. *LW* 37, 63 and *WA* 23. 142. 10.

44. *LW* 26, 95 and *WA* 40(I). 174. 3.

45. *WA* 48. 201. 5.

46. *LW* 13, 302 and *WA* 41. 104. 10; *LW* 14, 125–26 and *WA* 31(I). 447. 15; *LW* 27, 363 and *WA* 2. 586. 9; *WA* 37. 531 ff.; *WA TR* 4. 415. 1(No. 4664); *WA TR* 2. 497. 36(No. 2507b). See also, on this point, R. Bainton, "Luther on Birds, Dogs and Babies," in *Studies on the Reformation* (Boston, Beacon Press, 1966), pp. 67 ff., and H. Bornkamm, "The Picture of Nature," in *Luther's World of Thought* (St. Louis, Concordia, 1958), pp. 176 ff.

47. E.g., *WA TR* 1. 573. 31(No. 1160): "We are now living in the dawn of the future life, for we are beginning to regain a knowledge of creation a knowledge we had forfeited by the fall of Adam."

48. See, e.g., his description of Emser as one who "penetrates the Scriptures as deeply as a spider penetrates water." *WA* 2. 382. 20.

49. See R. Bainton, *Studies on the Reformation,* pp. 67 ff.

50. *WA TR* 1. 573. 31(No. 1160).

51. *WA TR* 4. 291. 1(No. 4391); cf. Sermon on John 6:32, *LW* 23, 33 and *WA* 33. 45. 3.

52. *The Bondage of the Will, WA* 18. 763. 1, English translation by J. I. Packer and O. R. Johnston (Westwood N.J., Revell, 1957), p. 282.

53. Exposition of Ps. 101, *LW* 13, 164 and *WA* 51. 214. 29.

54. *LW* 45, 113 and *WA* 11. 267. 31; *LW* 13, 224 and *WA* 51. 264. 6.

55. *LW* 13, 48 and *WA* 31 (I). 195. 30.

56. *Ibid.;* cf. Luther's exposition of Psalm 101:1, in which he pictures the Lord God contemplating the rulers who exercise authority without reference to his law, and saying to the angel Gabriel: "My dear fellow, what are these wise people doing in their Council chamber that they do not draw us into their deliberations? They must be wanting to build the Tower of Babel again. Dear Gabriel, go down there and take Isaiah with you, and read them a secret lesson through the window. . . ." (*LW* 13, 150 and *WA* 51. 203. 33.)

57. *LW* 13, 199 and *WA* 51. 242. 36.

58. J. Maritain, *Three Reformers* (New York, Scribner, 1932) pp. 28 ff.; B. Gerrish, *Grace and Reason* (Oxford, Clarendon Press, 1962), especially the Introduction and Chapters I and II.

59. Sermon, Oct. 25, 1522, *WA* 10(III). 380. 10.

60. An explanatory note on terminology is perhaps necessary here. The word "secular" has been employed in a way which must be sharply distinguished from "secularism." The latter is an ideology with an equally closed world view and an equally dogmatic outlook as the religious view which it tries to supplant. "Secular" is used here in the neutral sense, indicating an understanding of government as an open, human enterprise, free of religious validation or direction. Its nearest equivalent meaning is given in the word "human."

A "secular" understanding of government in this sense is threatened from two sides by attitudes which deprive government of its human character. On the one hand are sacral conceptions of government, which bring about the elevation of the ruler to the status of deity, or at least the attribution to him of divine qualities. This conception finds its clearest expression in the ancient Middle Eastern despotisms and is strongly echoed in the imperial cult of Rome. The same tendency appears in the medieval period in the extreme versions of Papal monarchist theory, with its assumption that the Pope is the direct representative of God who speaks with divine authority and beyond whom there is no appeal.

On the other hand, the understanding of government in secular or human terms is equally threatened by the secularistic ideologies of totalitarian regimes, since they elevate a particular political institution or figure to a position beyond correction or criticism.

61. Sermon on John 15:4, *LW* 24, 220 and *WA* 45. 661. 25.

62. Sermon on Luke 16:19–31 (June 22, 1522), *WA* 10 (III). 180. 13; cf. *WA TR* 4. 62. 5, 10 (No. 3993).

63. *LW* 31, 367 and *WA* 7. 65. 36.

64. *LW* 51, 77 and *WA* 10 (III). 18. 10; cf. *LW* 45, 67–68 and *WA* 8. 683. 18, 31.

65. *Smalcald Articles*, III, 12; *WA* 50. 250. 1. English translation in *The Book of Concord*, ed. by T. Tappert, p. 315.

66. *The Misuse of the Mass*, *LW* 36, 145 and *WA* 8. 491. 34; cf. *WA* 43. 507. 1; 3. 259. 18; 3. 139. 19; 3. 454. 25; 4. 173. 34; 4. 179. 14; 7. 721. 12; *LW* 41, 150 and *WA* 50. 629. 28; *LW* 51, 387 and *WA* 51. 190. 19.

67. *LW* 51, 306 and *WA* 47. 774. 32.

68. Sermon on Matthew 12:46–50 (1528); *WA* 28. 25. 6.

69. See the forty theses which Luther prepared in July, 1530, during the Diet of Augsburg, especially theses 5–7, *WA* 30 (II). 420. 17.

70. *Commentary on Galatians* 1:9(1535), *LW* 26, 58 and *WA* 40(I). 120. 22; cf. *The Babylonian Captivity of the Church, LW* 36, 107 and *WA* 6. 560. 33: "For the Church was born by the Word of promise through faith, and by this same Word is nourished and preserved. That is to say, it is the promise of God that makes the Church and not the Church that makes the promise of God. For the Word of God is incomparably superior to the Church, and in this Word the Church, being a creature, has nothing to decree, or- dain or make, but only to be decreed, ordained and made. For who begets his own parent? Who first brings forth his own maker?"

At this point also Luther comments on Augustine's statement that he had believed the Gospel because moved to do so by the au- thority of the Church. Luther interprets Augustine's statement in accordance with his own position here articulated—namely, that the Church does not judge the truth of Scripture but is taken captive by it. Cf. *LW* 35, 151–52 and *WA* 10 (II). 90 ff.

71. *WA* 47. 782. 10; *LW* 22, 442–43 and *WA* 47. 158. 17; *LW* 51, 305 and *WA* 47. 774. 4.

72. *Larger Catechism,* Part II, Art. III, *WA* 30(I). 188. 25. English translation in *The Book of Concord,* p. 416; cf. Luther's sermon on the same article of the creed, *LW* 51, 166 and *WA* 30 (I). 91. 19.

73. Exposition of John 14:25–6, *LW* 24, 172 and *WA* 45. 618. 20.

74. Exposition of Deuteronomy 4:29–31(1529), *WA* 28. 580. 32; Exposition of John 7:40–44, *LW* 23, 287 and *WA* 33. 459. 19.

75. *On the Councils and the Church, LW* 41, 144 and *WA* 50. 625. 5; *LW* 41, 143 and *WA* 50. 624. 18. The most useful discus- sion of Luther's terminology is to be found in Paul Althaus, *Die Theologie Martin Luthers* (Gütersloh, Gerd-Mohn, 1963), English translation by Robert C. Schultz, *The Theology of Martin Luther* (Philadelphia, Fortress, 1966), pp. 294 ff.

76. *WA* 45. 303. 2, 16.

77. *WA* 45. 303. 4, 19.

78. *LW* 41, 143 and *WA* 50. 624. 15.

79. Defense of the Thirteenth Proposition against Eck; *WA* 2. 190. 20.

80. *LW* 41, 143 and *WA* 50. 624. 16.

81. *LW* 41, 147–48 and *WA* 50. 627. 35.

82. *LW* 41, 144 and *WA* 50. 625. 22; cf. *LW* 12, 234 and *WA* 40(II). 521.

83. Luther sees this communion as stretching back into the time of the Old Covenant. The book of Psalms, in particular, was to him a picture book of "real, living, active saints" [*Preface to the Psalms, LW*, 35, 254 and *WA DB* 10 (I). 104.5]. "If you would see the holy Christian Church painted in living color and shape, comprehended in one little picture, then take up the Psalter. There you have a fine, bright, pure mirror that will show you what Christendom is." (*Ibid.*, 256).

84. *The Freedom of the Christian, LW* 31, 355 and *WA* 71. 57. 24.

85. *The Blessed Sacrament of the Holy and True Body of Christ, and the Brotherhoods, LW* 35, 70 and *WA* 2. 756. 20.

86. *LW* 51, 166 and *WA* 30(I). 91. 19.

87. Sermon on John 6:57, *LW* 23, 149 and *WA* 33. 232. 24; cf. *LW* 35, 50–51 and *WA* 2. 743. 7.

88. *Ibid., LW* 23, 149 and *WA* 33. 233. 9; cf. *Sermon on the Lord's Supper, WA* 12. 489. 9.

89. Sermon on John 17:11, *WA* 28. 149. 7, 33.

90. *Fourteen Consolations, LW* 42, 163 and *WA* 6. 132. 11.

91. *Sermon at Castle Pleissenberg, LW* 51, 305–306 and *WA* 47. 774. 15; cf. the exposition of Psalm 16:4 (1519–1521); *WA* 5. 451. 1, and Luther's defense of the thirteenth thesis against Eck (*WA*, 2. 190. 17), where he distinguishes clearly between the ecclesiastical organization and the *una sancta*.

92. *The Papacy at Rome, PE* 1, 349 and *WA* 6. 293. 3; cf. W. Pauck, *The Heritage of the Reformation* (Glencoe, Ill., Free Press, 1961), p. 40: "[Luther's] view of the Church as a spiritual-corporeal communion of believers was thus a Biblical-theological reinterpretation of the Roman Catholic idea of the Church as the mystical body of Christ. The correction of the impersonalizing that was implied in the Roman Catholic ecclesiology was of special importance to him."

93. It is true that Luther occasionally used the word "invisible" to describe the Church, but he clearly preferred the word "hidden" (*abscondita*). See, e.g., *LW* 27, 84 and *WA* 40(II). 106. The difference is significant because of the analogy between the Church's hiddenness and Christ's hiddenness.

94. *PE* 3, 394–95 and *WA* 7. 683. 9.

95. *Against Hanswurst, LW* 41, 211 and *WA* 51. 507. 14.

96. *LW* 35, 410 and *WA DB* 7. 418. 36, 7. 419. 36.

97. *PE* 3, 397 and *WA* 7. 685. 3.

98. *Lectures on Genesis* 21:1–3, *LW* 4, 6 and *WA* 43. 139. 37; cf. Sermon on Ps. 82 (Nov. 1, 1537), *WA* 45. 222. 26; Sermon on John 1: 46–51, *LW* 22, 194 ff.; Sermon on the Blessed Hope, *WA* 34(II). 129. 25.

99. *Lectures on Galatians* 5:19(1535), *LW* 27, 84 and *WA* 40(II). 106. 21. The Church was hidden, too, according to Luther, in the time of the old Covenant and under the Papacy. It was undoubtedly present but could not be clearly seen. *WA* 40(III). 505. 1; *LW* 4, 6 and *WA* 43. 139. 37.

100. "Die Entstehung von Luthers Kirchenbegriff," in *Gesammelte Aufsätze zur Kirchengeschichte,* I Luther (Tübingen, Mohr, 1921), pp. 245–78.

101. *WA* 4. 189. 17; *WA* 3. 124. 36; cf. Ps. 23:5, *LW* 12, 173 and *WA* 51, 290. 26; Ps. 110:1, *LW* 13, 241 and *WA* 41. 96. 34.

102. See, e.g., *The Ninety-Five Theses, LW* 31, 25 ff. and *WA* 1. 233–38; and the *Leipzig Debate, LW* 31, 313 ff. and *WA* 2. 158. 16; cf. Luther's letter to Spalatin (July 20, 1519), *LW* 31, 321–22 and *WA Br* 1. 422. 58(No. 187).

103. *Lectures on Genesis* 17:3–6, *LW* 3, 109 and *WA* 42. 626. 14.

104. E.g., *Commentary on John* 14:10, *LW* 24, 67 and *WA* 45. 522. 7; *WA* 47. 556. 27; *WA* 46. 707. 20.

105. *LW* 24, 67 and *WA* 45. 522. 7.

106. *LW* 41, 149 and *WA* 50. 629. 2. There is a play on words here. The word *Heiligthum,* translated "holy possessions," is the same as the word for "relic." See *LW* 41, 149, n. 385.

107. *Ibid.,* 152 and *WA* 50. 631. 29.

108. *Ibid.,* 153 and *WA* 50. 631. 36; cf. *LW* 36, 83 and *WA* 6. 544. 4. "If Baptism does not belong to Peter alone, then it is a wicked usurpation of power to claim the power of the keys for the Pope alone."

109. *LW* 41, 154 and *WA* 50. 632. 35; cf. Heinrich Bullinger's very similar account in the *Second Helvetic Confession,* in *Creeds of Christendom,* ed. by P. Schaff (New York, Harper and Bros., 1877), III, 872 ff.

110. *Lectures on Genesis* 28:16, *WA* 43. 597. 2; cf. *LW* 35, 201 and *WA* 30(II). 645. 21; *PE* 1, 361 and *WA* 6. 301. 3; *WA* 24. 149. 27; *WA* 11. 408. 8.

111. *WA* 7. 721. 9.

112. *WA* 25. 97. 32.

113. *WA* 47. 535. 15; cf. *WA* 45. 54. 12; *WA* 51. 520. 2.

114. *LW* 31, 31 and *WA* 1. 236. 22; *WA* 43. 597. 2.

115. *LW* 26, pp. 13, 19, 201, 378, 402, 407, etc.; *WA* 40(I). 52. 13, 62. 22, 327. 2, 576. 23, 610. 29, 617. 31, etc.; cf. Sermon on Ephesians 4:1–6, *WA* 22. 299. 38.

116. *WA* 22. 300. 2; *LW* 14, 92 and *WA* 30(I). 164. 15. Luther never discounted the importance of doctrinal formulation, however. In the treatise *De Servo Arbitrio,* he even declares that "one must delight in assertions to be a Christian at all." *WA* 18. 603. 10. English translation by Packer and Johnston, *The Bondage of the Will,* p. 66.

117. E.g., Sermon on Matthew 24:4–7, *WA* 47. 556. 27; cf. Sermon on John 1:47, *WA* 46. 707. 20; *LW* 24, 310 and *WA* 46. 11. 7.

118. Luther had in mind such imitations as holy water, which he regarded as the devil's imitation of baptism. "A popular proverb has it: Where God builds a Church, the Devil builds a tavern next door . . . the Devil is always the imitator of our Lord God, forever poses as divine and creates the impression that he is God." (Sermon, 1534, *WA* 52. 828. 14.)

119. *On Translating: An Open Letter, LW* 35, 201 and *WA* 30(II). 645–18.

120. Sermon on Ps. 72:14–15, *WA* 49. 41. 20; *WA TR* 4. 190. 4(No. 4190); see also Preus, "The Christian and the Church," in *More about Luther,* p. 147.

121. *Sermons on the Gospel of St. John* 15:2, *LW* 24, 206 and *WA* 45. 648. 15; cf. *LW* 14, 93 and *WA* 31(I). 166. 4.

122. *The Keys* (1530), *LW* 40. 371 and *WA* 30(II). 502. 22; *Sermon on the Ban* (1520), *WA* 6. 66. 13; cf. *WA* 1. 639. 2; *WA* 7. 236. 19.

123. Sermon on John 10:12–16, *WA* 21. 332. 34.

124. Packer and Johnston, *The Bondage of the Will,* pp. 122–23; *WA* 18. 652. 1.

125. *LW* 53, 63–64 and *WA* 19. 75. 3.

126. Bender, for example, in "The Anabaptist Vision," in Hershberger, ed., *The Recovery of The Anabaptist Vision,* pp. 40 ff., claims that the gathered Church was Luther's original aim. He cites a conversation of Luther with Schwenkfeld in 1525 (from *Corpus Schwenkfeldianorum* [Leipzig, 1911], 2.280 ff.) and a reference from Holl, *Gesammelte Aufsätze,* p. 359, to a statement of Luther, in 1522, in which he expressed the hope that "we who at present are well-nigh heathen under a Christian name might yet organize a Christian assembly." The implication of Bender's argument is that Luther compromised what was originally his fundamental in-

tention. Cf. J. Horsch, "The Rise of State-Church Protestantism," *MQR*, VI (1931), 189–91.

127. *LW* 53, 64 and *WA* 19. 75. 3.

128. *To the Christian Nobility of the German Nation* (1520), *LW* 44, 130 and *WA* 6. 409. 12; cf. Preface to the *Instructions for the Visitors of Parish Pastors in Electoral Saxony* (1528), *LW* 40, 271 and *WA* 26. 195 ff.

129. *LW* 53, 62 and *WA* 19. 73. 22.

130. *Ibid.*, and *WA* 19. 73. 25.

131. *Ibid.*, p. 61 and *WA* 19. 72. 6.

132. *PE* 1, 355 ff. and *WA* 6. 296. 39.

133. *Ibid.*, pp. 352 ff. and *WA* 6. 293. 3; cf. 4. 24. 35.

134. *WA* 7. 720. 2.

135. *Treatise on the Blessed Sacrament*, *LW* 35, 65–66 and *WA* 2. 53. 1.

136. *The Papacy at Rome*, *PE* 1, 353–54 and *WA* 6. 296. 5; cf. *WA* 4. 24. 35.

137. Letter to Amsdorf (1542), *WA Br.* 9. 610. 47(No. 3709): "The Church must appear in the world. But it can only appear in a veil, a mask, a shell, or some kind of clothes which a man can hear, see and understand, otherwise it cannot be found. But such a mask is a married man, a political or domestic person, John, Peter, Luther, Amsdorf, etc., yet none of these is the Church, which is neither Jew nor Greek, man nor wife, but Christ alone."

138. *LW* 13, 300–301 and *WA* 41. 162. 29.

139. *LW* 26, 97–98 and *WA* 40(I). 177. 22–181. 14.

140. *LW* 27, 87–88 and *WA* 40(II). 110. 14.

141. *LW* 4, 348–49 and *WA* 43. 387. 14.

142. *LW* 4, 343 and *WA* 43. 383–85.

143. *LW* 13, 301 and *WA* 41. 163. 8; cf. *LW* 26, 96 and *WA* 40(I). 175. 28; *PE* 1, 352 and *WA* 6. 294. 35.

144. *LW* 13, 300 and *WA* 41. 161. 32.

145. *Lectures on Galatians* 2:6, *LW* 26, 94 and *WA* 40(I). 173. 9; cf. *LW* 4, 347 and *WA* 43. 386. 8.

146. Reply to Ambrosius, *WA* 7. 719. 34; cf. G. Ebeling, "Luther: Theologie," *Die Religion in Geschichte und Gegenwart*, IV, 505.

147. *LW* 13, 301–302 and *WA* 41. 163. 30.

III. JOHN CALVIN

1. A brief but very good introductory account of the life and intellectual development of Calvin is found in F. Wendel, *Calvin:*

The Origins and Development of His Religious Thought, translated by Philip Mairet (London, Collins, 1963), Part I.

2. *De Aeterna Praedestinatione Dei, CR* 8(36), 294, translated by J. K. S. Reid, *Concerning the Eternal Predestination of God* (London, James Clarke, 1961), p. 97.

3. *Inst.* 1. 15. 1, *LCC* 183 and *CR* 2(30), 134.

4. *Inst.* 1. 14. 20, *LCC* 179–80 and *CR* 2(30), 131–32.

5. *Inst.* 1. 14. 22, *LCC* 182 and *CR* 2(30), 133.

6. *Inst.* 1. 14. 2, *LCC* 161–62 and *CR* 2(30), 118.

7. *Inst.* 1. 14. 20, *LCC* 179 and *CR* 2(30), 131.

8. *Inst.* 1. 16. 1, *LCC* 197–98 and *CR* 2(30), 144.

9. *Inst.* 1. 16. 2, *LCC* 198 and *CR* 2(30), 145; 1. 16. 4, *LCC* 202 and *CR* 2(30), 147; 1. 14. 14, *LCC* 174 and *CR* 2(30), 127; 1. 14. 17, *LCC* 176 and *CR* 2(30), 128; cf. Commentary on Psalm 135:6, *COT* 12, 174 and *CR* 32(60), 359.

10. Sermon on Deuteronomy 5:16, *CR* 26(54), 310; *Inst.* 4. 20. 4, *LCC* 1489 and *CR* 2(30), 1095; 4. 20. 24, *LCC* 1512 and *CR* 2(30), 1111–12; *Commentary on I Cor.* 15:24, *CNTC* 9, 324 and *CR* 49(77), 547.

11. *Inst.* 4. 20. 2; *LCC* 1487 and *CR* 2(30), 1093–94. Calvin adopted this conception of worldly rule as far back as the 1536 *Institutes* (*CR* 1(29), 230 ff). It is not, therefore, a justification of the system which developed in Geneva. Rather, the actual development there is an authentic expression of the view of the magistracy which Calvin had characteristically held from his early theological writings.

12. *Commentary on Jeremiah* 31:35–6, *COT* 20, 143 and *CR* 38(66), 699; Preface to the *Commentary on the Psalms, COT* 8, xxxviii and *CR* 31(59), 19; cf. Commentary on Psalm 115:3, *COT* 11, 344 and *CR* 32(60), 184; *Inst.* 1. 17. 1, *LCC* 210 and *CR* 2(30), 154; *Inst.* 1. 17. 6, *LCC* 219 and *CR* 2(30), 158.

13. *Commentary on the Psalms* 115:17, *COT* 11, 358 and *CR* 32(60), 192; cf. W. Niesel, *The Theology of Calvin* (London, Lutterworth, 1956), p. 64: "Not because the world exists do we attain a certain knowledge of God and then after a deepening of this knowledge an understanding of the Church; but just the opposite—because there is a Church, there is also a world. The will of the Creator is from the start directed toward the people who shall serve Him."

14. *Inst.* 2. 10. 2, *LCC* 429 and *CR* 2(30), 313; cf. 2. 10. 4, 5, *LCC* 431–32 and *CR* 2(30), 315.

15. E.g., George Tavard, in *Holy Writ or Holy Church* (New

York, Harper & Bros., 1959), speaks of Calvin's "overesteem for the Old Testament" and claims that for Calvin the differences between the two testaments "derive accidentally from the necessity of making revelation progressive" (p. 101). Cf. L. G. M. Alting von Geusau, *Die Lehre von der Kindertaufe bei Calvin* (Bilthoven, 1963), pp. 171 ff.

16. *Commentary on Exodus* 12:14, COT 3, 463 and CR 24(52), 290; cf. *Commentary on Hebrews* 8:6, CNTC 12, 108 and CR 55(83), 99; and *Commentary on Ezekiel* 16:61, COT 23, 178 and CR 40(68), 396.

17. *Inst.* 2. 11. 2, LCC 451 and CR 2(30), 330.

18. *Ibid.* cf. 2. 11. 5, LCC 455 and CR 2(30), 333; 4. 1. 24, LCC 1037 and CR 2(30), 764.

19. For a full discussion of this concept of "suspended grace," see J. Hesselink, "Calvin and Heilsgeschichte," in Felix Christ, ed., *Oikonomia: Heilsgeschichte als Thema der Theologie* (Hamburg-Bergstedt, Herbert Reich, Evang. Verlag, 1967), pp. 163 ff.

20. *Commentary on Genesis* 49:10, COT 2, 453 and CR 23(51), 598 (there is an error in pagination in the *Corpus Reformatorum;* page 598 is printed in the text as 958); cf. *Commentary on Colossians* 2:14, CNTC 11, 335 and CR 52(80), 108.

21. *Commentary on Acts* 13:32, CNTC 6, 375–76 and CR 48(76), 299.

22. E.g., Wendel, *Calvin,* pp. 263–84; Niesel, *The Theology of Calvin,* pp. 159–81.

23. *Inst.* 3. 21. 1, LCC 922–23 and CR 2(30), 680.

24. *Commentary on John* 6:40, CNTC 4, 162 and CR 47(75), 147.

25. *Inst.* (1536), II, 4, CR 1(29), 71.

26. *TT* 2, 41 and CR 9(37), 71.

27. *Inst.* (1539), VIII (1544: XIV), CR 1(29), 861 ff.

28. Wendel, *Calvin,* p. 268.

29. E.g., *De Aeterna Praedestinatione Dei,* CR 8(36), 313 ff.; Reid, *Concerning the Eternal Predestination of God,* pp. 120 ff.

30. *Inst.* 3. 24. 5, LCC 970 and CR 2(30), 716; cf. Sermon on Ephesians 1:4–6, CR 51(79), 282; Sermon on Daniel 12:1–2, CR 42(70), 127, 131. Calvin emphasizes the positive purpose of the Gospel for salvation, and accordingly reprobation is described as "accidental" in relation to God's purpose.

31. Actually, Book III ends with a chapter on the last resurrection, but this does not refute the point made; for the last resur-

rection itself is integrally related to election as the goal of the Christian life is related to its origin.

32. Emil Brunner, *The Misunderstanding of the Church* (Philadelphia, Westminster, 1953), p. 9.

33. *Dogmatics*, Vol. III, *The Christian Doctrine of The Church, Faith and the Consummation* (Philadelphia, Westminster, 1962), p. 19.

34. E. A. Dowey, in *The Knowledge of God in Calvin's Theology* (New York, Columbia University Press, 1952), p. 41, maintains that the really significant ordering principle is the *duplex cognitio Domini* rather than the Creed, but he allows that the structure of the *Institutes* is too rich to be restricted to one rationale of organization and points out that Calvin himself (1.16.18) claims to be employing the Creed in this way.

35. See, e.g., *Commentary on I Corinthians* 1:5, CNTC 9, 21 and CR 49(77), 310; *Commentary on Galatians* 2:20, CNTC, 11, 42–43 and CR 50(78), 199; cf. *Commentary on John* 6:35, CNTC 4, 159 and CR 47(75), 145.

36. *Commentary on Romans* 6:11, CNTC 8, 128 and CR 49 (77), 110.

37. *Commentary on Hebrews* 10:14, CNTC 12, 138 and CR 55(83), 126; Sermon on Mark 1:23–4 CR 46(74), 736; *Commentary on Hebrews* 7:25, CNTC 12, 101 and CR 55(83), 94.

38. *Inst.* 3. 1. 1, LCC 537 and CR 2(30), 393.

39. *Commentary on John* 6:35, CNTC 4, 159 and CR 47(75), 145; cf. *Commentary on Ephesians* 5:31, CNTC 11, 209 and CR 51(79), 226.

40. *Commentary on Romans* 6:5, CNTC 8, 124 and CR 49(77), 106; cf. *Commentary on I John* 2:6, CNTC 5, 247 and CR 55(83), 312. "Yet He does not simply exhort us to the imitation of Christ but, from the union we have with Him, proves we should be like Him. He says that a likeness in life and action will prove that we abide in Christ." That is to say, it is the reality of abiding in Christ which alone makes possible the ethical response of imitating Christ's example. Cf. also *Psychopannychia, TT* 3, 436 and CR 5(33), 191.

41. *Commentary on I Corinthians* 11:24, CNTC 9, 246 and CR 49(77), 487.

42. *Commentary on I Peter* 4:1, CNTC 12, 298 and CR 55(83), 270.

43. *Commentary on Romans* 6:5, CNTC 8, 124 and CR 49(77),

106; *Inst.* 2.16.13, *LCC* 521 and *CR* 2(30), 380; *Commentary on John* 17:19, *CNTC* 5, 146 and *CR* 47(75), 385.

44. *Commentary on I Corinthians* 1:5, *CNTC* 9, 21 and *CR* 49(77), 310; *Commentary on Galatians* 2:20, *CNTC* 11, 42–43 and *CR* 50(78), 199; *Inst.* 3.1.1, *LCC* 537 and *CR* 2(30), 393.

45. *Commentary on 2 Timothy* 1:9, *CNTC* 10, 296 and *CR* 52(80), 352.

46. *Commentary on I Corinthians* 1:13, *CNTC* 9, 28 and *CR* 49(77), 316.

47. *Commentary on Hebrews* 10:24, *CNTC* 12, 144 and *CR* 55(83), 94; cf. *Inst.* 3. 20. 19, *LCC* 876–77 and *CR* 2(30), 645; 3. 20. 24, *LCC* 883 and *CR* 2(30), 649–50; *CNTC* 9, 264 and *CR* 49(77), 501. This emphasis in Calvin is not restricted to his interpretation of the "body of Christ" image but informs also his understanding of the other images of the Church. See, e.g., the *Geneva Catechism* discussion of the *communio sanctorum. TT* 2, 51 and *CR* 6(34), 39.

48. *Psychopannychia, TT* 3, 463 and *CR* 5(33), 211.

49. *Commentary on John* 20:18, *CNTC* 5, 200 and *CR* 47(75), 434–35; cf. *Commentary on Colossians* 3:1, *CNTC* 11, 345 and *CR* 52(80), 117–18.

50. *Inst.* 3. 2. 24, *LCC* 570–71 and *CR* 2(30), 418. The comparison with Luther ought not to be made absolute. Luther does deal with the Christian's growth into Christ in the context of his doctrine of baptism. The point is simply that the notion of growth does not have the same significance for Luther as it has in Calvin's theology.

51. *Inst.* 2. 16. 16, *LCC* 524 and *CR* 2(30), 383; cf. 3. 25. 1–4, *LCC* 987 ff. and *CR* 2(30), 728 ff.; *Commentary on Hebrews* 6:19, *CNTC* 12, 86–87 and *CR* 55(83), 80–82.

52. *Commentary on Titus* 3:5, *CNTC* 10, 382 and *CR* 52 (80), 430; cf. *Inst.* 3. 25. 10, *LCC* 1004 ff. and *CR* 2(30), 741–42.

53. See, e.g., E. Buess, "Prädestination und Kirche in Calvins Institution," in *Theol. Zeitschrift,* 12 (1956), 347–61; A. Ganoczy, *Calvin: Théologien de l'Eglise et du Ministère* (Paris, Les Editions du Cerf, 1964); A. Lecerf, "La Doctrine de L'Eglise dans Calvin," in *Revue de Théologie et de Philosophie,* IX (1929), pp. 256–70; W. Mueller, *Church and State in Luther and Calvin* (Nashville, Broadman Press, 1954); H. Quistorp, "Sichtbare und Unsichtbare Kirche bei Calvin," in *Evangelische Theologie,* 9(1949–1950), 83 ff.

54. *Commentary on Hebrews* 6:1, CNTC 12. 72 and CR 55 (83), 68.

55. *Inst.* 3. 9. 5, LCC 718 and CR 2(30), 527.

56. *Commentary on I Thessalonians* 5:1, CNTC 8, 367 and CR 52(80), 168; cf. CNTC 9, 343 and CR 49(77), 562; CNTC 8, 396 and CR 52(80), 194.

57. *Inst.* 4. 8. 7, LCC 154–55 and CR 2(30), 850; *Commentary on Micah* 4:1 f., COT 28, 255 and CR 43(71), 339; *Commentary on John* 12:48, CNTC 5, 53 and CR 47(75), 304.

58. *Commentary on I Corinthians* 15:57, CNTC 9, 347 and CR 49(77), 565; *Commentary on Luke* 19.12, MML 2, 440 and CR 45(73), 568.

59. *Commentary on Philippians* 2:10, CNTC 11, 252 and CR 52(80), 29; cf. MML 3, 145 and CR 45(73), 666; *Psychopanny-chia*, TT 3, 455 and CR 5(33), 205.

60. *Commentary on I Peter* 4:12, CNTC 12, 307–308 and CR 55(83), 278–79; *ibid.*, 1.5, CNTC 12, 233 and CR 55(83), 211; MML 2, 404–405 and CR 45(73), 544; MML 3, 142, 174 and CR 45(73), 664, 685.

61. *Commentary on Acts* 1:3, CNTC 6, 24 and CR 49(77) 4.

62. *Commentary on Colossians* 3:3, CNTC 11, 347 and CR 52(80), 118–19; *Commentary on John* 5:24, CNTC 4, 129 and CR 47(75), 116; cf. *Inst.* 2. 15. 3, LCC 497–98 and CR 2(30), 363; *Inst.* 2. 16. 16, LCC 524–25 and CR 2(30), 383; CNTC 12, 132 and CR 55(83), 121; CNTC 10, 332–33 and CR 52(80), 385.

63. MML 2, 441 and CR 45(73), 568; *Commentary on I Corinthians* 15:57, CNTC 9, 347 and CR 49(77), 565.

64. MML 2, 406 and CR 45(73), 545; *Commentary on John* 13:31, CNTC 5, 68 and CR 47(75), 317; cf. CR 46(74), 908.

65. MML 2, 212 and CR 45(73), 425; cf. CNTC 7, 35 and CR 49(77), 346.

66. *Inst.* 3, 9. 4, LCC 716 and CR 2(30), 526.

67. *Inst.* 3. 9. 3, LCC 714 and CR 2(30), 525.

68. *Inst.* 3. 9. 4, LCC 716 and CR 2(30), 526.

69. *Inst.* 3. 9. 3, LCC 714 and CR 2(30), 525; *Commentary on I Timothy* 4:5, CNTC 5, 42 and CR 47(75), 293.

70. *Commentary on John* 12:31–32, CNTC 5, 42 and CR 47(75), 293.

71. *Commentary on Jeremiah* 31:35–36, COT 20, 143 and CR 38(66), 699; cf. COT 8, 163 and CR 31(59), 123.

72. *Commentary on Genesis* 3:3 ff., *COT* 1, 146 and *CR* 23(51), 57; cf. *COT* 8, 99 ff. and *CR* 31(59), 90–91.

73. *Inst.* 1. 15. 4, *LCC* 189 and *CR* 2(30), 138–39; cf. *CNTC* 11, 311 and *CR* 52(80), 87; *MML* 3, 334 and *CR* 45(73), 788.

74. *Commentary on Ephesians* 1:8, *CNTC* 11, 129 and *CR* 51(79), 151; cf. *MML* 3, 175 and *CR* 45(73), 686.

75. *MML* 2, 14 and *CR* 45(73), 303.

76. *Inst.* 4. 1. 1, *LCC* 1011 and *CR* 2(30), 745.

77. *The Misunderstanding of the Church*, pp. 9 ff.

78. *Inst.* 4. 1. 4, *LCC* 1016 and *CR* 2(30), 750.

79. *Inst.* 4. 1. 9, *LCC* 1023 and *CR* 2(30), 753; 4. 1. 11, *LCC* 1025 and *CR* 2(30), 755; cf. *Geneva Confession, CR* 9(37), 698.

80. *Inst.* 4. 2. 4, *LCC* 1046 and *CR* 2(30), 771; cf. *TT* 1, 49 and *CR* 5(33), 403; *CR* 53(81), 311; *CR* 35(63), 600; *Inst.* 4. 2. 3, *LCC* 1043–44 and *CR* 2(30), 769–70.

81. *Inst.* 1. 7. 2, *LCC* 75 and *CR* 2(30), 57.

82. *TT* 1, 215 and *CR* 6(34), 521; *TT* 1, 107 and *CR* 7(35), 33; *TT* 3, 264 and *CR* 7(35), 610; *CR* 50(78), 455.

83. *Commentary on Acts* 2:42, *CNTC* 6, 85 and *CR* 48(76), 57.

84. *Reply to Sadolet, TT* 1, 36–37 and *CR* 5(33), 393–94.

85. *Remarks on the Letter of Paul III, TT* 1, 259 and *CR* 7(35), 259.

86. *Inst.* 4. 1. 5, *LCC* 1018 and *CR* 2(30), 750.

87. *MML* 2, 121 and *CR* 45(73), 369; *Inst.* 4. 1. 22, *LCC* 1035–36 and *CR* 2(30), 763; 4. 2. 10, *LCC* 1051 and *CR* 2(30), 775; Homily No. 42 on I Samuel, *CR* 29(57), 705.

88. *Brief Form of a Confession of Faith, TT* 2, 129; cf. *MML* 3, 28–29 and *CR* 45(73), 592.

89. *Confession of Faith in the Name of the Reformed Churches of France, TT* 2, 150.

90. *Reply to Sadolet, TT* 1, 38 and *CR* 5(33), 394.

91. *Inst.* 4. 8. 4, *LCC* 1152 and *CR* 2(30), 848; 4. 1. 11, *LCC* 1025 and *CR* 2(30), 755; *MML* 2, 110 and *CR* 45(73), 362; cf. *CNTC* 5, 295 and *CR* 55(83), 357.

92. Sermon on Deuteronomy 7:5–8, *CR* 26(54), 515; cf. 506.

93. *Commentary on I Peter* 3:21, *CNTC* 12, 295 and *CR* 55 (83), 267–68; *Inst.* 4.2.6, *LCC* 1047–48 and *CR* 2(30), 772; *CNTC* 12, 210 and *CR* 55(83), 192; *COT* 8, 116–17 and *CR* 31(59), 99.

94. *Inst.* 4. 1. 5, *LCC* 1019 and *CR* 2(30), 751.

95. *Inst.* 4. 10. 30, *LCC* 1207 and *CR* 2(30), 889.

96. *Letter to M. Le Curé de Cernex* (1543); *Letters* I, 364–65 and *CR* 11(39), 485.

97. *Reply to Sadolet, TT* 1, 37 and *CR* 5(33), 394; Calvin's understanding of the true and ancient form of the Church is not limited to apostolic times but embraces such figures as Chrysostom, Basil, Cyprian, Ambrose, and Augustine, all of whom are seen as predating the ruin of the Church of the Papacy. Moreover, even within the Papal institution, some vestiges of the true Church remain (*Inst.* 4. 2. 11–12, *LCC* 1051–52 and *CR* 2[30], 775–76).

98. *The Necessity of Reforming the Church, TT* 1, 146 and *CR* 6(34), 474.

99. *Inst.* 4. 10. 30, *LCC* 1208 and *CR* 2(30), 889; cf. *CNTC* 9, 310 and *CR* 49(77), 535; *Inst.* 4. 10. 27–28, *LCC* 1205–1206, and *CR* 2(30) 887–88.

100. *Commentary on Acts* 6:1; *CNTC* 6, 157–58 and *CR* 48(76), 117–18.

101. *Inst.* 4. 1. 7; *LCC* 1021 and *CR* 2(30), 752–53.

102. *Ibid., LCC* 1028 and *CR* 2(30), 757; cf. *Inst.* 4. 1. 2, *LCC* 1013 and *CR* 2(30), 747; *MML* 2, 121; *CR* 45(73), 369.

103. *Inst.* 4. 1. 17, *LCC* 1031 and *CR* 2(30), 760; *Reply to Sadolet, TT* 1, 67 and *CR* 5(33), 415.

104. *Inst.* 4. 1. 15, *LCC* 1029–30 and *CR* 2(30), 757–58. Calvin had in mind particularly the Anabaptists; cf. *Inst.* 4. 1. 16; *LCC* 1031 and *CR* 2(30), 759; 4. 1. 19, *LCC* 1033 and *CR* 2(30), 761.

105. *Commentary on Romans* 16:21, *CNTC* 8, 328 and *CR* 49(77), 292; *Inst.* 3. 20. 42, *LCC* 905 and *CR* 2(30), 667; *CR* 53(81), 161; *CNTC* 11, 258 and *CR* 52(80), 35; *COT* 9, 303 and *CR* 31(59), 521; *CNTC* 12, 144 and *CR* 55(83), 132.

106. *Letter to Nicholas Radziwill, Letters* III, 133, *CR* 15(43), 429.

107. *Commentary on Daniel* 2:40, *COT* Dan. 1, 178 and *CR* 40(68), 601; cf. *CR* 53(81), 35–36.

108. *Inst.* 4. 1. 7, *LCC* 1021 and *CR* 2(30), 753.

109. *Ibid., CR* 2(30), 752; cf. *Inst.* 4. 1. 2, *LCC* 1012–13 and *CR* 2(30), 746–47.

110. *Inst.* 4. 1. 3, *LCC* 1015–16 and *CR* 2(30), 748. Calvin, like Luther, allows for a "judgment of charity" in recognizing membership of the Church (*Inst.* 4. 1. 8, *LCC* 1022–23 and *CR* 2[30], 753).

IV. MENNO SIMONS

1. There is now a substantial scholarly consensus concerning what ought to be regarded as mainline "evangelical Anabaptism," in distinction from groups like the Spiritualists (e.g., Denck, Schwenkfeld) and the Revolutionaries (eg., Münzer, Jan of Leyden, etc.). Evangelical Anabaptism, thus defined, includes such figures as Menno Simons, Konrad Grebel, Pilgram Marpeck, Dirk Philips, and many others of lesser stature. Their chief distinguishing characteristic (for which baptism was the outward symbol) was a withdrawal from the world, including the Catholic and Reformed Churches, into closely knit brotherhoods stressing Biblical faith and the regenerate life of discipleship. See on this point Franklin Littell, *The Anabaptist View of the Church* (Boston, Beacon Press, 1952), and G. H. Williams, ed., *Spiritual and Anabaptist Writers,* Library of Christian Classics, Vol. XXV (Philadelphia, Westminster, 1957), Introduction, pp. 19 ff.

2. Menno provides a rather full and detailed autobiographical account of his spiritual development in the *Reply to Gellius Faber* (*CW*, pp. 668 ff). See also the biography by Bender, in *CW*, pp. 3 ff.

3. The word "radical" needs to be stressed in order to make clear the difference from the limited and qualified dualism evident in Luther's thought.

4. Since this phrase is more commonly used in reference to the problem of the divinity and humanity of Christ, it needs to be made clear that this is not its meaning within this context. The point being made is that the vital center of Menno's Christology—the doctrine of regeneration—is expounded in such a way as to postulate a radical dualism between the regenerate and the unregenerate, and that this dualism, underlined by a parallel development in his eschatology, is crucial to his interpretation of the institutional Church.

5. Harold S. Bender, "The Anabaptist Vision," in G. Hershberger, ed., *The Recovery of the Anabaptist Vision* (Scottsdale, Pa., Herald Press, 1957), pp. 42–43.

6. Krahn, "Menno Simons' Concept of the Church," in E. J. Dyck, ed., *A Legacy of Faith* (Newton, Kan., Faith and Life Press, 1962), p. 17; cf. F. Littell, "The Anabaptist Concept of the Church," in Hershberger, pp. 119 ff.; F. Heyer, *Der Kirchenbegriff der Schwärmer* (Leipzig, 1939).

7. *Christian Baptism* (1539), *CW* 271 and *Op.* 423; cf. *CW* 693 and *Op.* 270; *CW* 553 and *Op.* 501.

8. *The Spiritual Resurrection, CW* 57, 60 and *Op.* 182, 184; *Why I Do Not Cease Teaching and Writing, CW* 318 and *Op.* 454.

9. *The New Birth, CW* 96 and *Op.* 127.

10. *Foundation of Christian Doctrine* (hereafter abbreviated as *Foundation*), *CW* 124 and *Op.* 14; cf. *CW* 241 and *Op.* 404; *CW* 245 and *Op.* 407; *CW* 410 and *Op.* 632; *CW* 521–22 and *Op.* 473.

11. *Christian Baptism, CW* 234 and *Op.* 399; cf. *CW* 208 and *Op.* 60; *CW* 527 and *Op.* 328; *CW* 274 and *Op.* 425; *CW* 774 and *Op.* 320.

12. *Foundation, CW* 145–46 and *Op.* 26; cf. *CW* 558 and *Op.* 504.

13. *CW* 232 and *Op.* 397; *CW* 410 and *Op.* 632; *CW* 55–58 and *Op.* 180–82.

14. *The New Birth, CW* 95 and *Op.* 126.

15. *Christian Baptism, CW* 245 and *Op.* 406; *Reply to Gellius Faber, CW* 654 and *Op.* 248; *Confession of the Distressed Christians, CW* 506 and *Op.* 463; cf. *CW* 1053 and *Op.* 434.

16. *A Tribute to Menno Simons* (Scottsdale, Pa., Herald Press, 1961), pp. 33–34. Littell points to passages such as *CW* 189 and *Op.* 50 and *CW* 654 and *Op.* 248.

17. *CW* 563–64 and *Op.* 507–508.

18. *The New Birth, CW* 94 and *Op.* 125–26; cf. *CW* 146 and *Op.* 26; *CW* 416 and *Op.* 636; *CW* 441 and *Op.* 535; *CW* 645 and *Op.* 240.

19. *Foundation, CW* 222 and *Op.* 68; cf. *CW* 416 and *Op.* 636; *CW* 324 and *Op.* 73.

20. *Why I Do Not Cease Teaching and Writing, CW* 299–300 and *Op.* 442; cf. *CW* 402 and *Op.* 118.

21. *The New Birth, CW* 92–93 and *Op.* 125.

22. *CW* 310 and *Op.* 449.

23. E.g., *Instruction on Excommunication, CW* 968 and *Op.* 194.

24. *A Pathetic Supplication to All Magistrates, CW* 528 and *Op.* 329; cf. *CW* 572 and *Op.* 514; *CW* 626 and *Op.* 228; *CW* 181 and *Op.* 46; *CW* 417–18 and Op. 637.

25. *The Blasphemy of John of Leiden, CW* 46–47 and *Op.* 629–30; cf. *CW* 90 and *Op.* 123; *CW* 54 and *Op.* 179.

26. *Foundation, CW* 109 and *Op.* 6; cf. *CW* 544 and *Op.* 495; *CW* 584 and *Op.* 137; *CW* 581–82 and *Op.* 125–26.

27. *Foundation, CW* 109–10 and *Op.* 6.

28. By a "pious error," the Verduin translation here prints the word "souls" instead of "soles."

29. *The Cross of the Saints, CW* 613 and *Op.* 154; cf. *CW* 585–87 and *Op.* 138–45.

30. *CW* 554 and *Op.* 502.

31. *Why I Do Not Cease Teaching and Writing, CW* 300 and *Op.* 442; cf. *CW* 91 and *Op.* 124.

32. *Confession of the Distressed Christians, CW* 522 and *Op.* 473; cf. *CW* 273 and *Op.* 424; *CW* 734 and *Op.* 295; *CW* 99 and *Op.* 129.

33. *Why I Do Not Cease Teaching and Writing, CW* 295–96 and *Op.* 439; cf. *CW* 117 and *Op.* 10; *CW* 35 and *Op.* 662; *CW* 117 and *Op.* 10.

34. *The Cross of the Saints, CW* 595 and *Op.* 144; cf. *CW* 81 and *Op.* 135; *CW* 592 and *Op.* 143; *CW* 667 and *Op.* 255.

35. Friedmann, "The Doctrine of the Two Worlds," in Hershberger, pp. 105–18. Friedmann's essay is not specifically on Menno, but it is an apt description of his essential position.

36. Bender, "Church," in *ME* I, 594–98; Littell, *A Tribute to Menno Simons,* Ch. II.

37. *Reply to Gellius Faber, CW* 679 and *Op.* 262; cf. *CW* 745 and *Op.* 302; *CW* 748 and *Op.* 303.

38. *Foundation, CW* 158–59 and *Op.* 33; cf. *CW* 181 and *Op.* 46.

39. *Reply to Gellius Faber, CW* 750 and *Op.* 304; cf. *CW* 98–99 and *Op.* 128–29; *CW* 269 and *Op.* 422. In a sense, Menno may have had a valid exegetical point in identifying the field as the world. Nevertheless, the parable seems to imply a radical intermingling of wheat and tares in the present age which does not really correspond to Menno's understanding of the complete separation of the regenerate and the unregenerate.

40. The combination of the principle of total separation with an attitude of confrontation and challenge is maintained largely because of the situation of persecution. In later periods, when persecution abated, the ideal of separation often lost this sense of active confrontation and led instead to a sterile withdrawal from contact with the world.

41. *The True Christian Faith, CW* 345 and *Op.* 85.

42. *Foundation, CW* 200 and *Op.* 56–57; *CW* 83 and *Op.* 175; *CW* 118 and *Op.* 11; *CW* 397 and *Op.* 116; *CW* 549 and *Op.* 498.

43. *Foundation, CW* 181 and *Op.* 46; cf. *CW* 80 and *Op.* 173; *CW* 303 and *Op.* 444; *CW* 185 and *Op.* 48.

44. *Instruction on Excommunication, CW* 962 and *Op.* 188.

45. *Ibid., CW* 967 and *Op.* 192; cf. *CW* 990 and *Op.* 208; *CW* 471 and *Op.* 347.

46. *Reply to Sylis and Lemke, CW* 1003 and *Op.* 482; *CW* 413 and *Op.* 634; cf. *CW* 471 and *Op.* 347.

47. *CW* 413 and *Op.* 634. In the *Instruction on Excommunication,* Menno insists that the word about forgiving one's brother seventy times seven applies literally only to the brotherhood of the regenerate and does not include carnal sins (*CW* 981 and *Op.* 202).

48. *Reply to Sylis and Lemke, CW* 1006–1007 and *Op.* 484.

49. *A Clear Account of Excommunication, CW* 457 and *Op.* 339.

50. *Reply to Gellius Faber, CW* 723 and *Op.* 288.

51. *CW* 467 and *Op.* 344.

52. Franklin Littell, for example, makes this understanding of history in terms of paradise, fall, and restitution the central core of the Anabaptist doctrine of the Church. See *The Anabaptist View of the Church.*

53. *Why I Do Not Cease Teaching and Writing, CW* 300 and *Op.* 442.

54. *Meditation on the 25th Psalm, CW* 85 and *Op.* 176.

55. *A Pathetic Supplication to All Magistrates, CW* 529 and *Op.* 329.

56. *Reply to Gellius Faber, CW* 630 and *Op.* 232; cf. *CW* 234–37 and *Op.* 399–401.

57. *CW* 713 and *Op.* 282; cf. *CW* 962 and *Op.* 188.

58. *CW* 739–41 and *Op.* 299–300.

59. *CW* 743–44 and *Op.* 301.

60. *The New Birth, CW* 89 and *Op.* 123.

61. *Foundation, CW* 192 and *Op.* 51–52; cf. *CW* 62 and *Op.* 184; *CW* 65 and *Op.* 163; *CW* 81 and *Op.* 174; *CW* 91 and *Op.* 124. While the reference to 1,500 years seems to indicate a belief in the continuity of the true Church, Menno probably had in mind a remnant of true believers within or without the corrupt Catholic institution. Menno consistently regarded the latter as the body of the Antichrist.

62. *The True Christian Faith, CW* 404 and *Op.* 119.

63. *The New Birth,* CW 97 and *Op.* 127; cf. *CW* 548 and *Op.* 497–98.

64. *Reply to False Accusations,* CW 544 and *Op.* 495.

65. See, e.g., *The Incarnation of Our Lord,* CW 792 and *Op.* 358; *Brief and Clear Confession,* CW 428 and *Op.* 525; *Instruction on Excommunication,* CW 967 and *Op.* 194.

V. THE REFORMATION HERITAGE

1. This latter view was very strongly asserted by Ernst Troeltsch. See *Die Bedeutung des Protestantismus für die Entstehung der modernen Welt,* 2nd. ed. (Munich, R. Oldenbourg, 1911), translated by W. Montgomery as *Protestantism and Progress: A Historical Study of the Relation of Protestantism to the Modern World* (Boston, Beacon Press, 1958), pp. 85–86. On the other hand, Karl Holl, for example, has attributed to the Reformation an immense significance in shaping distinctive aspects of modern society. See "Die Kulturbedeutung der Reformation," in *Gesammelte Aufsätze zur Kirchengeschichte* I (Tübingen, Mohr, 1948), translated by K. and B. Hertz and J. Lichtblau as *The Cultural Significance of the Reformation* (New York, Meridian, 1959), pp. 55–56, 72, 129.

2. The description of the Church as an "event" was enunciated most clearly by Karl Barth in his address to the first Assembly of the World Council of Churches in 1948. Barth wished to indicate by the term not that the Church has no visible form but that it does not define its essential nature by that form. Rather, the Church comes into being when the Word is preached and heard. ("The Church: The Living Congregation of the Living Lord Jesus Christ," in *The Universal Church in God's Design,* London, SCM, 1948, pp. 67–76.) While this emphasis is, in a way, particularly characteristic of some representatives of contemporary Protestant ecclesiology, it is not exclusively so. Indeed, J. L. Leuba, in *L'Institution et L'Evènement* (Neuchâtel, Delachaux, 1950), finds the tension between "institution" and "event" rooted in the New Testament and expounds it in relation to New Testament Christology, Apostolicity, and Ecclesiology. English translation, *New Testament Pattern* (London, Lutterworth, 1953).

3. E.g., Rom. 12:2; Gal. 6:14.

4. Gabriel Vahanian, *The Death of God* (New York, George Braziller, 1957), p. 196.

5. H. Richard Niebuhr, *Radical Monotheism and Western Culture* (New York, Harper & Bros., 1943), p. 52.

6. Gabriel Vahanian, *Wait without Idols* (New York, George Braziller, 1964), pp. 24–26.

7. Vahanian, *The Death of God*, p. 10.

8. This is not to say that the Reformers did not criticize the various Roman institutions on the basis of Scripture, only that the crucial issue was not the existence of these phenomena as such but the idolatry with which they were regarded.

9. Vahanian, *The Death of God*, p. 147.

10. Dietrich Bonhoeffer, *Letters and Papers from Prison*, rev. ed. (London, SCM Press, 1967), pp. 209–10.

11. R. Gregor–Smith, *Secular Christianity* (London, Collins, 1966), p. 124.

SELECTIVE BIBLIOGRAPHY

I. THE MEDIEVAL PERIOD

Augustine, Saint. *De Civitate Dei.* Edited by P. Schaff. Volume II of *A Select Library of the Nicene and Post-Nicene Fathers.* New York, Christian Literature Company, 1886–90.

——. *The City of God.* Translated by Marcus Dods. New York, Random House, 1950.

Dietrich of Niem. *De Modis Uniendi Ac Reformandi Ecclesiam.* Edited by H. Heimpel, in *Dietrich von Niem über Union und Reform der Kirche,* 1410. Leipzig and Berlin, Teubner, 1933.

——. *Ways of Uniting and Reforming the Church.* Translated by James Kerr Cameron, in *Advocates of Reform,* edited by Matthew Spinka. Volume XIV of the Library of Christian Classics. Philadelphia, Westminster, 1953.

Hus, John. *Tractatus de Ecclesia.* Edited by S. H. Thompson. Boulder, Colo., University of Colorado Press, 1956.

——. *The Church.* Translated by D. Schaff. New York, Scribners, 1915.

Marsilius of Padua. *Defensor Pacis.* Edited by G. W. Previté-Orton. Cambridge, Cambridge University Press, 1928.

——. *The Defender of Peace.* Translated by Alan Gewirth. 2 vols., text in Volume 2. New York, Columbia University Press, 1951 and 1956.

Thomas Aquinas, Saint. *Compendium of Theology.* Translated by C.O. Vollert. London, Herder, 1948.

——. *Compendium Theologiae, Opera Omnia,* XXVII. Paris, 1871–80.

——. *Summa Theologiae.* Latin text and English translation. Edited by Thomas Gilby. London, Eyre and Spottiswood, 1964.

——. *Theological Texts.* Translated and edited by Thomas Gilby. London, Oxford University Press, 1955.

Wyclif, John. *Tractatus De Ecclesia.* Edited by Johann Loserth. London, Wyclif Society, 1886.

——. *The English Works of John Wyclif.* 3 vols. Edited by F. D. Matthews. London, Wyclif Society, 1880.

II. MARTIN LUTHER

A. Texts

Luther, Martin. *D. Martin Luthers Werke: Kritische Gesamtausgabe.* Weimar, Böhlau, 1883–

——. *D. Martin Luthers Werke: Deutsche Bibel.* Weimar, Böhlau, 1906–1961.

——. *D. Martin Luthers Werke: Tischreden.* Weimar, Böhlau, 1912–1921.

——. *D. Martin Luthers Werke: Briefwechsel.* Weimar, Böhlau, 1930–

B. Translations

Luther, Martin. *Luther's Works* (American Edition). Edited by Helmut Lehmann and Jaroslav Pelikan. Philadelphia, Fortress Press and St. Louis, Concordia Press, 1955–

——. *The Precious and Sacred Writings of Martin Luther.* Edited by J. N. Lenker. Minneapolis, Lutherans in all Lands Co., 1903.

——. *Works of Martin Luther* (Philadelphia Edition). Edited by H. E. Jacobs. Philadelphia, Holman, 1915–1943.

——. *The Bondage of the Will.* Translated by J. I. Packer and O. R. Johnston. New Jersey, Revell, 1957.

C. Critical Works

Althaus, Paul. *Die Theologie Martin Luthers.* Gütersloh, Gerd-Mohr, 1963.

——. *The Theology of Martin Luther.* Translated by Robert C. Schultz. Philadelphia, Fortress, 1966.

——. *Communio Sanctorum. Die Gemeinde im lutherischen Kirchengedenken.* I, München, Kaiser, 1929.

Cranz, F. Edward. *An Essay on the Development of Luther's Thought on Justice, Law and Society.* Harvard Theological Studies, XIX. Cambridge, Mass., Harvard University Press, 1959.

Ebeling, Gerhard. *Luther: Theologie,* in *Die Religion in Geschichte und Gegenwart.* 7 vols. Edited by Kurt Galling. Tübingen, Mohr, 1957–1965. Vol. IV.

——. "The Necessity of the Doctrine of the Two Kingdoms." Translated by James W. Leitch, in *Word and Faith.* London, SCM Press, 1963.

Heckel, J. "Die Zwei Kirchen: Kirche, Staat und Recht zum Widerstand bei Martin Luther," in *Zeitwende,* 25 (1954), 156–68.

Holl, Karl. "Die Entstehung von Luthers Kirchenbegriff," in *Gesammelte Aufsätze zur Kirchengeschichte.* I, Tübingen, Mohr, 1921.

Kinder, Ernst. "Die Verborgenheit der Kirche nach Luther," in *Festgabe für Joseph Lortz.* Edited by Erwin Iserloh and Peter Manns. Baden-Baden, Grimm, 1958. I, 173 ff.

——. "Sichtbare und Unsichtbare Kirche," in *Zeitwende,* 19 (1948), 559 ff.

Lau, F. *Luthers Lehre von den beiden Reichen.* Berlin, Lutherisches Verlagshaus, 1952.

Marchand, L. "Le Mystère du Christ et de L'Eglise," in *Foi et Vie,* New Series, No. 1 (1946), 376–403.

Olsson, H. "Sichtbarkeit und Verborgenheit der Kirche nach Luther," in G. Aulen, a.o., *Ein Buch von der Kirche.* Göttingen, Vandenhoeck & Ruprecht, 1950, pp. 338 ff.

Pauck, Wilhelm. "Luther's Conception of the Church," in *The Heritage of the Reformation.* Glencoe, Ill., Free Press, 1961.

Preus, H. "The Christian and the Church," in *More About Luther.* Decorah, Iowa, Luther College Press, 1958.

Rietschel, E. "Luthers Anschauung von der Unsichtbarkeit der Kirche," in *Theologische Studien und Kritiken.* 1900, pp. 404 ff.

Rupp, Gordon. "Luther's Doctrine of the Church," and "Luther on the True and False Church," in *The Righteousness of God.* London, Hodder & Stoughton, 1953.

Saanivaara, U. "The Church of Christ According to Luther," in *Lutheran Quarterly* 5 (1953), 134 ff.

Strohl, H. *La Notion de L'Eglise chez les Réformateurs.* Paris, Alain, 1936.

Torrance, T. F. *Kingdom and Church.* Edinburgh, Oliver and Boyd, 1956.

III. JOHN CALVIN

A. Texts

Calvin, John. *Iohannis Calvini Opera Quae Supersunt Omnia.* 59 volumes. Edited by G. Baum et. al. *Corpus Reformatorum.* Vols. 29–87. Braunschweig, Schwetschke, 1863–1900.

——. *Iohannis Calvini Opera Selecta.* 5 vols. Edited by Peter Barth and W. Niesel. München, Kaiser, 1926.

B. Translations

Calvin, John. *Calvin's New Testament Commentaries.* 12 vols. Edited by D. W. and T. F. Torrance. Grand Rapids, Mich., Eerdmans, 1959– .

——. *Calvin's Tracts and Treatises.* 3 vols. Edinburgh, Calvin Translation Society, 1844. Reprint edited by T. F. Torrance. Grand Rapids, Mich., Eerdmans, 1958.

——. *Commentary on a Harmony of the Evangelists: Matthew, Mark and Luke.* 3 vols. Edinburgh, Calvin Trans. Society, 1845–1846.

——. *Commentaries on the Old Testament.* 30 vols. Edinburgh, Calvin Trans. Society, 1845–1855.

——. *Concerning the Eternal Predestination of God.* Translated, with Introduction, by J. K. S. Reid. London, James Clarke, 1961.

——. *Institutes of the Christian Religion.* Edited by J. T. McNeill, translated by F. L. Battles. Vols. XX and XXI of the *Library of Christian Classics.* Philadelphia, Westminster, 1960.

——. *Letters of John Calvin.* 4 vols. Edited by Jules Bonnet. Philadelphia, Presbyterian Board of Publications, 1858.

——. *Theological Treatises.* Translated, with Introductions and Notes, by J. K. S. Reid. Volume XXII of the *Library of Christian Classics.* Philadelphia, Westminster, 1954.

C. Critical Works

Barth, Peter. "Calvins Verständnis der Kirche," in *Zwischen den Zeiten,* 8 (1930), 216–33.

Bohatec, J. "Calvins Lehre von Staat und Kirche" (*Untersuchungen zur deutschen Rechtsgeschichte,* 147). Breslau, Marcus, 1937.

Buess, E. "Prädestination und Kirche in Calvins Institution," *Theol. Zeitschrift,* 12 (1956), 347–61.

Courvoisier, J. "Calvin and Covenant Theology," in *Church History,* XXV (1956), 136 ff.

——. "La Dialectique dans l'Ecclésiologie de Calvin," in *Révue d'Histoire de Philosophie Religieuse*, 44 (1964), 348–63.

Fröhlich, Karlfried. *Gottesreich, Welt und Kirche bei Calvin*. München, Reinhart, 1930.

Ganoczy, Alexandre. *Calvin, Théologien de L'Eglise et du Ministère*. Paris, Les Editions du Cerf, 1964.

Kolfhaus, Wilhelm. *Christusgemeinschaft bei Johannes Calvin*. Neukirchen, Erziehunsverein, 1938.

Kromsigt, P. J. "Calvins Lehre von der Kirche," in *Bib. Zeugnisse*, 22 (1924), 45–76.

Krusche, Werner. *Das Wirken des Heiligen Geistes nach Calvin*. (*Forschungen zur Kirchen-und Dogmengeschichte*, Vol. 8). Göttingen, 1957.

Lecerf, A. "La Doctrine de L'Eglise dans Calvin," in *Revue de Théologie et de Philosophie*, IX (1929), 256–70.

MacGregor, Geddes. *Corpus Christi: The Nature of the Church According to the Reformed Tradition*. Philadelphia, Westminster, 1958.

McDonnell, Kilian. *John Calvin, The Church and the Eucharist*. Princeton, Princeton University Press, 1967.

McGiffert, A. C. "Calvin's Theory of the Church," in Charles A. Briggs, ed. *Essays in Modern Theology and Related Subjects*. New York, Scribners, 1911.

McNeill, J. T. "The Church in Sixteenth-Century Reformed Theology," *Journal of Religion*, 22 (1942) 251–69.

Mueller, W. *Church and State in Luther and Calvin*. Nashville, Tenn., Broadman Press, 1954.

Niesel, W. *The Theology of Calvin*. London, Lutterworth, 1956.

——. "Wesen und Gestalt der Kirche nach Calvin," in *Evangelische Theologie*, 3 (1936), 308–30.

Pearcy, H. R. *The Meaning of the Church in the Thought of Calvin*. Chicago, Chicago University Press, 1941.

Petry, R. C. "Calvin's Conception of the Communio Sanctorum," in *Church History*, V (1936), 227–38.

Quistorp, H. "Sichtbare und Unsichtbare Kirche bei Calvin," in *Evangelische Theologie*, 9 (1949–1950), 83–101.

Strohl, H. *La Notion de L'Eglise chez les Réformateurs*. Paris, Alain, 1936.

Torrance, T. F. *Kingdom and Church*. Edinburgh, Oliver and Boyd, 1956.

Walker, G. S. M. "Calvin and the Church," in *Scottish Journal of Theology,* 16 (1963), 371–89.

Wendel, François. *Calvin: The Origins and Development of His Religious Thought.* Translated by Philip Mairet. London, Collins, 1963.

Werdermann, T. "Calvins Lehre von der Kirche in ihrer Geschichtlichen Entwicklung," *Calvin-Studien,* 1959, edited by Jürgen Moltmann. Neukirchen, Erz-Verlag, 1960.

IV. MENNO SIMONS

A. *Texts*

Simons, Menno. *Opera Omnia Theologica of Alle de Godtgeleerde Wercken van Menno Symons.* Edited by Hendrick Jansz Herrison. Amsterdam, Joannes van Veen, 1681.

B. *Translations*

Simons, Menno. *The Complete Writings of Menno Simons.* Translated by Leonard Verduin. Edited by John Christian Wenger. Scottsdale, Pa., Herald Press, 1956.

C. *Critical Works*

Bainton, Roland. "The Sectarian Theory of the Church," in *Christendom,* II (1946), 382–87.

——. "The Church of the Restoration," in *Mennonite Life,* 8 (July, 1953), 136–43.

Bender, H. S. "Church," in *Mennonite Encyclopedia,* I, 594–98. Scottsdale, Pa., Herald Press, 1956.

——. "The Anabaptist Vision," in *The Recovery of the Anabaptist Vision,* edited by Guy Hershberger. Scottsdale, Pa., Herald Press, 1957.

Fast, H. "Die Bedeutung der Gemeinde für die Taüfer," in *Der Mennonit,* 13 (1960), 133 f. 149 f.

Friedmann, R. "The Doctrine of the Two Worlds," in *The Recovery of the Anabaptist Vision,* edited by G. Hershberger. Scottsdale, Pa., Herald Press, 1957.

Garrett, J. L. "The Nature of the Church According to the Radical Continental Reformation," in the *Mennonite Quarterly Review,* XXXII (1958), 111 ff.

Heyer, Fritz. *Die Kirchenbegriff der Schwärmer.* Leipzig, Heinsius, 1939.

Krahn, Cornelius. "Menno Simons' Concept of the Church," in

A Legacy of Faith. Edited by E. J. Dyck. Newton, Kan., Faith and Life Press, 1962.

Littell, F. H. "The Anabaptist Concept of the Church," in *The Recovery of the Anabaptist Vision.* Edited by G. Hershberger. Scottsdale, Pa., Herald Press, 1957.

——. "The Anabaptist Doctrine of the Restitution of the True Church," in *Mennonite Quarterly Review,* XXIV (1950), 33 ff.

——. *The Anabaptist View of the Church.* Boston, Beacon Press, 1952. Revised and reissued as *The Origins of Sectarian Protestantism.* New York, Macmillan, 1965.

——. *A Tribute to Menno Simons.* Scottsdale, Pa., Herald Press, 1961.

Price, T. O. "The Anabaptist View of the Church," in *Review and Expositor,* 51, 1954.

Toews, J. *The Anabaptist Conception of the Church.* Dissertation, United College of Winnipeg. Winnipeg, Man., 1950.

Waltner, E. "The Anabaptist Conception of the Church," *Mennonite Quarterly Review,* XXV (1951), 5 ff.

Wray, F. J. "The Anabaptist Doctrine of the Restitution of the True Church," *Mennonite Quarterly Review,* XXVIII (1954), 185 ff.

Zijpp, N. van der. "The Conception of Our Fathers Regarding the Church," *Mennonite Quarterly Review,* XXVII (1953), 91 ff.

PERMISSIONS

ACKNOWLEDGMENT is gratefully made to the following publishers for permission to quote material from copyrighted works: Charles Scribner's Sons, for *The Church* by Jan Hus, translated by D. Schaff (Scribners, 1915); The Clarendon Press, for *English Works of John Wyclif*, edited by Thomas Arnold (Oxford, Clarendon Press, 1871); Concordia Publishing House and Fortress Press, for *Luther's Works*, edited by Helmut Lehmann and Jaroslav Pelikan (Philadelphia, Fortress Press, and St. Louis, Concordia Press, 1955–   ); Fortress Press, for *Works of Martin Luther*, edited by H. E. Jacobs (Philadelphia, Holman, 1915–1943); W. B. Eerdmans Publishing Company, for *Calvin's New Testament Commentaries*, edited by D. W. and T. F. Torrance (Grand Rapids, Mich., Eerdmans, 1959–   ); *Calvin's Tracts and Treatises* (Edinburgh, Calvin Translation Society, 1844; reprint edited by T. F. Torrance, Grand Rapids, Mich., Eerdmans, 1958); *Commentaries on the Old Testament* (Edinburgh, Calvin Translation Society, 1845–1855); *Commentary on a Harmony of the Evangelists: Matthew, Mark and Luke* (Edinburgh, Calvin Translation Society, 1845–1846); Fleming H. Revell Company and James Clarke (Cambridge, England), for *The Bondage of the Will* by Martin Luther, translated by J. I. Packer and O. R. Johnston (New Jersey, Revell, 1957); George Braziller, Inc., for *Wait Without Idols* by Gabriel Vahanian (copyright © 1964 by Gabriel Vahanian) and *The Death of God* by Gabriel Vahanian (copyright © 1957, 1959, 1960, 1961 by Gabriel Vahanian); Harper and Row, for *Secular Christianity*, by R. Gregor-Smith (London, Collins, 1966); Lutterworth Press and Westminster Press, for *The Theology of Calvin* by W. Niesel (London, Lutterworth, 1956); The Macmillan Company and SCM Press, Ltd., for

Letters and Papers from Prison by Dietrich Bonhoeffer (London, SCM Press, 1967); Mennonite Publishing House, for *The Complete Writings of Menno Simons, c 1496–1561,* edited by John Christian Wenger (copyright © 1955 by Mennonite Publishing House, Scottdale, Pa.).

Acknowledgement is also made to the Westminster Press for permission to quote from:

Calvin: Institutes of the Christian Religion, Vols. XX, XXI, The Library of Christian Classics, edited by John T. McNeill and translated by Ford Lewis Battles. Published in the U.S.A. by The Westminster Press. Copyright © MCMLX, by W. L. Jenkins.

Advocates of Reform, edited by Matthew Spinka. Vol. XIV, The Library of Christian Classics. Published simultaneously in Great Britain and the United States, by S.C.M. Press, Ltd., London, and The Westminster Press, Philadelphia. First published in 1953.

The Misunderstanding of the Church, by Emil Brunner. Translated by Harold Knight. Copyright © MCMLIII, by W. L. Jenkins, The Westminster Press.

The Christian Doctrine of the Church, Faith, and the Consummation, Dogmatics Vol. III, by Emil Brunner. Translated by David Cairns and T. H. L. Parker. Published in the U.S.A. by the Westminster Press, 1962. © 1960, Zwingli-Verlag, Zurich. English translation, copyright © 1962 Lutterworth Press.

INDEX